David Marcus: Editing Ireland

David Marcus: Editing Ireland

Edited by Paul Delaney and Deirdre Madden

The Stinging Fly

First published in Ireland by The Stinging Fly Press in 2024.

ISBN 978-1-906539-34-4

Introduction copyright © Paul Delaney and Deirdre Madden, 2024

© Copyright on all other material remains with
the individual authors, 2024. All rights reserved.

The Stinging Fly Press
PO Box 6016
Dublin 1
www.stingingfly.org

Set in Palatino
Cover Design: Eimear Gavin
Printed in Ireland by Walsh Colour Print, County Kerry.

The Stinging Fly Press gratefully acknowledges the financial support
of The Arts Council/An Chomhairle Ealaíon.

Contents

Paul Delaney & Deirdre Madden	Introduction	vii

I

Dermot Bolger	David Marcus: A Life	3
David Marcus	A Visit to Drishane House	15
Louis Marcus	My Brother David	25
Katrina Goldstone	David Marcus's Cultural Forebears	31
David Marcus	A Jolson Story	37
Eiléan Ní Chuilleanáin	*Poem:* David Marcus: on a bridge	49
George O'Brien	Found in Translation	53
Brian Merriman	*from* The Midnight Court	63
Mary O'Malley	*Poem:* The Irish for Knife	67

II

Tim Pat Coogan	*Interview:* David and *The Irish Press*	73
Gerard Smyth	A Golden Age	79
Ita Daly	A Meeting in Spring	87
Frank McGuinness	Two poems	95
Michael Harding	Dining on Dreams	99
Neil Jordan	Sand	105
Desmond Hogan	*Story:* The Mourning Thief	107
Mary Leland	We Are What We Give	119
Sebastian Barry	*Story:* The Beast	125
Mary Morrissy	The Art of Rejection	137
Eoin McNamee	*Poem:* Intensive Care	143

CONTENTS

| Éilís Ní Dhuibhne | David Marcus the feminist? | 147 |
| Harry Clifton | *Poem:* The Has-Beens | 157 |

III

Colum McCann	Expanding the Lungs of Irish Literature	161
Anthony Glavin	A Treasured Friendship	167
Ciaran Carty	Life with David, Almost	171
Jo O'Donoghue	That Rooted Man	179
David Marcus	The Joyce of Yiddish, the *Oy Vay* of Irish	183
Carlo Gébler	A Story's Worth	189
Mary Dorcey	*Story:* Another Glorious Day	199
William Wall	Remembering David	227

IV

Angus Cargill	David and Faber	233
Claire Keegan	*Story:* The Ginger Rogers Sermon	237
Declan Meade	More is More	253
Kevin Barry	*Story:* Miami Vice	257
Lucy Caldwell	On Being Various	269

V

| Sarah Marcus | Love, Always | 281 |
| Ita Daly | Still Beautiful | 283 |

David Marcus: Bibliography	291
Notes on Contributors	293
Acknowledgements	299

Paul Delaney and Deirdre Madden

Introduction

David Marcus was the most influential literary editor in Ireland in the twentieth century. His working life spanned sixty years, beginning in 1946 with the magazine *Irish Writing*, and ending in 2007, with the publication of the second volume of *The Faber Book of Best New Irish Short Stories*. In between, he edited or published a distinguished range of Irish fiction writers and poets. Marcus is probably best remembered for his association with 'New Irish Writing' in *The Irish Press*, a literary page which he edited from its inception in 1968 until his retirement in 1986. 'New Irish Writing' was a weekly sheet in this national newspaper, given over to the publication of contemporary Irish writing. The page had an open submissions policy, and it frequently set established authors (such as John McGahern, Edna O'Brien, or William Trevor) alongside previously unpublished writers. This simple idea revolutionised Irish literature, providing an accessible platform for a generation of writers to utilise, and ensuring that their work was introduced to an enormous readership. Under Marcus's editorship, 'New Irish Writing' raised the profile of new and emerging talent, and many of those then-younger writers have gone on to become major literary figures. Sebastian Barry, Patrick McCabe, Éilís Ní Dhuibhne, Desmond Hogan, and Mary Morrissy are just a few of the many people to first appear on this fabled page under Marcus's care.

'New Irish Writing' was typical of Marcus's ambition. It was not his first literary adventure, though. Twenty years earlier, as a young man in Cork, he co-founded *Irish Writing* with his friend, Terence Smith. Together, they co-edited twenty-eight issues of this magazine (with Marcus doing much of the textual work), before passing it on to Sean White in September 1954. Marcus also launched the first iteration of *Poetry Ireland* in 1948, editing it as a standalone paper before folding it as a supplement into *Irish Writing*. When Marcus stepped down from *Irish Writing* in the mid-1950s, it was because he was compelled to move—like so many Irish people of the time—to England for work. Taking up a job in an insurance company, it must have seemed as if his literary career had ended. Those dreams were revived in the late 1960s, however, on his return to Ireland. Over the four decades that followed, and in addition to overseeing 'New Irish Writing', Marcus edited thirty anthologies of Irish poetry and short fiction, starting—appropriately—with *New Irish Writing 1* (1970), a selection of original work from the first year of *The Irish Press* page.

Marcus was a prolific anthologist, and some of his selections were published by major international publishing houses; others were produced by independent Irish presses. As a creative artist his output was modest, and comprised three novels (*To Next Year in Jerusalem* [1954], *A Land Not Theirs* [1986], and *A Land in Flames* [1987]), a volume of short stories (*Who Ever Heard of an Irish Jew?* [1988]), and a scattering of poems and translations from Irish. The most important of his translations was a version of Brian Merriman's eighteenth-century poem, *Cúirt an Mheán Oíche* (*The Midnight Court*), which was produced in a beautiful, limited edition by Dolmen Press in 1953, and which included headpieces and vignettes designed and cut by Michael Biggs. Marcus also wrote two volumes of autobiography, including the intimate *Oughtobiography: Leaves from the Diary of a Hyphenated Jew* (2001). Many of these works were well received but few have survived the passage of time. Conversely, Marcus's significance as an editor remains palpable. In addition to his anthologies and his work

INTRODUCTION

with 'New Irish Writing', Marcus co-founded Poolbeg Press (with Philip McDermott) in 1976, playing a vital role in its operations for over a decade. He helped to establish the long-running Hennessy Award for Irish literature in 1971; he served as literary editor of *The Irish Press* during the mid-1980s; and he acted as a scout for several publishing houses in London, working closely with the likes of the legendary literary agent, the late Giles Gordon. In the process, Marcus provided a conduit for many Irish writers hoping to place their work. By any stretch, his was a remarkable career.

'Editors are often shadowy creatures,' Marcus's wife, the writer Ita Daly has noted. Their names are generally unknown to the public, their involvement in the process of publication is typically undervalued or misunderstood, and the traces that they leave on published texts are—or at least should be—invisible to everyone but the authors concerned. This anonymity appears to have suited Marcus. By temperament, he was a quiet, unassuming man who was happy to shun the limelight. His personal shyness was possibly accentuated by feelings of being an outsider, as the grandson of Lithuanian immigrants who fled persecution in the late nineteenth century, as a non-drinker in an often sodden industry, but also as a Jew in an overwhelmingly Catholic State. A consequence was that he tended to keep to himself, corresponding with writers, fellow editors, publishers, and agents by letter rather than in person. In addition, though, Marcus valued the idea of the unobtrusive editor, understanding his role as someone whose job was to enable and assist in the creation of art. In this respect, his natural qualities—his reserve and sense of discretion, his modesty and generosity of spirit, his attentiveness to people and to literary texts—were well-matched to the position that he fashioned for himself. Above all, Marcus had exceptional judgement and instinct. 'A nose for literature, just as rare as a nose for wine—that's what David had,' Ita Daly succinctly put it in her memoir of her life with her husband, *I'll Drop You a Line* (2016). 'Great editors instantly recognise the voice, even at the stage where it is struggling to emerge.'

David Marcus: Editing Ireland commemorates this talent and celebrates its legacy. It does so in Marcus's centenary year (he was born on 21 August 1924) by bringing together a selection of people who knew him, who worked with him, or who were published by him over an extended period of time; it also includes contributions by a few people who continue to be inspired by the ideas which underpinned his work. 'It is too early yet to assess or evaluate the influence of this novel form of literary periodical on contemporary Irish writing,' Marcus wrote in 1970, as he reflected upon the early achievements of 'New Irish Writing'. 'But there is every indication that its existence alone has acted as a spur to scores of young writers who would otherwise have fallen silent. That'll do for a start.' It was a characteristically understated assessment that simultaneously spoke to Marcus's objectives as a literary editor. Those objectives would continue to shape his thinking for the duration of his career, and many of them can be found in embryo in his earliest work, in the initial pages of *Irish Writing*.

'Irish writing is a great deal more than writing *done* in Ireland,' the young Marcus announced in the first issue of that magazine. Rather, he stated, it is literature that partakes of the world. It includes writers from different backgrounds, who engage with various genres and competing ideas, and it encompasses people who live on and beyond the island of Ireland. 'To "live out" is not for an artist one of the Seven Deadly Sins,' Marcus continued, and Irish writers—and writers of Irish descent—can be found in nearly every corner of the world. It is an invigorating claim with which to begin a new journal, and it is all the more refreshing when its context—the anxious isolationism of mid-1940s Ireland—is recalled. It was also a bold assertion for a young Jewish man to make in the immediate aftermath of the Second World War. For Marcus, though, Irish literature evolved out of the relationship between the national and the international, and diversity of practice was—and still is—central to its health as a creative art. This was part of the rationale for *Irish Writing*. 'Our concern lies entirely with what is vital in Ireland,' he explained in his foreword to the first issue, 'and this we hope to give—may our symbol be the cornucopia!—in all its abounding variety.' In the process, Marcus identified a principle that would become central to his work as a literary editor over the next six decades.

When the second issue of *Irish Writing* was published in June 1947, Marcus introduced another idea that he would also develop in the years that followed. 'We are happy to include the work of writers who have only begun to make their way, and in placing their work side by side with that of writers of widely recognised gifts, we hope to encourage them to more sustained flight.' The commitment to emerging writers was a crucial factor in the establishment of the new magazine. Not only was it underscored by Marcus's decision to publish lesser-known writers in *Irish Writing*, it also resulted in occasional competitions being held for new and promising talent. Some of the early volumes of the magazine featured advertisements for *Irish Writing*'s first Literary Award, for instance, with the fifth issue publishing the winning story, 'She is Far from the Land', by the long-forgotten Valentine Clery. The encouragement of such talent would become a hallmark of Marcus's editorial career, resulting, among other things, in his curation of a special volume of *Irish Writing* called 'Young Writers' Issue' in September 1953. Amongst the contributors to that issue, Marcus included early work by Val Mulkerns, Seán Lucy, and Thomas Kinsella, together with the first published work by Eugene McCabe, a short story, 'The First Term'.

The following year, in April 1948, Marcus raised a further point that he would remain faithful to in the decades that followed. 'We will continue to publish writers from over the border,' he wrote, mindful that trade restrictions between Britain and Ireland had impacted on the availability of *Irish Writing* in the North. 'In literary Ireland there is no partition.' Michael McLaverty, who was included in that issue, was one of many Northern writers to consequently feature across the eight years of Marcus's involvement with *Irish Writing*. Writing a few years later, in the contemporaneous journal *The Bell*, Mary Beckett—another Northern writer whom Marcus championed—identified a partitionist mentality that was espoused by many people in the South in the mid-twentieth century. 'Catholics in the Six Counties are in the peculiar position of being unwanted both north and south of the border,' Beckett wrote in the autumn of 1951. 'Here we are alienated by our religion and politics; in Dublin, it would seem, by our accent.' This sense of alienation bled into many programmes and cultural events, in and outside Ireland, and would become pronounced during the dark years of the Troubles, when the North was routinely considered 'a place apart' (to recall Dervla Murphy's still evocative phrase). It is something that Marcus consciously resisted.

A final commitment of Marcus's, which is evident from his early involvement with *Irish Writing*, is his determination to publish literature by women. Mary Lavin, Teresa Deevy, 'Temple Lane' (Mary Isobel Leslie), and Blanaid Salkeld were all regular contributors, as was Norah Hoult, who contributed nonfiction and three stories to the magazine. Hoult was also one of several writers to contribute to a 'Women Writers' Issue' of *Irish Writing* in 1954, along with Elizabeth Bowen, Lavin, Beckett, K. Arnold Price, Mulkerns, and Kate O'Brien. This idea for a special issue was progressive for its time, and the quality of work that it generated was—and remains—stimulating. It is important, of course, not to interpret this as evidence of something that Marcus was not. As a man born into a conservative community in the mid-1920s, he was very much a product of his times and could hardly be considered feminist in a contemporary sense. Truer would it be to say that Marcus was impartial—or rather, as impartial as anyone can be—in his appraisal of literature, and that he was primarily interested in the quality of writing, regardless of provenance or preconceptions about its authorship. His guiding principles as an editor were rigorous but inclusive, and he was receptive to changing energies and to new voices. It is for this reason, perhaps, that Éilís Ní Dhuibhne has elsewhere remarked that 'Marcus democratised—and, by the way, feminised—Irish literature.'

INTRODUCTION

*

With the sixth issue of *Irish Writing*, Marcus ceased writing regular forewords to his magazine. Thereafter, he only added occasional prefaces to a few issues of this periodical. A double volume in 1952, marking the twentieth and twenty-first issues, for example, saw him reflect on all that *Irish Writing* had accomplished, taking particular pleasure in the fact that 'we have published again and again the work of the talented unknown,' and that 'we have [also] given some indication of the bounty, the persistent vitality and scope of Irish writing.' Meanwhile, a special 'non-Irish' issue, which was designed to celebrate the convening of the International Congress of PEN in Dublin in June 1953, prompted him to decry 'the existence of a certain spiritual isolationism' in Irish society. 'Not being another planet,' Marcus complained, people in Ireland must think beyond the parochial and recognise their place in the world: 'we must share, after all, the fate of the world in which we live.' Comments such as these were expressive of Marcus's core beliefs. For the most part, though, Marcus refrained from editorialising in later issues of *Irish Writing*. This change in policy was never explained, but it meant that most of the texts that he published were unglossed, as authors were left to speak for themselves. This, in turn, allowed Marcus to conceptualise his responsibilities as an editor in a way that was different to his exemplar, Sean O'Faoláin, as the younger man began to craft a role for himself that was deliberately less conspicuous, and controlling, than it might have otherwise been.

In many respects, this set a template for Marcus to follow. Once 'New Irish Writing' was established in the late 1960s, Marcus only rarely included editorial comments in his page in *The Irish Press*. Similarly, the vast majority of anthologies that he edited only carried short forewords in which Marcus refrained from commenting upon the writers or the texts that he had collected. Thus, for instance, the *Phoenix Irish Short Stories* series, which Marcus edited almost annually between 1996 and 2003 (for some reason no volume appeared in 2002), included brief prefaces with pithy reflections on such issues as the optimum length for short fiction (*Phoenix Stories 1997*), the pressures on contemporary writers to desist with the short form (*Phoenix Stories 1999*), the demise of venues for the publication of short stories (*Phoenix Stories 2000*), and the importance of revision in short-story writing (*Phoenix Stories 2001*). Similar observations could be made about each of the popular anthologies that he curated for Bloomsbury in the mid-to-late 1990s—*Irish Christmas Stories* (1995), *Irish Christmas Stories II* (1997), and *Mothers and Daughters* (1998)—as they all contained forewords of a couple of pages, at most, that were not directly related to the republished stories. (The first of those books, incidentally, included a story by the then-largely forgotten Maeve Brennan, 'Christmas Eve'.) Marcus's two Faber anthologies of Irish short fiction—*The Faber Book of Best New Irish Short Stories, 2004–5* (2005), and *The Faber Book of Best New Irish Short Stories, 2006–7* (2007)—were also prefaced with succinct introductions, which did not describe the stories that were included. Instead, in the first of those prefaces, Marcus celebrated the fact that all of his contributors had written stories that spoke to the now. 'Today's world has found new frontiers,' he enthused, 'as indeed has today's short story.' In the second, Marcus pressed the significance of the history of Irish women's writing.

Reading Marcus's prefaces today, it is striking to note the consistency with which they expound the same ideas. The championing of neglected or emerging authors, the support of women's writing, enthusiasm for new work, the desire to see Ireland through an international lens, belief in cultural pluralism and inclusion, and the commitment to aesthetic standards: these are just some of the points that recur time and again in Marcus's forewords, and that helped to determine the choices that he made as a literary editor. Those prefaces, in turn, gave way to some remarkable anthologies, such as the highly influential *State of the Art: Short Stories by the New Irish Writers* (1992), which comprised a collection of stories by writers whose debut volumes of short fiction were published in the 1970s and 1980s. Aside from the quality of work that was included, one of the things that made *State of the Art* especially significant was the fact that half of its contributors—or seventeen of the thirty-four authors—were women. This careful gender balance was intentional on Marcus's part and ran counter to the traditional composition of Irish anthologies; it was a point that Marcus addressed in his uncharacteristically lengthy introduction to that volume. Another example was *Alternative Loves: Irish Gay and Lesbian Stories* (1994), published within a year of the decriminalisation of homosexuality in the Republic, at a time when homophobic attacks and prejudices were still rife in Irish society. Marcus proudly accepted the commission to edit that anthology but judiciously invited the scholar and activist, Ailbhe Smyth, to write its preface. 'One of the many strengths of [this] collection is the expansive range and variety of the voices it invites us to listen to,' Smyth, in turn, commended. 'For there is no such thing as the "definitive" lesbian or gay experience—or story. Why should there be?' Many other instances could be cited which speak to the diversity of writers that Marcus supported, and to the variety of stories that he helped to see into print over a long career. And it was a long career: lest it be forgotten, Marcus's earliest work saw him publish very late work by Edith Somerville and James Stephens; over half a century later, he was amongst the first to recognise the talent of the then-emerging Claire Keegan and Kevin Barry.

David Marcus: Editing Ireland provides the first major retrospective of that extraordinary career. It comprises a miscellany of work by various cultural and literary figures, and it includes poems, stories, reflections, and critical essays; it also reproduces a few selections from Marcus's own creative writing. To assist readers, the book is divided into several sections.

The first section opens with an overview of Marcus's life by Dermot Bolger. This leads into a chapter from *Oughtobiography*, which depicts Marcus's visit as young man to one of his literary heroes, Edith Somerville, in the mid-1940s. A personal reflection by Marcus's brother, the filmmaker Louis Marcus, follows, recalling life in Cork in the late 1930s and 1940s, and discussing the family's Jewish heritage. The latter theme is developed by the historian Katrina Goldstone in her analysis of Marcus and a lineage of Irish Jewish artists and intellectuals in the early-to-mid twentieth century. Some of the tensions arising from Marcus's complex cultural identity are illustrated in his short story, 'A Jolson Story', which was first published in *Irish Writing* in 1955, and which is reprinted here for the first time. This section also features new poems by Eiléan Ní Chuilleanáin and Mary O'Malley, each of which is accompanied by a personal note by the respective poet, testifying to Marcus's importance for their own work and touching on his significance as a translator from Irish. An excerpt from Marcus's most famous translation—his 1953 edition of *The Midnight Court*—is included, as is an essay by George O'Brien, which explores Marcus's version of that celebrated, controversial poem. As O'Brien suggests, in addition to being an act of linguistic importance, translation can be understood in metaphorical terms as an attempt to bring together different cultures, times, and ways of thinking; consequently, it can provide a means to reconcile what Marcus once described as 'the ongoing trauma of having to juggle a hyphenated heritage.'

The second section concentrates on Marcus's involvement with 'New Irish Writing'. It opens with an interview with the person who played a decisive role in the establishment of that literary page, Tim Pat Coogan. Not only did Coogan give permission for 'New Irish Writing' to begin publication in 1968, as former editor of *The Irish Press* he ensured that Marcus was able to work independently without compromising his principles or needing to secure funding. This interview is complemented with an essay by the former managing editor of *The Irish Times*, Gerard Smyth, remembering the Dublin newspaper world of the late 1960s and 1970s. This, in turn, is succeeded by the first of two pieces by Ita Daly, describing the early stages of her own emergence as a writer, and interweaving the story of her romance with her future husband with her refinement of technique and style. 'When David asked me out to dinner,' she wittily recalls, 'he may have seen it as a date but I saw it more as a workshop.'

Ita Daly and Gerard Smyth each cut their teeth as young writers in 'New Irish Writing', and they are two of twelve writers who are included in the second section who either debuted in or had very early work published by Marcus in *The Irish Press*. The section includes original copies of two of those texts—Sebastian Barry's short story 'The Beast', and Eoin McNamee's poem 'Intensive Care'—which are reprinted precisely as they first appeared in 'New Irish Writing'. Both of these texts are accompanied by notes by Barry and McNamee, looking back to those early acts of publication. Several other writers also feature who testify to the sense of validation that came from having their work accepted by Marcus, including Neil Jordan, Mary Leland, and Michael Harding. Mary Morrissy, meanwhile, reflects upon the experience of having work rejected (as well as accepted) by 'New Irish Writing', and attests to the care Marcus took to explain his reasons for turning down material. 'David honed and refined the art of rejection,' she explains. 'This meant that he was conferring status and respect on you, even when he was saying no.' The section also features an essay by Éilís Ní Dhuibhne, which engages with Marcus's commitment to the publication of work by women writers, and considers how this was manifest in the work that he incorporated into 'New Irish Writing'. Poems by Frank McGuinness and Harry Clifton are included, as is Desmond Hogan's short story 'The Mourning Thief', which Marcus himself chose to anthologise in the volume *Irish Christmas Stories*.

The third section begins with a triptych by Colum McCann, which focuses attention on three stages of Marcus's career: his precocity as a young editor of *Irish Writing*; the friendship he subsequently shared with McCann's father, the writer and editor, Sean McCann; and, later still, the part he played in the development of McCann's own career, beginning with the publication of a story in the *Phoenix Irish Short Stories* series. When

Marcus retired from 'New Irish Writing' in 1986, the page was briefly edited by Anthony Glavin before it passed over to Ciaran Carty. Section three includes essays by Glavin and Carty, in which both men consider their part in the ongoing history of this page. In addition, Carty traces the nearly fifty-year association of the Hennessy Literary Awards with 'New Irish Writing', beginning in 1971 and running through to 2019. Jo O'Donoghue ponders Marcus's involvement with Poolbeg Press, and remembers a few instances where she worked with Marcus—initially as a young editor at Poolbeg, and later as a seasoned publisher with Marino Books/Mercier Press. A second chapter from *Oughtobiography* is included, in which Marcus further considers issues of cultural identity, and in which he movingly announces—as someone who followed the atrocities of the Second World War from an uncomfortable distance—that 'while being Irish may provide the tinder for my everyday passions, the Jew in me is branded on my soul as indelibly as the numbers on the arms of the Holocaust victims and survivors.'

Carlo Gébler reprises Mary Morrissy by recalling the experience of having work both rejected and accepted by Marcus; he also provides a link across the generations, as he remembers the admiration his parents—the writers Edna O'Brien and Ernest Gébler—also had for Marcus. Gébler was one of a number of writers who were commissioned to contribute to Marcus's last work, *The Faber Book of Best New Irish Short Stories, 2006–7*, and his essay describes this experience, including a gentle description of Marcus as an ailing figure in his early eighties. Mary Dorcey also wrote for this anthology, and the story that she contributed, 'Another Glorious Day', is reprinted here. It is a poignant choice given that it is narrated from the perspective of an elderly person with a literary imagination who is suffering from dementia. An extended note is added to this story, in which Dorcey attests to the support Marcus gave to her own writing, and in which she praises the spirit of inclusion which underwrote Marcus's ambitions as an editor. The section ends with a tribute by William Wall, beginning with an account of Marcus's funeral in 2009 before stretching back to reminisce about aspects of a life, and a friendship, all the while stressing Marcus's enduring love for his native Cork.

The penultimate section explores aspects of Marcus's legacy in a contemporary context. It includes essays by fellow editors Declan Meade and Angus Cargill (from The Stinging Fly and Faber & Faber, respectively), each of whom reflects upon Marcus's importance as an editor but also considers the imprint he has left on Irish literature. One of Marcus's defining characteristics was the ability to spot talent, and to offer opportunities to younger authors who might otherwise have never seen their work published. Amongst the many people he helped in this way are two of the most acclaimed contemporary Irish prose writers, Claire Keegan and Kevin Barry. The fourth section includes original versions of two stories that Marcus first published in the *Phoenix Irish Short Stories* series: Keegan's 'The Ginger Rogers Sermon' and Barry's 'Miami Vice'. Short notes are appended to each of these stories, in which Keegan and Barry speak to the importance of Marcus for their emergence as writers. The section concludes with an essay by another celebrated contemporary author, Lucy Caldwell. Unlike Keegan or Barry, Caldwell never met or was published by Marcus. However, her short story anthology *Being Various* (2019) is suffused with what she calls 'the David Marcus sensibility', which she defines as a quality 'which searches for new ways of telling old stories, and for stories entirely new, that sees the energy of creative change as being brought about when the traditional meets the cutting edge.' *Being Various* is the most recent iteration in the occasional Faber *Irish Short Stories* series that Marcus initiated— and Angus Cargill commissioned—in 2005. To date, this series has run to six volumes, with two books curated by Marcus and the other anthologies edited by Joseph O'Connor, Kevin Barry, and Deirdre Madden.

The book ends with a final short section, or a postscript, comprising a personal reflection by Marcus's daughter, Sarah, as well as a second contribution from Ita Daly. These two pieces give added detail about Marcus's life—his passion for classical music, for instance, as well as his love for literature and for family. They also portray his final years, and include an affecting description by Daly of her husband's struggles with dementia, his illness, and his death. Daly's essay—and the larger book—concludes with an image of sunlight after death. The cover of *David Marcus: Editing Ireland* picks up on this, with Eimear Gavin producing a striking design of an open book, with one hundred page leaves symbolising Marcus's centenary year. Each of those pages represents Marcus's commitment to literary practice, with the book standing for the many texts and people that he encouraged over a long career. In addition, though, Gavin's design could be taken to resemble a sunburst, and so understood to denote light, vitality, and creativity. It is a fitting symbol for someone who did so much to promote Irish writing, and whose legacy remains strong and energising. In this centenary year, it is important that that legacy is remembered, and that Marcus's contributions to Irish literary culture, and to the Irish book industry, are celebrated. As Tim Pat Coogan has inferred, 'he was that extremely valuable figure, an enabling man.'

David Marcus: Editing Ireland

I

Dermot Bolger
David Marcus: A Life

In the eyes of most Irish citizens who lived in what was called the Irish Free State, the Second World War was an inconvenience that was occurring off-screen. Strict censorship laws meant that the majority of the Irish public (assured by *The Irish Press* that what was happening to Jews in Europe was no worse than what was happening to Catholics in Northern Ireland) had little sense of the realities of that conflict—even if the Belfast Blitz in April 1941, and the smaller scale bombing of Dublin's North Strand in May the same year, gave some indication of the war's horrors. Attitudes might be summed up by the stopover of Irish government minister Frank Aiken in Portugal, en route to a disastrous diplomatic visit to Washington in the spring of 1941. In Portugal, Aiken bizarrely agreed with the dictator Salazar that, amid the devastation in Europe, the real victims were 'the neutrals who were paying for the war'.

In 1942 *The Cork Examiner* castigated 'uninformed citizens' for 'paying too much attention to the war'. But not all Irish people could afford this studied indifference. As a young Jewish man growing up in Cork, David Marcus—a future poet, translator, novelist, short story writer, editor extraordinaire, starter of literary journals and indefatigable champion of new Irish writers—recalled how he and his fellow four hundred Jews in Cork 'knew from letters and messages smuggled out what was happening to their co-religionists in Germany', and 'that the five thousand Jews of Ireland had been marked down for slaughter in due course'.

In later life, Marcus still recalled childhood nights 'when hour after hour I stayed awake listening for the tramp of Nazi boots on Cork's innocent streets and for the panzer divisions raging through the Mardyke.'

But thankfully when outside forces did prise Marcus away from Cork's close-knit Jewish community, they were not German tanks. Those influences came from the books that he eagerly read as a young man. The ideas in these novels propelled him into starting to write poems and then into establishing, from a remarkably young age, a succession of outlets to let Irish writers—established and unknown—have a new platform to be heard in their own land. When he passed away in Dublin in May 2009, Ireland lost a great encourager of generations of Irish poets and prose writers, someone who was alert to, and adept at, creating the space for work by new writers to appear in a time of official and unofficial censorship and financial austerity.

Marcus was just 22 when he launched a literary quarterly called *Irish Writing*, which he ran from 1946 to 1954. As is often the case with people who have a major impact on Irish life, he was an outsider. Not only was he unknown when he started out, but he was based in what literary circles in Dublin and London viewed as a provincial city. Indeed, when he began to edit the first issue of *Irish Writing*, he was still so closeted in Cork's small Jewish community that he had never set foot under a non-Jewish roof. Furthermore, he was a teetotaller during a period when most literary circles revolved around pubs, where the vindictiveness which passed for repartee meant that—as the poet, Patrick MacDonogh wrote—'For the quick coinage of a laugh / We cut, to make wit's reputation / Our total of two friends by half.'

Yet, undeterred by his outsider status, Marcus wanted not just to find new writers but to provide an Irish platform for established writers who were published abroad and banned at home. Reading that Liam O'Flaherty (at the height of his fame following John Ford's adaptation of his novel, *The Informer*) had arrived home from America to stay at the Gresham Hotel in Dublin, Marcus hesitantly called to the hotel's reception. He did not expect to be summoned up to the writer's room, let alone to be instantly promised a new story. When the subject of payment came up, O'Flaherty (his face covered in lather as he shaved) told the apprentice editor that 'whatever you're paying the others will do me'. Three weeks later O'Flaherty sent a telegram from his native Aran Islands: '*Story ready. Send money.*' With borrowed money Marcus paid for the story and received one of O'Flaherty's masterpieces, 'The Touch'.

Another unexpected manuscript arrived by post. James Stephens—the diminutive working-class Dubliner to whom was entrusted the task of finishing *Finnegans Wake*, if Joyce did not live to do so—sent Marcus 'A Rhinoceros, Some Ladies and a Horse'. The accompanying note suggested that the story 'wasn't half-bad', but if the young editor did not like it he was free to send it back. The young Corkonian loved it and arranged to meet Stephens in London to present him with a copy of the inaugural issue of *Irish Writing*. Stephens laughed when Marcus asked in a phone conversation how he would recognise him when they arranged to meet outside a café in Piccadilly. 'That's simple,' Stephens said. 'I'll be the smallest man you've ever seen.'

Even Samuel Beckett (whose 1934 collection *More Pricks than Kicks* was admired by Marcus) replied to a letter, sent via his French publisher, to generously say that as soon as he wrote anything reasonable the young man could have first refusal. In private, Beckett's spirit of generosity did not extend to his opinion of the first issue of *Irish Writing*, with Beckett rather grouchily complaining to his French publisher that 'I do not feel like giving them anything. The whole thing is genuinely sickening. A short story by James Stephens, that you would not wipe yourself with. Despicable old gnome.'

Seeing as the only Irish poetry that Beckett championed at this time was the bold modernism of Brian Coffey and Denis Devlin, it is unlikely that Marcus's editorial (which described Irish poetry as 'half a gypsy as she goes her way, with a pose of wildness, into the world') would have appealed to Beckett. But, despite his reservations, Beckett soon sent Marcus an extract from his unpublished novel, *Watt*, telling his French publisher: 'I could find nothing less scandalising, and yet I do not think that it will ever get taken on there.' Beckett was wrong to think that Marcus would not publish it, and despite his initial misgivings, he was still willing to support the new magazine. The only Irish writer to refuse the young Corkonian was the cantankerous George Bernard Shaw, whose postcard in reply contained one single word written in huge letters: 'NO'.

Others were more forthcoming, and Marcus successfully solicited work from writers as diverse as Kate O'Brien, Mary Lavin, James Plunkett, a young Mary Beckett, the now unfairly neglected Mervyn Wall, Valentin Iremonger, Patrick Kavanagh, Flann O'Brien, Michael McLaverty, Donagh MacDonagh and numerous others. He was fortunate in being assisted by a business partner and co-editor—his sometimes overlooked friend, Terence Smith. The 28 issues they edited included one issue devoted to women writers—a rare gesture in an era when casual misogyny was the norm in Dublin literary circles.

The manuscript that the young Marcus most wanted came from Edith Somerville, then aged eighty-eight and living in Drishane House in Castletownshend. He was invited to visit her to collect it. The ninety-mile journey from Cork took four hours, with fuel so scare that Marcus later claimed that the freezing train ran on 'a mixture of coal-dust, peat and splinters of wood borrowed from the more outlying parts of the third-class carriages'. Not only was it his first time in a Big House, it was his first time inside a non-Jewish house. The host who met him—Somerville's nephew—was welcoming, but Marcus was so scared that he felt he could refuse nothing offered to him—including non-kosher meat and whiskey. Marcus had only ever seen whiskey drunk in cowboy films, so he drank the proffered drink in one gulp, startling his host and nearly knocking himself out. But he came away with the precious short story because many Irish writers recognised that, in a land of writers, Marcus was a rarer miracle—a fine editor who would champion them.

Two years after founding *Irish Writing*, Marcus started another journal, *Poetry Ireland*. The aim of this journal was to give Irish poets the type of platform he was already providing for fiction writers with *Irish Writing*. *Poetry Ireland* ran as a quarterly and consisted, on average, of approximately 26 pages; in total 19 issues were produced. The magazine was cognisant of national and international trends: issue 7 was devoted to American poets, while even Beckett would have approved of issue 10—a facto collection by Denis Devlin. Emerging names appear in other issues, including Pearse Hutchinson, Patrick Galvin, Thomas Kinsella, Richard Kell, Seán Lucy, Valentin Iremonger, Val Mulkerns and Anthony Cronin. Older writers like Samuel Beckett, Ewart Milne, Cecil Day Lewis and Blanaid Salkeld were happy to appear here, and foreign poets included e. e. cummings and William Carlos Williams.

It is hard to imagine the difficulties of keeping not one but two magazines afloat at that time, long before Arts Council subventions, in an era of paper shortages. At one stage the contemporary journal, *The Bell*, was printed on paper so badly recycled that the original print was visible beneath the new typesetting. This prompted its former editor, Sean O'Faoláin, to encourage readers to sell on their copies after reading them to help him reach a wider readership, because he could only print a limited number. *Poetry Ireland* also needed to cope with a crippling British trade ban, which meant that no copies of the magazine could be sold there, and to contend with censorious printers who would only agree to print a translation of Brian Merriman's acclaimed eighteenth-century poem, *The Midnight Court*, if three cuts were made to the text.

Print runs were small but publication allowed for a certain status. Anthony Cronin later recalled a fraught encounter with a hostile official in Franco's fascist Spain who only accepted his explanation that he was a visiting writer after a search of his possessions unearthed a copy of *Poetry Ireland* containing one of his poems. By 1952 finances were so grave that Marcus was forced to cease publishing *Poetry Ireland* as a separate entity; however he was able to keep the magazine's name alive by issuing nine more issues of it as a supplement in *Irish Writing*. Two years later, though, he was forced to give up *Irish Writing* also and to move to England.

By this time, Marcus's own stories had started to be published abroad, and in 1954 his debut novel, *To Next Year in Jerusalem*, appeared in London. Marcus moved to London in the same year, using any royalties from his novel to pay off the accumulated debts of *Irish Writing*. After years of scraping by while trying to keep *Irish Writing* afloat, he needed to seek employment and a steady wage. Thus, for the next thirteen years, he worked in an insurance company. Marcus's *Irish Writing* had lacked the crusading zeal of *The Bell* and it never gained the mythological status of John Ryan's better-resourced magazine, *Envoy*. But as late as 1982, Pearse Hutchinson wrote in *The Sunday Tribune* that 'There is a special small heaven for editors who pay their writers really well and promptly, and for that heaven, where there isn't ever likely to be any great lebensraum problem... the founders of *Irish Writing* are surely bound.' Not only did Marcus treat writers as professionals, and pay them on time (despite receiving little financial support to do so), he created several legacies that continue to this day.

Firstly, starting in 1962, the Dolmen Press (who published Marcus's translation of *The Midnight Court* in 1953) released seven annual editions of *Poetry Ireland*, with its editor, John Jordan, stressing the link with Marcus's magazine. This iteration of the magazine had the sort of financial backing through advertisements that Marcus could only have wished for. But despite this support, the journal petered out in 1968. A decade would pass before John F. Deane (another selfless crusader for poetry) rekindled the magazine name in 1978 with what was, at first, little more than a typed, photocopied newsletter. In time, this helped to launch the organisation that is now called Poetry Ireland, which has published the vibrant quarterly journal, *Poetry Ireland Review*, since 1981.

It is a step too far to say that if Marcus had not started his tiny poetry magazine in Cork in 1948, there would not now be a national poetry organisation of the same name. Deane is a dynamo who founded The Dedalus Press and undoubtedly others would have stepped into the breach. But my favourite line in *Ulysses* is where Bloom says that 'a revolution must come on the due instalments plan'. Marcus was among those who paid the early instalments.

And secondly, *Irish Writing* didn't simply die out after Marcus left for London in the mid-1950s. In 1968 he returned to Ireland, with an even more radical plan to transform the magazine into its most famous incarnation, 'New Irish Writing'. His plan was simple and ingenious. It allowed someone like me, growing up in a working-class area, which back then did not even possess a public library, to be exposed to new stories by writers like Edna O'Brien and John McGahern. It also allowed me to dream not only of being a writer, but of becoming a published one.

This standalone page within a national newspaper would not have had the same impact if Marcus had succeeded with his initial plan to persuade the more exclusive, upmarket *Irish Times* to carry it. Although my seafaring father read *The Irish Times* avidly in his later years, in the 1970s it was a bird of rarely spotted plumage in Finglas. Most working-class families read either *The Irish Press* or *Irish Independent*. Thankfully Marcus was intercepted by two forward-thinking *Irish Press* journalists, Tim Pat Coogan and Sean McCann, who offered him the space in which 'New Irish Writing' thrived from 1968 to 1988.

Marcus's 'New Irish Writing' launched a new generation of

prose writers as diverse as Neil Jordan, Patrick McCabe, Deirdre Madden, Anne Devlin, and the superb, Ita Daly, whom Marcus later married. It also provided a crucial weekly outlet for new generations of Irish poets. The late Gerald Dawe appeared in its pages when barely out of his teens, with work published under the name G. C. Dawe. And I can still the recall the excitement of having an early poem of my own published in 1976, while I was still a schoolboy.

In addition to the spur that only publication can bring, though, 'New Irish Writing' proved a good education for me in the necessity of learning to accept rejection as part of a writer's life. Having published one of my early stories and a poem, Marcus rejected everything I sent for years afterwards. Indeed, it was only after his retirement in 1987, when Anthony Glavin briefly steered the page before *The Irish Press* capsized, that my name appeared in the 'New Irish Writing' page again. Rereading the early work I sent Marcus, I think he was largely right, and it never affected our friendship.

'New Irish Writing' disappeared from *The Irish Press* in 1988, but once again the flame that Marcus lit as a young man in Cork continues to burn. The mantle of editor has been taken up for the past thirty-five years by another great enthusiast and nurturer of new talent, Ciaran Carty. I have acted as an advisor to Ciaran for most of this period, during which, despite innumerable difficulties, the seed that was planted by Marcus continues to grow. Our initial home was *The Sunday Tribune*. When that paper collapsed in 2011 we moved to the *Irish Independent*. Then, under pressure from Hennessy cognac, who sponsored an award associated with the page, we moved to *The Irish Times*. However, when Hennessy changed from being a wine-geese family with Irish roots to simply becoming another international brand, they diverted their sponsorship elsewhere. *The Irish Times* pulled the plug and our long journey seemed finally to be over.

But there is a magic and serendipity to the 'New Irish Writing' page. When we lost our space in *The Irish Times*, I had a phone call from Tom Coogan—an *Irish Independent* journalist, and the son of Tim Pat Coogan. Tom followed in his father's footsteps by working behind the scenes to create the conditions that allowed us to return to the *Irish Independent*. That paper has been hugely supportive to Ciaran as he continues to edit the latest incarnation of the magazine that Marcus founded nearly eighty years ago.

As for David Marcus, after *The Irish Press* folded, he continued to edit numerous anthologies of Irish writing. His last anthology from Faber, *The Faber Book of Best New Irish Short Stories, 2006–7*, showed that, even if in poor health in his early eighties, he remained a connoisseur of excellence and an astute encourager of talent.

He published two successful novels in the 1980s (one set in Cork's small Jewish community during the War of Independence), a short-story collection, and two volumes of autobiography, including *Oughtobiography: Leaves from the Diary of a Hyphenated Jew*, in which he explored the complexities of balancing his Jewish and Irish heritages. He also continued to love meeting writers.

In his final decade I met Marcus on many occasions, generally for coffee in Wynn's Hotel in Dublin. I have vivid recollections of always finding this elegantly dressed elderly gentleman patiently waiting on the front steps, umbrella and black leather gloves in hand, smiling shyly in greeting. Often he spoke of the stroke, some years previously, that had started to curtail his life. He had been meeting another writer when that writer had noticed that something was amiss and urged him to go straight home and to see a doctor. The damage caused by the stroke gradually impeded Marcus's daily life. Yet, when it came to literature, he could still bring his old focus to words on the page. During one meeting, he said he had underestimated the amount of material he had commissioned for what was to be his last anthology, and he asked if I had something for him to consider. I gave him a very short short story. When we met again, not only had he read the story and liked it, but he had a page of notes with suggestions for small, judicious edits. It revealed the same attention to detail that he had shown when accepting a story of mine when I was a schoolboy. I had published various novels in various languages in the intervening decades, yet that moment of completing the circle, with Marcus once again making tiny edits to a story of mine, thirty years on, felt as satisfying as any of those publishing deals.

Perhaps this was because he was such a fixture of my childhood and the childhood of writers of my generation, the person we bombarded with our early stories and poems and dreams. As the poet Eiléan Ní Chuilleanáin noted after his death, Marcus 'published the work, especially the early work, of, it seems, almost every poet now publishing in Ireland'. She remembered him as 'always gracious, interested especially in promoting the unknown, sometimes the unformed, writers of the future. His courage, patriotism, his glad quest for the unorthodox and unexpected, his dedication, set a standard for the literary life.'

Each time we met was a pleasure, but—because of his stroke—on each occasion he could recall fewer of his remarkable memories. Yet he openly confronted the fact that his memory was fading with absolute honestly and characteristic dignity, acceptance and intelligence. In 2005, as part of an event for Cork City Libraries, I brought Marcus to Cork and, during a long dinner conversation, established what stories he still remembered. This allowed us to have a flawless public conversation the next day. This so mesmerised the City Librarian that she commissioned the film maker Pat Collins to travel to Dublin and record us recreating this conversation. Sadly, during the six months it took to set up this film, many of those memories were lost. Once the cameras began to roll, I realised that we needed to make an entirely different film.

In Pat Collins's short, moving film, Marcus holds a volume of his autobiography and confesses to having no recollection of writing it. With another person it might have felt like a tragic moment, but there was such innate dignity within Marcus that this felt like a rich human moment. He was showing us by example how to accept—with steadfast intelligence and humility—the fact that this is how life's journey might go, not just for him but for thousands of us who, as we grow old, will find familiar words slipping away. What began as a film about his memories of youth became a film about the dignity of ageing.

But Marcus had one last discovery to make. For six decades he loved to experience the thrill of encountering a fresh voice, a new writer who lights up your imagination with a shock of recognition and a sense that the essence of your inner self has been captured by another. It was sad but in another sense joyful and fitting that his last literary discovery, made in the closing years of his life, were the poems of a poet who spoke directly to him: a young Jewish poet growing up in Cork during the war.

While sorting through his study, Marcus found an envelope untouched for years that contained a hundred typewritten poems. They read like the work of a young man. He had no idea who the author was, although the poems moved him deeply. Only after reading them all did he discover, from the typed name on the last page, that the author was in fact himself. These were the poems he wrote when he was young.

His stroke had robbed him of any recollection of having written these poems. But, having discovered so many other writers, he could now discover himself: the Jewish boy fearing a Nazi invasion; the young man determined to establish a magazine for Irish writers; the nervous youth once dispatched to *The Irish Times* offices by Frank O'Connor with instructions to tell the literary editor that O'Connor was demanding that the newspaper publish a poem that had shyly been shown to him.

I can recall Marcus's excitement when he showed me these poems, his trademark smile after reading one aloud. In 2007 I arranged for this treasure trove of lost poems to be published by New Island, under the title *Lost and Found*, with an introduction by George O'Brien. If their discovery was wonderful for an old man who found his younger self in an envelope tidied away years before, it was also wonderful for poets who had been aided by Marcus to discover this other side of him—the sensitive young wordsmith dreaming of fame who would generously spend his life helping others to achieve it.

It was impossible to be in his company and not feel enriched. It was impossible not to visit the home he shared with his wife, Ita Daly—who cared for him so well in those difficult years—without feeling the love that existed between them. Life stripped away his memories, but literature has preserved them. His words live on in his books. But his generosity and dedication means that the words of dozens of other writers also live on, young poets who sent him work for sixty years, writers whom he encouraged by giving them the courage to push on with their dreams.

His death robbed Ireland of a champion of literature, an encourager of generations of Irish writers, someone who created space for writers in times of censorship and financial austerity. But the continued existence of *Poetry Ireland Review* and 'New Irish Writing' carries on the journey of that young man who nervously set out for Castletownshend to seek out a story from Edith Somerville, with no idea of the great odyssey he was embarking on.

David Marcus

A Visit to Drishane House

from Oughtobiography, *Chapter Eight*

High on my list of favourite Irish short stories ever since I had first read them were the Somerville and Ross *Irish R.M.* collections, and there was no doubt in my mind that if I could have a contribution from Edith Somerville in the first issue of *Irish Writing*, it would be the jewel in the crown. But she was then eighty-eight and I had no idea what her state of health might be, so when I wrote to her at her Castletownshend home, Drishane House, I was fully prepared for a polite refusal. The reply, however, was not from her but from her nephew, Sir Neville Coghill, the Chaucer authority and Oxford don, who was at the time on holiday at Castletownshend. He wrote that his aunt would be happy to discuss my request with me and he invited me to Drishane House to meet her. He went on to say that if I were travelling by train I would have to stay with him overnight as the only train arrived at Skibbereen, the nearest station, at an hour after Dr Edith would have retired. I didn't have a car, and anyway couldn't drive, so the train and an overnight stay it would have to be.

The prospect appalled me. It had never occurred to me that my letter could lead to having to meet and talk with such a literary icon as Edith Somerville, but as the purpose of the visit was only to get her to contribute to the inaugural issue of *Irish Writing*, after a few days the prospect became more exciting than daunting. Unfortunately, the lapse of time allowed the other prospect—

the overnight stay with such an august literary personage as Neville Coghill—to become the real terror. How would I possibly maintain any extended, serious conversation with an Oxford don and authority on Chaucer, of whose work I was totally ignorant? He would not be expecting. to have on his hands a mere callow youth presenting himself as the editor of a projectedly important literary periodical. I would be exposed as an impostor, a humbug, a charlatan. And altogether apart from conversation, what about comportment? How did one behave in such surroundings? What was the protocol at table? What should I wear, for God's sake? I, who had never in my life been inside a non-Jewish home, and here I was, galloping headlong into the Big House of Irish literature. It was a situation which Leopold Bloom, with some help from Joyce, might have handled, but Leopold Bloom I was not. However, there was no alternative. I had had to write to Sir Neville accepting his kind invitation.

From my home in Cork the train journey to Skibbereen was only ninety miles but it took almost four hours. World War II might have ended, but the Emergency, Ireland's ironic euphemism for that little altercation somewhere off its shores, was still in force, so fuel was scarce and trains were running on what the wags called a mixture of coal-dust, peat, and splinters of wood borrowed from the more outlying parts of the third-class carriages. It was a long and very cold four hours; which I made longer by spending the whole time worrying. The only consolation I could think of—and to call it consolation was a triumph of self-delusion—was that once I was met at the station by Sir Neville, I would be so busy trying to create an impression that I'd have no more time for angst.

Immediately the train puffed to a stop I was out on the platform looking for my host. But this, surely, couldn't be Sir Neville—a small, jarveyish man, touching his cap and stretching his hand out for my little travelling case?

'Mr Marcus?' he enquired in a soft, country voice.

I nodded uncertainly.

'Follow me, sir,' and he led the way.

Ah, of course, the car, with Sir Neville, would be waiting outside the station.

But there was no car there, only a small, round, horse-and-trap affair, like a tub on wheels—and no Sir Neville in it. My guide opened the little door, put in my bag, handed me up and hopped onto the seat in front. Jogging the horse into motion, he said, 'Sir Neville is waiting for you in the house, sir.'

As we jolted and bounced over the miles I tried to keep calm but panic mounted inside me as we drew nearer our destination. I essayed a few conversational sentences. The weather allowed a speculative comment or two. Then our conveyance—'I bet the horse is used to this journey. He seems to take it easily,' I said. It was an even more inane remark than I suspected. 'Aye,' was the considered reply, 'she's a good oul' mare, is Nancy.' I said no more.

At last we turned into the drive of Drishane House and eased to a stop at the open door where my host immediately materialised. Though I had, of course, seen many pictures of Edith Somerville, I had never seen one of her nephew. I had imagined a dryish, donnish, smallish man. I found before me a giant, large-boned, long-handed, big-headed—a man so tall that his shoulders seemed slightly rounded from continued bending to communicate with his fellow-men.

Even more striking was his face—I couldn't help immediately bringing to mind that old Frankenstein of the cinema, Boris Karloff; a warm, friendly, smiling, even good-looking Boris Karloff, to be sure, but withal a Boris Karloff. Sir Neville betrayed no surprise at my extreme youth but politely showed me to my room, intimating that as soon as I was ready I could come down for a spot of food.

I was now so worried that I had to sit on the edge of the bed to cool off. How long should I delay? Three minutes? Five? Ten? Even before I could decide, there was a knock on the door. 'Ready?' said my host, as he opened it and stooped in. I sprang up and accompanied him, feeling as if I was taking my last walk. Going downstairs he told me that his mother, Lady Coghill, and the other guests and family were in the village, attending the cinema, and would be back late. I heaved a sigh. At least that was something I did not have to face immediately. We entered the dining room. 'I've eaten already,' he said, 'so I'll just sit and talk with you while you have your dinner.'

Dinner, I could see, was cold meat—and that faced me with my first dilemma. As an orthodox Jew I had never eaten non-kosher meat. What should I do? The ordeal of having to keep up a literary conversation with Sir Neville was giving me enough to think about without affronting him at the outset by rejecting his food. I decided to swallow the meat along with one of the fundamental taboos of my upbringing.

If only that had proved to be my only problem! No sooner was I seated at the table than my host's first words struck terror into my very entrails.

'You'll have a drink?' he murmured, and for the first time I spotted a tumbler flanked by a bottle of Paddy, its regimental stance and golden glitter played on by the vying lights of a palatial chandelier and sparklingly reflected in the array of highly polished silver, like rows of Royal Horseguards, on either side of the placemat before me. The bottle was already in Sir Neville's hand. 'You'll have a drink?' had really been more statement than question, a conventional politeness to which—so his manner suggested—an affirmative answer was taken for granted.

But, alas, I was an exception. Not only had my Jewish home been strictly kosher as regards food, it had also been strictly non-alcoholic. When I was eight I had found an empty stout bottle and, smelling it, had recoiled almost in a dead faint. The memory never left me and resulted in my never taking a drink in my life. I had never even seen the inside of a pub!

But this was one challenge I couldn't dare reject. I might look a mere youth but I was now playing the role of a literary bloke, and I knew that by reputation any literary bloke worth his salt was supposed to be able to take his liquor. Here was a chance, perhaps the only chance I might have in this company, to separate the man from the boy in me. The whole success of my venture into the Big House would surely depend on the impression I created on Dr Edith's nephew. I couldn't fail for the want of a bit of stomach lining.

The bottle was still being held over the glass. 'Thank you,' I said, trying to suggest by my tone that Sir Neville's hesitation hadn't really been necessary.

The whiskey began to chug into the tumbler.

'Say when,' I heard.

The instruction froze my already panic-stricken mind. When was 'when'? I didn't know. How much would be seemly as well as making the right effect? A quarter tumbler was surely too little, a half tumbler too much. Something in between? 'When,' I jerked out, by which time I had rather more than half a glass.

I pretended nothing but nonchalantly started my meal. Inwardly, however, I was frenziedly debating the next nerve-wracking problem: At what stage does one drink the whiskey? At the start of the meal? At the end? In the middle?

Sir Neville gave me what I thought might be a clue. 'Some water?' he enquired. If the drinking were to be later, he would have delayed that, I told myself. Then I must drink now. But water? Did one take water with whiskey? Surely only immature novices would dare insult such an ancient and aristocratic beverage. In a moment of inspiration I casually covered the glass with my hand and shook my head.

'Certain?' asked Sir Neville. I should have been warned by the strange note in his voice but I was too distracted by yet another dilemma. How did one drink whiskey—in sips or in one swallow? My memory was full of tough-looking, guntoting screen. cowboys who jerked their heads back and drained their glasses at a gulp. Naturally, that was it. Sir Neville was eyeing me. I steeled myself, raised the glass to my lips and downed the drink in a single swallow—then bent to resume my meal.

Nothing happened for perhaps two and a half seconds and I was beginning to congratulate myself on the discovery of a wonderful, unsuspected talent. Then I seemed both to feel and hear something strike the wall behind me. It was the back of my head.

While it was slowly resuming its normal shape I sat speechless, almost transfixed. I could have been one of those Pompeian inhabitants, overtaken even at his meal by the stream of lava and fixed for ever in that common posture. A fountain of fire was shooting up inside me and my face burned like a radiator: I couldn't move—I dared not move! It was as if the room and everything in it were held steady only by my paralytic stillness, and that the very slightest motion on my part would set the whole place in a mad whirl. I could apprehend my host looking at me with a close, wide-eyed stare, evidently wondering if I was still conscious. I was—but only just. By a supreme effort of will I was hypnotising myself into maintaining sobriety. It was the only thing I could think of doing.

Slowly a modicum of self-control returned. I choked back a desire to cough, manfully prohibited my eyes from watering, and offhandedly resumed my meal. Sir Neville's own responses were not, for a few moments, altogether smooth, and he seemed in some doubt. Then after a pause he lifted the bottle again and said, 'Care for another?' But like every good magician, I knew better than to perform one's *pièce de résistance* twice before the same audience. I politely declined, managing, I think, to imply that I really could do it again but wouldn't be such a hog as to do so on his whiskey. Sir Neville didn't press me. He replaced the bottle with a somewhat regretful expression, as if he was sorry he hadn't observed more closely when he had the chance.

Not surprisingly, I have absolutely no recollection of the rest of our conversation. Presumably some conversation of sorts did take place, but whatever remained of my mental processes had other things to worry about. What further terrors would I have to undergo when Lady Coghill and her guests would return from the village? O bedtime, bless├⌐d bedtime! Could I survive until then, or would I collapse in the middle of the house-party festivities and be ignominiously packed off first thing in the morning without even seeing Dr Edith?

The return of Lady Coghill and her guests was akin to an invasion. They seemed to number anything up to thirty people between young and old, but possibly in my still muzzy state I was seeing double. Lady Coghill greeted me with friendliness and even a touch of deference, a mixture no doubt calculated to put me at my ease but in fact having the very opposite effect. The resemblance between her and Sir Neville was striking, the same big build and the same Karloffian appearance, without Sir Neville's stoop but including his charming smile. She didn't burden me with introductions, simply throwing my name out to the general assembly. But Sir Neville included me in older conversation groups that immediately came together, seeming to be made up mostly of family members. He would quietly identify for me whoever held the floor at any one moment. More often than not it was a Somerville from the Royal Navy, giving me in my confused state the impression that the place was awash with Admirals of the Fleet. In keeping me from the younger guests I suspect that, having during the few hours we had spent together gauged my limitations and knowing what diversions were planned, he was saving me embarrassment.

Certainly I could not have made any contribution to the histrionics that followed, a succession of erudite charades based largely on classical allusions, Greek to me, sometimes literally as well as metaphorically. This went on to general hilarity and applause with apparently inexhaustible energy and imagination until Sir Neville bent to whisper in my ear that breakfast would be at nine o'clock, after which he would take me to Dr Edith, adding that the high spirits would probably continue for some time, so if

I was tired after my long journey no one would mind if I slipped quietly up to bed. Feeling overcome with relief and gratitude, I thanked him for his consideration and bade him goodnight. Boris Karloff he certainly was not.

I slept heavily through the night, remembering just before I dropped off to repeat to my mind the order, 'Wake at eight, wake at eight,' hoping my newly found gift of self-hypnosis wouldn't let me down. It didn't, and I was able to present myself in the breakfast room at exactly nine o'clock.

Sir Neville was sitting at the table, evidently not yet having eaten and with no food in front of him, though the handful of the older male family members present were happily munching away. I noted that none of the younger people had yet put in an appearance.

'Good morning,' my host greeted. 'Sleep well?'

'Yes, thank you. Capital!' I replied, hoping I was striking the right note.

'How about a little walk first?' he suggested. 'Give us an appetite.'

On one side of the room large French doors were open onto a very extensive garden with a beautifully manicured lawn. No doubt a pre-breakfast constitutional was *de rigeur*, so I stepped out with him, though to keep pace with his Gulliverian steps required unused-to effort on my part.

'I was re-reading the *Irish R.M.* stories recently,' I said, choosing my ground. I had a good knowledge of the stories, and had quickly decided to lead the conversation and play to my strength with my opening gambit. That should keep me out of deep water and possibly earn me some brownie points into the bargain. We exchanged views and preferences, did one circuit of the lawn and arrived back at the breakfast room. The array of food laid out in trays, bowls and covered dishes on a long sideboard, though momentarily taking me aback, presented me with no new problems.

'What do you fancy? There's...'

'No thank you, Sir Neville,' I cut in confidently, 'I never eat breakfast. Just tea and toast is all I ever have.'

My host raised his eyebrows at this non-breakfast—which in truth was my normal one—but made no comment, probably deciding that such exiguousness in the intake of food was no more freakish than might be expected from someone with the capacity for whiskey that I had demonstrated.

After breakfast Sir Neville accompanied me to meet Edith Somerville, who lived in a house of her own in the grounds. He brought me into her studio, introduced me and departed.

Though in her mid-eighties, Edith Somerville still possessed the brightness and mental agility of a woman in her prime, and her charm—evidently a family gift—was magnetic. She was ensconced in a large armchair at the far end of the studio, a long, wide, many-windowed room of brown panelling, the walls like those of a picture gallery prepared for an exhibition, so many were the pictures that covered them. Seeing me gaze about in some awe, she smiled and said, 'Look around, do, before we have our talk.'

I dutifully examined 'the pictures nearest me, paintings delicately coloured, drawings and sketches, photographs of streets and outdoor scenes.

'Now sit here.' She motioned with her stick to the chair opposite her.

'One could spend hours admiring all these,' I said quite sincerely, for though I had been aware that as a young woman she had studied art, I had never seen any of her work. Gracefully she inclined her head in acknowledgement of my appreciation. Obviously the subject was dear to her, for she was happy to spend almost the first hour of our conversation talking about art and music—at least she talking and I listening as she regaled me with stories of her days as an art student in Paris.

'Now tell me about this *Irish Writing* of yours,' she eventually invited. I told her about my love of literature, of my plans and ambitions, and named some of the famous Irish writers who had already agreed to support the periodical. She seemed happy with my outline and to my delight promised to send me something.

'Nothing very exciting, you understand. Perhaps a piece about my collaboration with dear Martin Ross. Not that there can be anything in it that I haven't said before. Would that suit you?'

I told her what it would mean to the success of *Irish Writing* to have such a distinguished contribution in the first issue. She waved my comment aside, then picking up a book from a small table beside her, opened it at its title page, took up her pen and said, 'I'll sign this as a present for you. One of my more recent efforts.'

As she finished signing I was about to hand her a blotter that was placed nearby, but she quickly forestalled me, saying, 'No, never blot a signature. Let it dry naturally, just like a sentence ending.' The book was *The Sweet Cry of Hounds*.

Then 'Come with me,' she said, rising and tapping me with her stick. 'It's such a lovely morning.'

She rang a bell, had her pony and trap brought out and took me on a descriptive tour through her beloved countryside. On our return, Sir Neville again materialised to greet us, and Dr Edith bade me goodbye, saying, 'I hope you enjoyed that. At least it should fortify you for your horrible journey back to Cork.' It did, it and my memories of a very kind and wonderful lady. I returned home knowing full well how fortunate I had been to have met and talked with a writer of such nobility and fame. I had the feeling that the future of *Irish Writing* could not be more promising.

Louis Marcus

My Brother David

There were five of us: three brothers, of whom David was the third, my sister Nella, and myself. We lived in an end-of-terrace three-bedroom house on the tree-lined Mardyke Walk, ten minutes on foot from the city centre. Across the road was a stream, then the green expanse of Cork's cricket ground backed by the heights of affluent Sunday's Well, its gardens sloping down to the River Lee. It was an idyllic setting.

David was twelve years older than me, and he used to complain jokingly that my arrival shortly before his thirteenth birthday robbed him of a proper Barmitzvah party. For we belonged to a small Jewish community of fifty or so families where everyone knew everyone else. That's usually called close-knit, though some could find it claustrophobic.

Our grandparents had come to Ireland from Lithuania in the 1880s as part of the massive flight of East European Jews from Czarist persecution. Our parents, one born in Dublin and the other in Limerick, were fully integrated into Irish life, but preserved the core of traditional Jewish observance. We kept a kosher home, and our father attended synagogue weekly. But, as he put it in his parents' Yiddish vernacular, we weren't *meshugah frum*—crazy religious.

David claimed that even as a boy he became sceptical about religion. Yet he preserved throughout his life a strong sense of Jewish identity, which infused two of his novels and his book of short stories. This was characteristic of our generation, reared as we were under the dark weight of historical Jewish persecution, reinforced by the contemporary horror of the Nazis.

Ireland had been the least antisemitic of European nations. The Limerick outbreak of 1904 that sent our mother and most of that community fleeing, while deplorable, was not comparable to the long and bloody history of pogroms elsewhere. Nevertheless, racist myths about Jews were then the norm throughout the Western world. And in a stagnant Ireland that looked with envy at the Fascist resurgence of Germany, antisemitic jibes were not uncommon. Also, in a country that was 95% Catholic, and conspicuously devotional at that, having a different Sabbath, holy days, dietary laws and language of prayer inevitably imposed a sense of otherness on a small religious minority.

Perhaps that also helped to make our house unusually liberal for its time. Like most of their generation, our parents had no more than primary education. But they had an innate openness of mind that made for free discussion. My brothers read *The New Statesman and Nation*, an English left-wing weekly of politics, ideas and the arts. And while our father devoured *The Cork Examiner* and *The Evening Echo*, we also took *The Irish Times*. I still remember the blazoned front-page headlines when Noël Browne broke the scandal of the Mother and Child Scheme's suppression.

Our father, a trained glass-cutter, worked with a man and a boy in a ramshackle former coach-house whence they supplied endless thousands of framed holy pictures to shops across Munster. Sacred Hearts, Perpetual Succours and Papal Blessings were among the favourites, and at one stage there was a vogue for images of the much-loved black saint, Martin de Porres.

At that time, we would probably have been called middle class. But we never had a car; I can remember when we finally got a fridge; and a phone was installed only when all my siblings had emigrated to London and our parents wanted to talk to them once a week. Maybe that is partly why my father was able to put us all through secondary school, not free in those days, and all the boys through UCC, which was also fee-paying.

Ours was a very musical home. Like many of their generation, our parents loved opera, and they came to know the repertoire well from the annual visits of two English touring companies to the Cork Opera House. My father would sometimes hum, and my mother sing, their favourite arias (she had a bit of a voice). In the kitchen, where we ate and mostly lived, there was a large valve radio that we called 'the wireless', and, apart from the news, it was constantly tuned to symphony concerts from around Europe. We also had a wind-up gramophone with steel needles, and a large collection of shellac 78rpm records—classical, operatic and Jewish cantorial.

We were all given the opportunity to learn one or more instruments, and there was a baby grand piano in the drawing room. Despite a certain nervousness in performance, David became an accomplished pianist. His lifelong favourite was Mozart's D Minor Piano Concerto, of which he mastered the first two movements. My sister Nella, studying to be a music teacher, scored the orchestral accompaniment for two violins. With her on First Violin and me on Second, we performed the Mozart piece with David several times for our own private pleasure.

One thing that both David and I inherited from our father was a passion for sport, though I didn't share their interest in horse racing. They weren't gamblers; the stakes were always modest. But they loved the daily flutter that challenged the probabilities of horses' form, and the schemes of trainers.

Even in sport, however, the sectarian norms of the time prevailed. In the cricket ground across the road from us, most of the teams were Catholic; one, called C of I, was for Protestants; and I played for a club which accepted all sorts. This voluntary ghettoisation arose from a universal dread of intermarriage, whereby at least one of the families involved would feel the pain of tribal loss.

The Cork Jewish Youth Association tried to observe this norm, even in a dwindling community. We put together a motley soccer team to play a few friendlies in preparation for our annual game against the much stronger Dublin Jewish club, a match that often proved to be less than friendly. Only two or three of our team looked like footballers, and David was one of them. With his good looks and athletic build, he claimed the glamour position of centre forward—nowadays called the striker. I don't recall him scoring many goals, but he had one distinctive feature to his play. After five or ten minutes of each game, he would leave the pitch to be noisily sick on the side-line. He would then return, and play the rest of the match as though nothing had happened.

His role in table tennis was quite different. Our Jewish club had a team just about good enough to play in one of the lower Cork leagues. But David was well above that standard. He joined St Nick's, a club that must have accepted everyone, and became a regular Munster interprovincial. He also entered the national administration of the game, and ended as non-playing captain of Ireland. His choice not to play for the Jewish club would have taken a strong sense of independence at that time.

There were a lot of books in our house. Among them I still recall several bound volumes of a weekly part-series called *The Great War... I Was There!*, with horrific photos of trench misery and carnage. My mother had used gift coupons to buy uniform editions of Shakespeare, Dickens and H.G. Wells. My brothers, Bram and Elkan, as well as David, had a huge bookcase of paperbacks, mostly by modern authors. And there was regular traffic to and from the Cork City Library.

We knew that David had literary aspirations. So it was no surprise when, having declined to practise as a qualified barrister, he became a literary editor by founding *Irish Writing*, and later *Poetry Ireland*. He operated from a tiny room in our house, with just enough space for a table with a typewriter, and a few shelves.

He continued to write poetry, some of which was published— either original poems or translations from Gaelic poets of the eighteenth century. Then he discovered Seán Ó Ríordáin, an employee of Cork Corporation, and came to believe that here was a major modern poet who should be brought to the English-reading public. This enthusiasm was shared by Revd Coslett Quin, and it is ironic that the two main translators of this leading Irish language poet were a Protestant clergyman and a Jew.

Another highlight was David's racy translation of Brian Merriman's long poem of the eighteenth century, *Cúirt an Mheán Oíche / The Midnight Court*, in a sumptuous edition published by Liam Miller's Dolmen Press in 1953. We were particularly pleased that one of the first subscribers for the poem was Seán T. O'Kelly, then President of Ireland. The book would certainly have been banned, as Frank O'Connor's earlier version had been in 1945, but its high price and limited distribution kept it from the attentions of the Censorship of Publications Board.

In spite of the enormous prestige of *Irish Writing* and the publication of his first novel, *To Next Year in Jerusalem*, David had to face the reality that as a writer, or as an editor, he could not make a living in the Ireland of the 1950s, from which scores of thousands were emigrating. So he left for London where three of his siblings had already settled, two of them doctors and our sister in music administration. I was still at school in Cork, but we learned from his letters, and later by phone, that his law degree had helped him get a job in insurance. He studied in night classes, and rose to be a claims manager. There was no further talk of literature.

By 1960 I had settled in Dublin, in an Ireland where Seán Lemass had succeeded Éamon de Valera, where the economy was looking up, and where the winds of change were blowing. As I began to mix in artistic circles, everyone introduced to me would brighten when they heard I was David's brother—though none of them had ever met him! Then my parents left Cork and settled in London to be near the family. And whenever I went to see them, David was clearly vegetating.

In 1967, my wife, Chookie, and I urged him to visit us in our recently acquired house, and get a feel for the changed Ireland. He came, and such was the abiding reputation of *Irish Writing* that everywhere we went he was received as a kind of living legend. On one of these excursions we had lunch in Neary's of Chatham Street with Seán Mac Réamoinn. (I had a feeling it was maybe David's first time in a pub.) Seán was a master broadcaster, renowned for meeting last-minute deadlines, and a compassionate man. As we were finishing our chat, he asked if David could do him a favour. Seán had to edit that evening a radio programme of talks he was producing, and was short one piece. Could David write three or four minutes on anything at all, and a studio would be available to record it at five o'clock? When we left, an excited David raced to a nearby newsagent, bought an exercise book and a pencil, and repaired to St Stephen's Green to do his piece. I think that was the moment when he realised he could probably earn a living in Ireland as a freelance writer. So he took the plunge, settled back here, and got the inspired idea of a weekly newspaper page of 'New Irish Writing', which Tim Pat Coogan leapt at in *The Irish Press*. The rest is literary history.

Sometime later, I asked Seán about his appeal to David to write that radio talk. Did he really need the piece so urgently? Or was he shrewdly throwing David in at the deep end after years of inactivity? He gave me an enigmatic smile and said, 'A little bit of both.'

Katrina Goldstone

David Marcus's Cultural Forebears

One of my favourite toys as a child was a large teddy bear, which emitted a fake growl every time you patted its back. For years, I trailed that bear round with me on my various moves from country to country. The bear was given to me by my father's friend, Maurice Fridberg. He was a funny uncle in the best sense, one who goofed and clowned and always tried to make children laugh, being something of an overgrown child himself, with a special affection for Niall Tóibín. Sometimes, as a young girl, I would retreat to my father's den and leaf through a large book of moody black-and-white photography by 'Uncle Maurice', with scary photos of trees, twisted boughs like mythical creatures frozen in amber. It was an early attempt at eco-art, I suppose.

It was only when I was researching my book *Irish Writers and the Thirties* that I discovered 'Uncle Maurice's' other history as a promoter of culture and literature with his Hour-Glass Library. This was a short-lived imprint of the 1940s, which published Norah Hoult, Frank O'Connor, and Elizabeth Bowen, among others, between the covers of simple fleur-de-lis embossed boards. Like a number of Irish Jewish cultural figures in the 1930s, 1940s and 1950s, he promoted established and little-known writers, and introduced new strands of thinking; in 1962, he produced his book of tree photography *Life from the Trees: Photographic Impressions*. People like Maurice Fridberg, writer and anthologist Leslie Daiken, screenwriter and journalist Michael Sayers, gallery owner Victor Waddington, artists Estella Solomons and Harry Kernoff, and critic and cultural commentator A.J. (Con) Leventhal, they all preceded or overlapped with David Marcus. And they furnished Marcus with a distinguished and eclectic cultural lineage.

Michael Sayers and Leslie Daiken were Dublin-born Jewish writers who were anti-fascist through the 1930s and 1940s, and who sought to express their identities as Jews on the Left in very different ways, whilst also engaging with the broader cultural movements connected to anti-fascism and internationalism. Daiken was very much influenced by the American Jewish radicals, Joseph Freeman and Michael Gold, in his ideas about socially committed literature. His friend, Michael Sayers, a protégé of T.S. Eliot, moved to the United States in 1937, and, with Albert E. Kahn, published investigative reporting books in the war years, revealing the extent of prior Axis infiltration and antisemitic activity. Sayers later fell victim to the blacklisting fervour of the McCarthy years, which curtailed a promising career as a pioneer of television drama at NBC.

Daiken's 1936 anthology *Goodbye Twilight, Songs of the Irish Struggle* fused the idea of American socially conscious verse and Irish ballads, and gave an opportunity for first-time publication to Irish poets such as Charles Donnelly, Ewart Milne, Thomas O'Brien and Eileen Brennan. The collection was excoriated by some, and faintly praised by others. In the 1930s and 1940s, he turned to the vexed question of minority literary representation, resisting what Declan Kiberd, in another context, has described as 'the experience of being perpetually described and defined by others'. In 1939, Daiken began the first of many attempts to write about his Dublin Jewish childhood in a semi-autobiographical form, and the first of three extracts from this work was published in the influential Irish cultural periodical, *The Dublin Magazine*. Daiken sought to depict his own community on his own terms and to create an insider account which moved beyond condescension, whilst also seeking to combat antisemitic imagery.

Daiken was later encouraged by Samuel Beckett and Austin Clarke in his bid to write the Irish Jewish novel. Daiken and 'Con' Leventhal were both, in different ways, asserting a creative intellectual identity, and countering reductive, demeaning ideas about Jews, with their own representations of nuance. Leventhal's seminal essay, 'What It Means To be A Jew', was held over because of wartime censorship. It was therefore not published in Sean O'Faoláin's *The Bell* until 1946, just as the full horrors of the Nazi extermination programme were appearing in Pathé newsreels and in Irish newspapers.

In an obituary tribute to Daiken, Brian O'Neill of *The Irish Press* wrote, 'He was always busy, always trying to give some Irish writer a hand.' Daiken's obituaries, with scant mention of his leftwing past, cast him as a 'Dublin-Pickwickian' character, or an ersatz Leopold Bloom, though Yiddish Micawber seems more apt. Only one obituarist succeeded in capturing the many facets of Leslie Daiken's life, remembering him as 'a poet in the world of art, as a writer and worker in the political and social spheres'. None referred to Daiken's 30-year on–off struggle to write the definitive Irish-Jewish novel. So David Marcus got there first.

Sayers, Daiken's childhood friend, was an anti-fascist investigative reporter during the Second World War, and wrote on Fifth Column activity and antisemitism for publications in the United States and in Ireland. He also wrote a strange semi-allegorical short story about wartime Ireland and political allegiances, entitled 'The Neutrals', for *Harper's Bazaar*. Sayers roomed for a time with Eric Blair, better known under his penname George Orwell, and he was, like Orwell, a contributor to the *New English Weekly*. During the 1930s, he wrote reviews in culturally significant literary publications, like *The Criterion*, and he was part of the vibrant cultural scene of London in the interwar years. He not just shared accommodation with Orwell, he also mingled in Orwell's broader social circle. Sayers wrote an early review of Orwell's work for *The Adelphi*, in which he emphasised the brutalising aspects of British imperial rule as delineated by Orwell. He was one of the first critics who detected that fledgling development of Orwell's prose—the one that would become a defining feature of his writing—its 'limpid windowpane' quality.

Sayers and Daiken, both Dublin Jews on the Left in the era of fascism, sometimes disagreed politically, but in his diary in the post-war years Sayers wrote a touching pen portrait of his friend, admiring his integrity in the face of hostility.

Harry Kernoff's leftist roots were more proletarian, as his cabinet maker origins dictated: in this, he was following a tradition from the Bund to other strands of Jewish socialism. His visit to the USSR in the early 1930s with Hanna Sheehy Skeffington, on an official trip with the Friends of Soviet Russia, further opened him up to ideas about political art, and coincided with his production of a series of stark woodcuts on labour and anti-capitalist themes. En route to the USSR, he presented a woodcut of James Connolly to the crew of the *SS Cooperatizia*. With the woodcut 'Unemployed' he portrayed the stark tragedy of the man without work, and he supplied similar woodcut illustrations and portraits, including one of Roger Casement, to the left-wing *Republican Congress* newspaper.

Daiken and Sayers, Estella Solomons, and Leventhal, were all older than David Marcus, but they each represented different facets of an alternative cultural milieu for Leftist and liberal Jews who might find the conservatism of both Irish Catholic literary culture and the conformity of the Irish Jewish community somewhat stifling. They were also looking to broad European schools of thought and cultural pluralism at a time when the barbarians were at the gate. In the 1930s, in particular, dehumanising stereotypes of the rapacious 'capitalist Jew' or 'Bolshevik Jew' circulated not just in Nazi Germany but in the pages of Irish newspapers, religious publications, and sometimes in the course of Dáil debates.

It is no exaggeration to say that without the likes of Daiken and Leventhal, gallerist Victor Waddington, and David Marcus, the Irish cultural landscape in the mid-twentieth century would have looked very different, and much less diverse. Waddington not only represented modernist masters like Jack Yeats and Colin Middleton, he also brought the works of Jacob Epstein to Dublin in the 1940s. Leventhal also opened up the area of literary and theatre criticism and brought in European influences, both in his translation work and as a key champion of Beckett, penning one of the first reviews of *En Attendant Godot*. He expressed reservations about Marcus's novel *To Next Year in Jerusalem*, when he reviewed it in 1954. In the end, for people like Daiken and Sayers, exile was the answer to being a minority within a minority in the Irish Free State and that, in part, contributed to their erasure from the Irish cultural record.

Although Estella Solomons is repeatedly referred to as a portraitist of Republicans on the run, there is no appreciation of the significance of her own self-portraits, and their place among the canon of Jewish women daring to present and interpret themselves. As the stories of Jewish women are so rarely told in the context of Irish Jewish history, partly because there are so few archival sources, Solomons' paintings and drawings of herself must stand in as a temporary tribute to many other Jewish women in Ireland who are now lost to history. (Cork-born novelist Betty Miller and Hannah Berman can also feature on the too-brief cultural history of Irish Jewish women.) In addition, the salons she hosted with her husband, James Starkie, tapped into European models of intellectual exchange and café culture.

Solomons' and Kernoff's self-portraits, Leventhal's essay 'What It Means to Be A Jew', Daiken's autobiographical excerpts and radio play, *The Circular Road*: each of these texts, in their own way, played with ideas of Jewish representation. Although it might be forgotten today, this group of Irish Jewish writers and artists foreshadowed Marcus's extraordinary influence on Irish literary culture as a cultural enabler and a broker. Most, to a greater or lesser degree, sought to express an Irish Jewish viewpoint in all its complexity, presenting a resistance to the then pervasive dehumanising stereotypes of Jews, stereotypes so versatile in their 'plasticity' and in their shapeshifting adaptation to any political or economic context, whether it be anti-communism or Nazi ideology.

Marcus's enormous contribution to Irish literature has somewhat overshadowed his own attempts at Jewish self-expression, which rests not only with the three novels that he wrote (*To Next Year in Jerusalem, A Land Not Theirs,* and *A Land in Flames*), but also with various short stories, including the revealingly titled collection *Who Ever Heard of an Irish Jew?* In another of Marcus's stories, the early story 'A Jolson Story' (1955), which used the death of the singer Al Jolson as a catalyst for a Jewish boy experiencing doubt about faith, Marcus also created a pen portrait of the long-suffering sister which gives an albeit very brief insight into the fate of some Jewish women—voices and opinions we hardly ever hear in an Irish Jewish context. Within the pages of *Oughtobiography*, Marcus was clear-eyed about his own efforts, sanguine even, and he made crystal clear both his intent in writing his books, and his sense of failure:

> Primarily my material was my identity as a Jew and the subjective conflicts that engendered. Not—very definitely not—that I regretted the Jewishness of being a Jew. What I regretted was my inability to transform my material—my identity and its consequential ever-present feeling of rootlessness—into great literature.

Despite writing a best-seller, and even though he was popularly lauded, Marcus could not but judge himself harshly.

Today, with initiatives like Breaking Ground Ireland and Black & Irish, a new generation of hyphenated Irish writers are transforming their 'material', speaking up and staking a claim, just as, decades earlier, Leslie Daiken, Estella Solomons, Harry Kernoff, Michael Sayers, and Con Leventhal, and then Gerald Davis, Louis Marcus, Louis Lentin, and David Marcus did. In a contemporary context, Marcus's importance as a cultural visionary, and his legacy as an author and an editor, acts as both a beacon and an inspiration.

David Marcus
A Jolson Story

from Irish Writing 30 *(March 1955)*

When Mr Abrahams turned over a page of his evening paper and suddenly came on the paragraph reporting the death of Al Jolson, the shock made him lower the cup of tea in his hand so forcefully into its saucer that everyone looked at him.

'*Vos is de meisa?*' asked his father, speaking in Yiddish, the white strands of his beard almost brushing the table-top and the black skull-cap on his head skidding down even further towards the back of his creased neck.

'Jolson is dead,' announced Mr Abrahams, tragedy in his voice as if he had suffered a bitter, personal loss.

But his father, who was sitting at the opposite end of the table, and whose memory, and indeed other faculties too, had begun to deaden and slow down after nearly eighty years' use, could not quite place the name immediately, and so thinking that he must not have heard it aright, he pecked about for help. '*Vu? Vu?*' he said, in the anxious and irritated way of very old people who find it increasingly hard to keep up, and looking in turn to right and left at his daughter and grandson, '*vu hust ga starbin?*'

'Jolson,' Leah answered impatiently. 'Al Jolson—the singer.'

'Jolson?' he repeated in puzzlement, still at sea, the cracking red skin of his face shrinking and folding, as he grimaced with annoyance; and then suddenly, 'Ah, Jolson, de zinger,' his dry, blue lips opening wide in satisfaction and a momentary flash of childish triumph in his eyes like a light flicking on and off. Then his features became impassive again as he resumed his meal. He had succeeded in catching up with the memory of that name; he had recalled that it stood for a hoarse, rough voice and silly, unintelligible, *meshugganeh* songs that came out of many of the records his son constantly played. But the recollection was of no importance to him: Al Jolson was no one he knew and Al Jolson's music was not his kind of music: it was mad noise compared to real music—sacrilege beside the pure, winged notes of prayer that the Cantor sang in the synagogue during the *Shabbos* services every Friday and Saturday, and on the frequent high and holy festival-days. The name slipped easily out of his mind again as he handed his daughter a tall glass from beside his plate and watched her pour the black, strong tea into it. He took the glass back and dropped in a spoonful of sugar and a slice of lemon. This was the only way he ever drank tea, the way by which the drink was known to Jews all over the world as Russian tea, and as his old eyes, bent almost level with the glass, gazed at the crystal specks of sugar sinking down through the dark, shimmering liquid and the ring of lemon floating on the top, the sight reminded him, as always, of the endless, heavy skies and the thick tightly-closed drapery of cloud that made the sun weak and pale like a lemon-coloured moon, and the flakes of snow that seemed constantly to be falling, falling, when he had been a young man in his parents' home in Russia.

He sipped and savoured the tea as his son read aloud the details of Al Jolson's death. But no one was really interested in hearing it. Leah, two years older than her brother, who was himself turning forty, had long ago perfected the knack of closing her ears to people's voices. That was the result of what she called, in her own mind, her 'married spinsterhood.' Conscripted into her brother's large, echoing house to rear his baby son after the early death of its mother, her own youth and personality had been crushed and battered into herself by voices, almost as the talents and personalities of soldiers are drilled into uniformity under the parade-ground megaphone. First there had been her father, who had never dropped the habit of conversing in Yiddish, the tongue his family and fellow-Jews had used in their native Russia. But to Leah, who had gone to school not with Russian peasants' children but with the daughters of Irish farmers and small industrialists, Yiddish was a foreign language she did not need, and her father's babbling was something she never cared for and only very imperfectly understood. Then there had been her brother—a brother who in making money and a successful business-career early in life had taken himself off to a small Irish town where there was not another Jewish family and had gradually grown apart from her, but whose loss had brought him up sharp, making him turn again for help to his own blood. When she and their father had moved into his large house, the idea of rearing his son Lennie had appeared attractive and exciting. But she soon saw what a prisoning burden she had undertaken. The man with a glittering mansion, wealth, and a lifetime ahead of him, but who was already a widower with a baby son, was far different from the brother with whom she had grown up. His constantly-expressed anxieties and admonitions in everything relating to young Lennie's upbringing soon reduced her to sullen bitterness. Wanting to mother the child, she had been chilled and rebuked so much that she had come to feel more like its step-mother instead of the aunt she was. As a result there was little or no bond between Lennie and herself, and even the memory of the bond that once existed between her and her brother had quickly faded. Now that Lennie was no longer a schoolboy but already two years in his father's business, her functions in the house became more and more those of a maiden aunt and she craved for herself only peace and quiet in which to brood. But even of peace and quiet she could find little, for during the day she never knew when her father would break into his babble of Yiddish, and at night, more often than not, her brother would pass the time playing record after record on his radiogram.

For hours on end he listened to his music and much of it, in recent years, had consisted of Jolson songs. So while she sat now, as he read out the newspaper report, she could not bring herself to feel any interest in the news—except perhaps to recite in her own mind a small prayer of thanksgiving that at least there would be no more new Al Jolson records and a larger prayer of hope that her brother might soon tire of the ones he had.

Much the same thought occupied Lennie's mind, though for rather different reasons. To him Jolson was just another singer, his songs worthless panderings to sentimentality. He could never admire his father's taste in music; it was, he thought, so lacking in a sense of discrimination. One thing and one thing alone was sufficient to get almost any record, good or bad, into his collection—a Jewish artist. His father loved music—Lennie did not doubt that—but he never loved it more than when a Jew performed it. And it was that lopsidedness of judgement, that blind complex, which had gradually but surely succeeded in blocking the channel of understanding that should have joined Lennie and his father, closing between them like a door which neither knew how to open.

It was their circumstances as much as themselves that was to blame for the existence of such a barrier. Once Lennie, who from early childhood had shown a quick, eager, probing mind, had started his schooldays, the rift began: not only between him and his family but also between him and a great deal of what his family represented. Entering a school in which all his fellow-pupils were non-Jews, he entered a new world which seemed to have pattern and purpose. He began to lose patience with his rapidly ageing grandfather and to cease listening to his increasingly aimless Yiddishe chatter. The brusqueness of his father towards his aunt—which he had never previously noticed—was now irksome, and his aunt's all-suffering demeanour was something he tired of seeing. The ritual of his religious observances became uninteresting habits, devoid of meaning, and the static pointlessness of his home-life was contrasted, much to its disadvantage, with the flow and flux of events which coloured the background and talk of his school-friends.

The two factors which could have checked the tendencies he was developing and would have bound him to his family and his faith were just the two factors that were lacking—a mother and Jewish company. One of these factors alone might have been sufficient to preserve in him the formula of tradition his father and grandfather cherished. But without either—without a mother to act as a prop when the new world of school-life opened to him, and without Jewish friends to act as conductors of Jewish feeling and atmosphere outside his home—he slowly began to feel growing in himself a scepticism of Jewish ways and a corresponding enthusiasm for the life of the people and friends among whom he lived. The more his father emphasised the importance of preserving their Jewishness no matter what the dangers and the difficulties and the more he took pride in every Jewish achievement however small and irrelevant, the more Lennie was being pushed further and further away. It was a drift which made both of them unhappy since both recognised it, and in their own ways they tried to arrest it—Lennie by thought and argument with himself, and his father by increased harping on the values of their tradition. But their feeble efforts to reach out to each other only served to carry them further apart.

So it was that Lennie, in a curious, perverted way, almost derived some pleasure out of his father's sorrow at the death of Al Jolson. The silence of his grandfather and aunt, and of himself too, would disappoint his father who, he knew, would be aching either for someone to whom he could praise Jolson or at least for a respectful mourning comment which would encourage him to launch out into his own tribute. So Lennie purposefully continued to eat and pretended nothing until his father, baited into surrender, and trying to affect nonchalance, began to hum to himself one of his favourite Jolson numbers. But there was no response, and so cutting off the tune in the middle and closing his paper, he said aloud, 'A great loss, a great loss,' despairing almost as much for the absence of appreciation all around him as for the death of one of his firmest idols.

'What's the great loss?' said Lennie, not really meaning to speak but feeling a sudden pang of regret at his own hard-heartedness.

'Why, Jolson's death of course,' said his father, lighting up again into enthusiasm.

The swift dart of emotion that had prompted Lennie into speech had gone, and he was almost sorry for showing any interest, but knowing that he could not now stamp out the fire of thought he had quickened in his father's mind, even if he really wanted to, he casually poked at it with another question.

'And what's the loss of Jolson? People die every day.'

His father bent forward nearer him. 'But Jolson was such a singer.'

'So?' said Lennie. 'Singers die every day too, and there are still plenty left.'

His father leant back again in his chair and said, half to himself, 'But there's not another Jolson. A voice like his comes only once in a lifetime—no, once in a century.'

'A voice like his!' countered Lennie in amazement, 'but he had no voice. He croaked.'

'Ah, what do you know or care about it?' answered his father in disgust. 'It was the way he sang, the way he put it over. He was a real entertainer, "the greatest entertainer of them all" they called him. An artist! A great artist!'

Lennie and his father eyed each other, silently, challengingly. Lennie knew his father was holding something back, something he wanted to say that meant more to him than everything else, something that expressed the sum of his worship of Jolson. And his father knew that Lennie was waiting for him to say it, waiting for him to trot out his old chestnut, waiting to look at it and turn away from it in distaste, instead of holding his mind open to receive it, to fondle and cherish it in warm talk with him as a badge of their honour and greatness. Let him, thought his father. Let him shake his head and smirk over it, but it's true, true for me and for millions no matter what he says—Jolson was a great artist because of one thing. He was a great artist. Lennie's father leant forward again and spoke his thoughts loudly, daringly, 'He was a great artist.' He paused in the silence. 'And why?' He paused again as Lennie's eyes held him, a corner of ridicule showing in them, ready to flood his next sentence. But he was caught up now and had to carry on. 'Yes. Because he was a Jew. Because he sang with a Yiddishe heart.' He sank back once more and clasped his hands in satisfaction and relief.

Lennie sniffed and, looking up in resignation at the ceiling, drawled, 'Here we go again.'

'Yes, here we go again,' said his father, 'and despite what you think, that's the truth of it.'

'But what about all the other singers—the ones who aren't Jews?' asked Lennie. 'Some of them are quite good too, you know. How would you account for that?'

'I don't have to account for it,' his father rejoined. 'I am only accounting at the moment for Jolson, and the other great Jewish artists. They would not be where they are today if they hadn't been Jews.'

Such a frank expression of loyalty disgusted Lennie. He banged a knife on the table. 'That's sheer nonsense.'

'No, it is not nonsense. Being a Jew means something, same as being French means something, or Italian, or Irish. Every race has a talent for something in greater degree than any other race. That's human nature. Take the Irish—you should know about the Irish—what have they been distinguished for? Tell me what.'

Lennie thought a moment. 'Well,' he said, 'they're noted for their fighting qualities.'

'Exactly,' rapped his father, striking his open palm on his knee and looking in triumph to the other silent members of the family. 'There you are. They are great fighters and always have been because that's one of the things nature has inclined them to and circumstances have practised them in. Take the Italians, they paint. Take the British, the French, anyone you like. They all have their own speciality.'

'And take the Jews?' prompted Lennie.

'Take the Jews,' echoed his father reflectively. 'Take the Jews. They have a touch of magic, a talent for accepting the worst and making the best of it because they drain themselves of their injuries by expression. They feel—and they express with true, real feeling. That's what makes them so conspicuous as musicians and interpreters. The Jewish heart. That is what makes a Jolson.'

'Ah, how can you delude yourself so easily?' said Lennie. 'That's all just a lot of racial conceit. It's the kind of thinking and talking that makes people anti-Jewish, the contention that we are something special, that we have "a touch of magic".'

'But I'm telling you,' answered his father in exasperation, 'every race has its touch of magic. With us Jews it is just that our magic is the kind that glitters and attracts. We are simple, expressive, emotional, sentimental. How can I explain to you—we have something that can make people forget—forget themselves and forget us. We are children if you like, primitives, basic. There is a bit of a Jew in everyone.'

'My God!' said Lennie, sitting up with a start. 'What a thought!'

'And what's wrong with it?' answered his father, haughty, proud, righteous. 'Is being a Jew such a great burden? Does it mean nothing to you? Are you sorry already?'

Lennie, recognising the serious turn the discussion was taking, felt a little alarmed. He did not mean to upset his father so much and indeed, pushed by the jarred relationship between them, had expressed rather more opposition than he had intended.

'No, it isn't that, honestly,' he remonstrated. 'It is just that—' he looked around, trying to think of what it was he wished to express. He saw his grandfather, face lowered, head nodding up and down, as he recited to himself the grace after meals, and his aunt, oblivious of the conversation about her, scanning the paper which his father had discarded. There was no answer there, no help from either of them. They had no such problems, no such questions. It was not their argument—it was between himself and his father, and, deep down, Lennie felt that perhaps not even his father was really involved. Perhaps it was just a private, one-man struggle.

'Well, it is just what?' came the question.

'Oh, I don't know,' Lennie blustered. 'It is just that you forget all the Jews whose Jewish heart has done them no good, the Jews who have been persecuted, or the ones who have been lucky and were merely failures of their own volition. Being a Jew is just an accident of birth. You seem to forget that. No one by his own effort can be born a Jew so it's no special credit when it happens. Yet you think being a Jew is the only virtue.'

His father rose and pushed his chair back before he answered. Then, crushing his napkin into a ball and dropping it on the table, he said, 'No, Lennie, I don't forget that being a Jew is an accident of birth and I don't think it is the only virtue. But sometimes it can be a virtue to remain a Jew.'

Lennie sat motionless as his father paced out of the room. For some time he remained in that position, brooding, until his grandfather had finished grace and moved to a softer chair in the corner and his aunt commenced to clear away the table-ware. Then, standing up and undecided what to do, he suddenly heard the sound of a gramophone-record coming from the drawing-room. The clear, cutting edge of Jolson's voice singing the lush words of *Sonny Boy* enveloped him. Lennie wondered if his father were playing these records now just to taunt him or maybe to reproach him. And *Sonny Boy*? Why especially *Sonny Boy*? Was that deliberate? Was it to remind him of something—or was it being played by his father for himself alone, for his own entertainment and his own consolation? Lennie could not tell, but suddenly finding the press of questions too difficult to bear, he flung his coat about him and hurried out of the house to the nearest cinema.

Yet even there he was allowed no escape from his thoughts for, after only two or three shorts, and as the organ was rising from the pit in front of the stage, a notice came on the screen announcing to patrons that instead of the planned programme of songs the resident organist would play a selection from the music of Al Jolson, 'in tribute to the memory of that great artist'. Lennie cursed to himself and, leaving his seat, rushed out of the cinema while the audience applauded in appreciation.

Outside he smiled ruefully, thinking that there did not seem to be any place where he could be spared Jolson's particular brand of raucousness. It was too early to go home for in all likelihood his father would be up and still playing records. The only escape left to him was the local Social Club and he made his way there.

He went in and was greeted by the ten or twelve youths and girls already present, all of whom he knew and some of whom he had gone to school with. He joined a group in one corner where a game of darts was in progress and as soon as it finished and someone dropped out, he filled the empty place for the next game. But he was only preparing to throw his first dart when in another corner a girl wound the gramophone and put on a record—Jolson again. Lennie threw savagely, missing even the outer ring and embedding the dart deep in the board. He continued with the game until it was finished, hoping as each record came to an end that the next one would not be Jolson. But the rest of the members were now all grouped about the gramophone and the Jolson records had been weeded out and lay in a stack, each awaiting its turn. It was evidently to be an Al Jolson festival and as Lennie's companions moved to join the humming group, he was irresistibly drawn along with them. He stood listening, a companion's arm on each of his shoulders, and gazed at the spellbound faces. To him this adoration was unfathomable. What made it? What caused it? How could it be explained? During a pause while a record was being changed, someone turned to him, saying, 'What a personality! What a voice! Jolson was a Jew, Lennie, wasn't he?'

'Yes,' answered Lennie, 'he was. But do you really think he had a good voice?'

'Not a good voice,' came the reply, 'just a voice and a special way. But it's even more than that—it's a kind of magic in his style.'

Lennie was amazed. That was what his father had said, something about magic. And what else? That there was a bit of a Jew in everyone. Well, there seemed to a bit of something in all these different people that the voice, or the style, or the magic of Al Jolson appealed to. Lennie listened, standing with them for almost an hour, until the stock of records was finished and they began to go through them again. Then he quietly detached himself from the group, took his coat, and left.

All the way home he pondered on the enigma of the whole situation, trying to make sense out of it and to identify his own position and feelings. What was his duty? Where was his path? Was it really a virtue to remain loyal to one's blood and heritage no matter what they might be? Was there such an obligation on him? And anyway, what were his real feelings? How much was he influenced by circumstances and surroundings? How sure could he be in his opposition? He could no longer answer any of these questions.

He opened the door of his home and went in. Everyone was gone to bed but he was too restless to follow suit. He entered the drawing-room and idly wandered to the records piled beside the radiogram. They were evidently the ones his father had been playing for they were all of Al Jolson. He lifted them, one by one, reading the labels and recognising many of the titles he had heard earlier in the Club—*California, Chinatown, Swanee, Babyface, Rosy, April Showers, You Made Me Love You, The Anniversary Waltz*—he continued lifting them until he suddenly came on one he had not heard played for a very long time and the existence of which he had quite forgotten. It was Al Jolson's recording of *Kol Nidrei*, the most solemn prayer in the Hebrew liturgy, the prayer that is sung by the Cantor to herald the opening of the most hallowed event in the whole Jewish year, the Day of Atonement.

Lennie took the record in his hand, remembering many things from his past, how every year without fail his father shut up the home and the whole family travelled to Dublin to observe the fast, how they all spent the long day until sundown in synagogue, praying and making penance, how until his confirmation at the age of thirteen he had looked forward to being allowed enter the sacred company of adults and fast himself for the whole twenty-six hours, and how every year he had continued to observe that fast, perhaps unthinkingly, but still with some pride and even relish, and always feeling after it the mystery of such symbolic atonement that had point but no explanation. On a whim he opened the radiogram and put on the record. And as the words of the prayer floated out, imparted by Jolson with the special, characteristic, time-honoured flourishes of the Jewish Cantor, Lennie remembered the meaning and symbolism of the prayer; that all terrestrial ties of whatever sort which had been entered into for the future year were to be absolved completely and could have no force after the Day of Atonement unless renewed. He felt, within himself, the rightness of such a wholesale, clean-cut remission, and the perfectness of the implication that only spiritual bonds could last for ever, never to be broken, never to be eased out of, never to be completely forgotten. And as the last syllables of the *Kol Nidrei* came from the record and the sound of the music died away, he seemed to find something—in the prayer, or in his mood, or even perhaps a magic in Jolson's voice—that fitted in and made sense deep in his heart.

Eiléan Ní Chuilleanáin

David Marcus: on a bridge

So little of ourselves really belongs to us,
to our life, as it spills as we move, it rounds a likeness
to be pocketed by the next who crosses the trail
as herds migrate; it sweeps past in a flood.
A decade of our time is lit by a patent lamp
suddenly obsolete. A hall of reflections,
a man running through to the hastening sound,
beating drums near at hand.
                              Yet in spite of metaphor
something is left, almost a document
though hardly stable, an intriguing note
in the margin of someone else's story
that spins into view and claims the light,
opening up libraries and the plans of cities.

Look at our books, they are trampled full of people,
their histories never quite ours, languages
half ours, codes, the word *Technicolor*
in the Dolmen *Midnight Court*. Something remains,
from the Mardyke, from the linotype printing shop,
from Eileen O'Faolain's drawing-room where we met him
on Sean's seventy-fifth birthday and she gave us sherry
and the talk was all about how badly writers are paid
until Seán said 'This conversation is too literary';
but then there's that story from the nineteen-fifties, remember,
two young writers on their cheap honeymoon
who ran out of money for the last weekend—
so David met them by appointment on St Patrick's Bridge
in Cork, a cheque in his hand to pay for their work.

Time stands, the tidal river surprised
into reflective calm as it turns for the harbour.
She tells the story at the end of her long life,
how they were astonished to find that he was so young,
standing on the bridge with the payment, handing it over.

W.B. Yeats in 1926, in his introduction to Arland Ussher's translation of *Cúirt an Mheán Oíche*, wished for the intervention of 'some man of known sobriety of manner and of mind' who could speak more authoritatively than himself about the Gaelic original. Presumably such 'known sobriety' was missing from the CV of the later translator Frank O'Connor whose version of the same poem was banned—perhaps as much because of the writer's private life (he had married a divorced actress), as because of the scandalous nature of the translated text. But of David Marcus, whose translation was published in 1953 and (like Ussher's) was not banned, a certain sobriety of manner and mind could be predicated, though that quality was only one side of his character as a literary man. I suggest Cork supplied the sobriety but also helped to point him towards more surprising places.

Old as I am, I am just too young to remember him in Cork in the era of *Irish Writing*. His brother Louis was a presence, David was an offstage influence in the culture of the city in the early 1950s. But he seemed to me, when I met him later, to epitomise that culture. People who were inclined to a certain conservatism of habit—necessary, I suppose, in a society very likely to be shocked by small deviations from the conventional standard—combined with a mental and imaginative adventurousness. There was an edge to their desire to explore, a certain defiance. That at any rate is how I remember the people and their milieu, seen through the eyes of a young teenager.

In a small city, a small group shared with the citizenry as a whole a conviction of the importance of their own place. The small University College, the five bookshops each with its own ethos and identification, the amateur orchestra and its patrons, the film society, the painters and one distinguished sculptor, the Everyman Theatre, created a local network that was closer than anything I've seen since. Difference was valued, the Marcuses and Goldbergs, the German Fleischmanns, the Protestant Burrows (Rachel Burrows spoke French with my mother at Irish-language events rather than dropping into English), the Sanquests, seem to me now to have been recognised as making the city more complete.

It was then a natural setting for a literary journal to be created by a twenty-two year old, a home for voices much wilder than his own. I am particularly struck by the welcome he gave to the anarchic talent of Patrick Galvin. A working-class voice, which might have been rejected by the middle-class—even if sometimes impoverished—network I have described, found an outlet. Galvin's poem 'The Connie Ribbon' (published in *Irish Writing* in 1951), a quintessentially Cork poem, veers from realistic framing of the dire poverty of his docker family in the late 1930s to a quasi-folksong refrain celebrating the emblem of the school he had left, with the assistance of a forged birth certificate, at the age of eleven:

> Sitting on the quay wall with knees up
> Watching the still ghost of timber and corn sails
> Creep up the river from Roche's point.
> This was the gay lad wearing his Connie Ribbon
>
> And the quay slept while dockers warmed their hands with
>   stale breath,
> A bare quay empty as dockers' bellies
> And the air was stiff like Murphy
> As the Innisfallen blew farewell to the white clock…
>
> Hello, hello, O wear your Connie Ribbon,
> Wear it like the devil, far across the sea
> And if they ask you why you think to wear it,
> Say you wear it for a lassie, far far away.

The same response to a writer of wild energy seems to me to provide the impetus for Marcus's *The Midnight Court*. The poems recovered from his youth and published by New Island in 2007 are good, but the sparks really fly when he encounters Merriman's pulsating verse. By the second line he is translating '*an drúcht go trom*' as 'dew [...] as thick as chalk'. The chalk is there for the rhyme but its sheer oddity is a signal that the old poem has swallowed its translator whole and that a new power is emerging. A special talent that shows itself in such encounters underlies all of his long career, and we must be grateful that he began so early, and remained faithful to its commands.

George O'Brien
Found in Translation

There was a time when, as he tells us in *Oughtobiography*, David Marcus was 'convinced' that he was 'the best poet in Ireland under twenty-one'. Nor was he the only aspiring bard of his day with the same conviction, it is safe to say. But unlike the majority of minstrel boys, David retained a noteworthy attachment to poetry. There are, of course, more resonant strings to David's bow than that sounded by his work with, and for, verse. Still, that work can hardly be thought negligible. His *Lost and Found: Selected Poems and Translations* (2007) marks sixty years of poetic engagement, beginning with the landmark creation in 1948 of *Poetry Ireland* and including his revealing profile of 'an era and a generation not previously taken whole' in the 1975 anthology *Irish Poets 1924–1974*. And that engagement also ensured that, whenever possible, David's weekly 'New Irish Writing' page in *The Irish Press* included a poem or two. All this adds up to rather more than the enthusiasm of an aficionado, and should not be regarded as mere functions of the editor's office.

Rather, each achievement is an act of curation implicitly dedicated to reducing the distance between poems and their public, thereby supplying poetry with the oxygen of public hearings. The result is an economy of free speech, in which the singular activity of writing poetry is exchanged for, or balanced out by, an open-minded receptivity on the part of a well-disposed audience. And the terms and operation of such an economy come into focus more sharply than usual when they are overshadowed by the bully censor, as in the case of *The Midnight Court*, David's translation of Brian Merriman's eighteenth-century poem, *Cúirt an Mheán Oíche*, which may be seen not only as exemplifying his commitment to poetry's place in the republic of letters but also as an expression of compelling personal preoccupations.

Since the launch of his career as a published author with a version of 'An Bonnán Buí' ('The Yellow Bittern'), David's translations from the Irish have had a distinctive place amidst his various dealings with poetry. It might even be argued that translating was a natural expressive outlet for David, given translation's connotations of barrier-removal, distance-effacement and estrangement-reduction, and its intentions (however unstated) to establish approachability and parity of esteem. Translation is, in a sense, an ethic, and as such has an even more obviously public dimension than publications in the home language. This sense of translation emerged with particular cultural force in mid-twentieth century Ireland when David began his work of making the canon of Irish poetry more available to a general audience.

Not that his efforts bespoke a proselytiser's ambition—that would be not David's style at all, and besides, his translations appeared too fitfully to be considered a project as such. Nevertheless, as is all too well known, at the time—his 'Bonnán Buí' came out in 1945—the literature of the Irish language seemed so firmly in the keeping of officialdom as to be regarded by the majority of readers as remote, if not distasteful. David's echo in *Oughtobiography* of the writer Medb Ruane's statement that 'My generation was administered Irish the way we were administered cod liver oil' gives the flavour of the typical relationship between imbiber and provider.

And when David devoted the January 1949 issue of *Poetry Ireland* to translating from the Irish, Sean O'Faoláin concluded that 'All translations from the Irish now can be no more than either the occasional technical amusement of the poet, or a flower cast gratefully on a grave.' To which David made the only necessary response by continuing to translate, in part because of the 'spiritual' reward deriving from the intensity of his investment in the task itself. On how his endeavours align with the interest in versions from the Irish expressed by contemporaries such as Thomas Kinsella and Eoghan Ó Tuairisc, David is characteristically silent. But an additional way of appreciating his contribution to Irish writing is to acknowledge its place within the overall post-war impetus to generate a fresh relationship to the nation's poetic heritage, an impetus which has been sustained undiminished by virtually every noteworthy Irish poet of the past seventy-five years.

A generally liberating note may be detected in translation's work of retrieval and adaptation, as well as in its overtones of possibility, renewal and refreshment. Translating endows the original work with a two-fold existence, one which honours its primary place of linguistic residence while releasing it from that singular, unfamiliar habitation. Perhaps such reverberations of duality possessed a particular appeal for a translator conscious of the twin identities striving for reconciliation with each other in what David called the 'hyphenated' reality of being an Irish Jew.

By the time David published his 'Midnight Court' in 1953, the *kulturkampf* fomented by the O'Connor version had subsided. Yet, its shadow lingered. There was no guarantee that a new translation would not become the pretext for further iterations of the prevailing orthodoxy. Not that such a possibility was a deterrent, obviously. On the contrary, it might be seen as an incentive. Some of the most forceful language in *Oughtobiography* is directed at the 'culturally criminal nonsense' of banning O'Connor's rendition (particularly when the Irish original remained freely available). In addition, 'More or less as a one-man protest I decided to thumb my nose at the crass ukase of the establishment and frustrate it with an act of auto-pollution.'

Such a provocative statement of independence might suggest that David was taking up the cudgels in defense of the free-thinking 'Utopian' and child of nature that was O'Connor's Merriman. David was not a follower, however—'I knew what I wanted to do'. What this was, its importance to Irish cultural development, and what it says about the value of translation in David's imaginative life are not only distinctive articulations of literary value in their own right. They receive additional worth by virtue of the interdependence between them revealed in the Marcus 'Midnight Court'.

As O'Connor unmistakably showed, translating *Cúirt an Mheán Oíche* could be an occasion of outspokenness. The manner and degree of how O'Connor availed of the occasion, however, makes his sense of the original rather a rant. The Marcus version, on the other hand, is a romp. W.B. Yeats found the Merriman to be a 'vital, extravagant, immoral, preposterous poem', and though it is not as if David took his cue from Yeats, these are the characteristics that inform his treatment. Indeed, it may be his recognition of these all too human attributes that prompted David's view of the original as 'one of the great "survivor" poems of the western world'. And by translating with the human element to the fore, David greatly broadens the work's general appeal, thereby demonstrating that to regard Merriman as a pretext for ideological axe-grinding is to attenuate the energy that makes his poem live. By virtue of his approach, David makes the censor's interests seem parochial—a diminution of the heritage those interests are assumed to be safeguarding. As David's 'one-man' comment indicates, his is an individual treatment, and that, too, is an important dimension of the quietly radical human touch with which he handles the appellants, testifiers and the cases they make for themselves in Merriman's court as they seek to overcome the social constraints that have been placed between themselves and their natures.

A sense of freedom underlies this sense of the original, expressed primarily in David's 'irresistible' attraction to Merriman's 'raciness and musical mastery.' Freedom not only takes the form of an idea or a principle, it is an indispensable element of experiencing the poem. One of the original's greatest achievements is its subversive readiness to convey lamentable conditions in a jaunty tone, an approach which not only affects the poem's versification but also extends to the quasi-legal dream scenario which structures the work (the kind of court which would appeal to the David Marcus who had decided to exchange his law career for one in literature). One of the effects of the subversion is, as David found, to make music and meaning one. The playfulness with which this pairing is accomplished may be read as freedom's signature, a reading which also invokes the anti-puritanical, humanitarian ethos which David's version upholds and which is crucial to his view of the poem as a 'survivor'.

Play, pleasure, liberty and what David termed 'hilarity' constitute the intellectual and aesthetic complexity of *Cúirt an Mheán Oíche*, and one means he came up with of offering immediate access to the interplay between these elements that Merriman created was through the simple but telling decision to take verbal risks. As he wrote, 'I strove to make my version a translation in both senses: one that would be as faithful as possible to the spirit of the original as well as an attempt to present the poem as Merriman might have written it were he alive today and composing in English.' In translating Merriman as if he were a contemporary, David gives his work a certain directness, brings the original home, in a sense, and gives its vitality continuity while at the same time dispensing with hidebound historicity. And as David pointed out, such updating seemed prompted by the original's content: 'changes in the status of the priesthood and the clamour for women's rights make *The Midnight Court* almost as uncomfortably pertinent today as it was when Brian Merriman composed it.'

In addition to such thematic concerns, however, using—though not overindulging in—the vocabulary of his own day is in keeping with David's tacit desire to render the poem in as natural an idiom as possible, thereby encouraging readers 'to enjoy its thrusts and to savour its felicities'. As a complement to the pleasure-prompting 'sparkle [...] music [...] modernity' of the repertoire of David's linguistic and rhythmical effects, there is something of a devil-may-care air about using modern allusions and contemporary instances—'telephone', 'King Kong', 'action stations', 'a packet of fags'. But there is also something exemplary in the translator introducing such popular usages and terminology, a recognition that a classic can be deprived of its vigour by an excess of piety or by the pursuit of a supposedly 'ideal' language in which to render it. And, obviously, David's choice was his to make, and he was independent-minded enough to make it.

The impossibility of knowing what and how Merriman would have written if he were writing his masterpiece in the Ireland of the 1950s has been brought up as a criticism of David's verbal updating. Such an argument, however, cuts both ways. In a sense, impossibility impels the imagination. Admittedly, David does not conform to the letter of the original, and may also be called to pedantic account for some awkward versification—'His wife may have fooled him—but didn't he wrong her?/And—truly now—which of *us* would have been stronger?' is not the most felicitous of couplets, nor is it the only metrical sore thumb to stick out. But, as noted, it is the spirit of the thing that he wishes to render, not merely in homage to Merriman but also in the implicit belief that not just a local readership but Irish culture as a whole would be enlivened by becoming acquainted with the tonic transgressions of *Cúirt an Mheán Oíche*.

At the time of the first edition of David's *Midnight Court*, however, the way ahead was by no means assured. The Dolmen Press issued just two hundred copies, limited to subscribers—'perhaps', David has speculated, 'a [...] tactic to forestall another ban.' David had had his *Six Poems* (1952) published by Dolmen in a fine edition, and his *Midnight Court* also fully lived up to the press's lofty publication standards, the expense of which, rather than caution alone, may have been responsible for the small print-run. It may even be that the book's elaborate design—one of Dolmen's earliest efforts to keep alive Ireland's illustrious history of book production—was intended to honour the poem's standing as a cultural treasure, its elaborate effects counteracting the stains of salacity and immorality applied by the censor to the O'Connor translation. In any case, the time and care lavished on the production does seem a fitting tribute to Merriman's original and a proud announcement of its rebirth as a classic of Irish literature. Subsequent editions, as well as a popular dramatic adaptation by David and Sean McCann staged at the Gate Theatre in 1968, are further evidence that this translation was both welcome and worthwhile.

For translator, publisher, and the public at large, the Marcus *Midnight Court* was a triumph of recuperation. A sense of justice having been done—the very possibility that Merriman's poem dreams of—emerges. This outcome derives in the first place from a mutuality of interest and respect between the new version and the original, resulting in a form of reconciliation between them, as though strangers are talking at their ease to strangers and the past can coexist productively with the present. Demonstrating mutuality and the potential for reconciliation it offers may have been enough for David. But it may also be suggested, however tentatively, that something more may have been at play in his taking up the various challenges of the work, primarily that of making his way through such a complicated imaginative and linguistic landscape as that of Merriman's eighteenth-century East Clare. David's successful traversal of this landscape is all the more noteworthy for have been accomplished in addition to all his other different and demanding literary activities, and his worry as to whether his spoken Irish would be found wanting at the Dolmen launch.

One possibility as to what the 'something' might be is perhaps touched on by his discovery in Merriman of the 'two things' which formed, as he wrote in *Oughtobiography*, 'that inner me [...] music, and the ongoing trauma of having to juggle a hyphenated heritage of being both Irish and Jewish.' Music speaks for itself, in a sense, and, as noted, David responded with delight to the musicality of *Cúirt an Mheán Oíche*. To characterise, much less to interpret, David's 'trauma' in the context of the reconciliatory task of translation may risk depriving both the personal condition and the artistic work of their proper significance and weight. Nonetheless, perhaps a few preliminary thoughts regarding the worlds of others connoted both by translation and trauma will not seem out of place, if only in an effort to accommodate the isolation, vulnerability and dread that 'trauma' connotes. For it is not as if trauma's presence is a happenstance of history from which those who have not suffered it are disconnected. On the contrary, David's hyphenated identity has a salient place in our collective social and cultural awareness, acknowledgment of which is an enlargement of our shared humanity in a manner analogous to the way in which translation broadens our sensibilities and imaginations. Accessibility to these two human territories refines our sense of the place we're in, while the appearance of the two spheres in language makes all the more resonant the implications of 'the determined attempt to speak' made by the first appellant to plead her case at the midnight court.

Writing about the Cork City on which David drew in his novels *A Land Not Theirs* (1986) and *A Land in Flames* (1987), his uncle, the noted lawyer and public figure Gerald Y. Goldberg, has said that the city's Jewish community live 'a life subsumed by fear'. And one scholar has noted that the publication of Frank O'Connor's 'Midnight Court' by Maurice Fridberg (also an Irish Jew) 'raised the phantom of antisemitism'. In *Oughtobiography*, David juxtaposes 'the joke of national censorship, the Irish government's cordon sanitaire' alongside the fact that '[t]he population had been generally kept in the dark about the war engulfing Europe.' Though, David goes on, 'not all of us.' Ireland's Jews were in no doubt as to what Hitler's plans were for such as they, the nightmarish and (quite possibly impending) horror of which

David vividly recounts. The traumatising character of annihilation generated 'my own emergency', a state dramatically at odds with The Emergency as defined by officialdom.

Translations from the Irish seem a long way from such overwhelming concerns. Yet, David composed his translations at a time when, with a future for himself (and not him alone, of course) seeming to hang precariously in the balance, he was attempting to make what peace he could with his dual heritage, to reconcile the two sides of the hyphen, the Irish one of which remained mute while the Jewish one protested to high heaven. (Coincidentally, Merriman's refrain in *Cúirt an Mheán Oíche* is the question of what is going to become of us—'*Cad a dhéanamaid feasta gan síolrú?*', so to speak—and the poem ends with the Merriman persona escaping trauma by the skin of his teeth.) Marcus and Merriman agree: a fresh start is required. In effect, David tells us he thought so at the time, for it was in the aftermath of the war that he resolved some of his own conflict by turning from a career maintaining the letter of the law to the rather riskier one of upholding the spirit of the word. In his own words, 'I had a way to find, a new bridge to build.'

A future requiring a crossing point. A structure bringing two sides together, overcoming the distance they're initially apart. A landmark that wasn't there before. An opening of fresh means of access, a different line of communication. A suspension between (cultural) territories. A hyphen.

David's bridge metaphor is suggestive. And it contains, too, hints of what translation can at least have in mind to do. Care must be taken not to overstate the case, of course. Valuable matters can also be lost in translation. But it is at least a pleasing thought to imagine that when David was engrossed in his versions of the Irish, he was discovering that though that hyphen of his might signify division, it could also serve to connect, to conciliate, and to show a way forward.

Brian Merriman

from *Cúirt an Mheán Oíche /*
The Midnight Court

translated into English by David Marcus (1953)

The Third Part
*In which the poet hears further derogatory charges against the male sex
in general and the previous speaker in particular.*

The girl, by now, had heard enough
And up she started in a huff,
She read your man the Riot Act,
Paused for a breath and then attacked:

'Lucky,' says she, 'that I've a care
For the fact that you're old and a little queer,
And that Her Worship might object
Or soon I'd teach you some respect.
I'd quickly put you out of action
And beat you down to a vulgar fraction
Till, with a mighty final blow,
I'd send you on your way below.
It's certain no one takes as true
The stories of the likes of you,
But still I'll tell how you behaved
Towards the girl *you* say you saved:—

Reduced to begging from door to door
All she had were the rags she wore,
Exposed to every kind of weather
She'd all but reached the end of her tether—
Day after day, walking the street
With hardly a drink or a bite to eat.
And then this chancer happened by,
Fooled her up to the ball of her eye,
Promised her, if she'd be his wife,
Breakfast in bed for the rest of her life,
A separate banking account of her own,
A butler, a car, and a telephone,
And every month a brand-new gown,
With a country seat and a flat in town!
There wasn't a thought in anyone's mind
That it could have been love of the dimmest kind
Would make her consent as long as she'd live
Had she any better alternative.
Fat chance there was of a night's high jinks
With such a fossilised old sphinx;
What passion could a girl entice
From thighs as stiff and as cold as ice,
A hulk that a furnace couldn't heat,
A bag of bones, devoid of meat?
The saints themselves wouldn't expect
A wife to stand for such neglect
From a hog of a husband whom nothing would stir
To see was she feather, or fin, or fur;
Who, lure as she might, would never mate her
But lay like a human refrigerator.
Not that she set him too great a task
(Once per night wasn't much to ask!)
And don't imagine her modesty
Would scare a fellow from making free,

BRIAN MERRIMAN

A lady she was from stem to stern—
But where's the wick that, when lit, won't burn?
She'd work all night—you can bet on that—
And at dawn she'd still give him tit for tat.
She'd grant his pleasure whatever it be,
Her eyes aglaze with ecstasy,
She'd not ignore his eager questions
Or snap at him for his suggestions—
Down beside him she'd recline
Wound around him like a vine,
And trying to coax a flame to light
She'd kiss his lips and squeeze him tight.
His fancy she often attempted to tease
By rubbing against him from waist to knees;
She did her best to make him play
But there wasn't a move from that lump of clay,
He remained indifferent to all her tricks,
To kisses, caresses, scratches, and kicks.
I blush to reveal that he left her languish,
Gripping the bed-post, sobbing in anguish,
Bewailing the shame of a spotless sheet,
With frozen limbs and chattering teeth,
And she cried till dawn without cessation,
Tossing and turning in humiliation.

What neck he has, acting the critic,
That leprous, parlous paralytic;
His wife may have fooled him—but didn't he wrong her?
And—truly now—which of *us* would have been stronger?
What bear or badger, buck or beagle,
Leaping stag or wheeling eagle
Would gasp with thirst a single hour
And let the sweetest drink go sour?

I have the gravest doubt indeed
Whether a beast of any breed
Would look for food where nothing grows
And shun the meal beneath his nose.
Let's hear, you dolt, your fine defence
And see if it makes any sense
Was there anything missing that you can tell?
If not, then weren't you doing well?
Is a house devalued the slightest bit
If twenty million inspected it?
Don't be afraid, you poor old crock,
You wouldn't get in if you should knock.
Have you so large an appetite
That others shouldn't take a bite?
Don't fool yourself: it's plain to see
You couldn't exhaust a female flea!
Put your illusions well aside
Unless you want to be certified,
And don't be making such a fuss
Because the woman was generous—
She could handle a dozen a day, or more,
And toss *you* off as an encore!
Such jealousy would be no fault
In someone who was worth his salt,
A lusty lover, a proved romancer,
A fellow who wouldn't take 'no' for an answer,
Who'd not be stopped by etiquette,
Whose thrust would be sharp as a bayonet;
But there's more to fear from the prick of a thorn
Than from this old cow with a crumpled horn!'

Mary O'Malley

The Irish for Knife
for David Marcus

Is a dive clean as an arrow
tipped with poison from the yew,
is a sliver of a bay cast in steel,
with the edge of a swallow's flight.
I have no coins to give you, just this
small gift, forged with precision
to gut fish, calm dangerous waves
and lift the flap of our dimensions.

(*Scian* is the Irish for knife.)

— — —

Long before I had any contact with the Irish literary world, the name David Marcus was familiar. He was, for writers of my generation, as central to contemporary writing as The Dolmen Press and *Poetry Ireland* were to Irish poetry. I had first become aware of him through his translations of 'The Yellow Bittern' and *The Midnight Court*, but in that nebulous way of Patron Saints and recording angels, he was always in the ether. At some point I started reading the 'New Irish Writing' page in *The Irish Press*.

There I first read Desmond Hogan, Neil Jordan, Dermot Healy and Deirdre Madden. I have always loved the short story, in particular the Irish and American stories introduced to me early by the wonderful anthologies edited by Gus Martin and in the stories in my schoolgirl collection *Dúil* by Liam Ó Flaithearta. The stories in *The Irish Press* were fresh and varied, and owed as much to Carson McCullers and Anton Chekhov as they did to Máirtín Ó Caidhin or Brendan Behan. There was a kind of literary democracy behind the editing of the pages, in the breadth of subject matter from jazz to trawlers, from Wexford to London and beyond. I never sensed a censoring of either subject matter or style, though Marcus was a sharp and astute editor, with a brilliant ear for tone. It might have been in part due to his choices that I became aware of the importance of tone, and started to pay it attention.

I was introduced to him once, at one of those events in Dublin where everyone but me seemed to belong. What I remember isn't being introduced, but seeing him across a room and realising who he was. I felt as if I was in the room with John Lennon or Bob Dylan, as if with one of the beings so remote and indispensable that you believe they can't be real. The moment remains clear as a photograph, his slightly old-fashioned look, his sharp attentive gaze, his attention to whoever was talking to him. And me, standing at the edge of the gathering, starstruck. Someone took pity on me and introduced me in that kind way some writers have with newcomers.

Looking back now, I don't regret my shyness. If anything, my admiration for him has grown. David Marcus didn't just start most of Ireland's important magazines and outlets for new writing, he stayed the course. Again and again, generation after generation, he kept turning up, and where many intimidated new writers, he measured and encouraged their work. Somewhere, at some stage, long before I was ready to submit anything anywhere, permission was given by a quiet Jewish Corkman who broke the mould of the hard-drinking, gregarious literary type so beloved of Irish anecdote and so alien to a nervous outsider. Something about the range and democracy of 'New Irish Writing' gave me the idea that I had permission. I was living abroad, teaching, rearing kids, reading Latin American, Spanish and Portuguese poetry, and whatever novels came my way in English. I was not writing. Deliberately. Unfortunately for me, this wasn't working very well. Somewhere around 1982, I started reading poetry in English again. I didn't want to write in English. My voice was stuck in another language. We moved back to Ireland from Lisbon in 1986. In 1987 or 1988, I started writing poems again.

I never submitted to David Marcus because I was waiting until I thought I had something worth consideration, by which time he had stopped editing the page that had provided me with a new generation of short-story writers. Luckily for me, the page continued in *The Sunday Tribune*, edited by the other great Irish editor, Ciaran Carty, quietly encouraging, exacting and generous, so generous that I felt it would have been unfair to call on his time for advice. Sometime in 1989, a friend got me an envelope, addressed and stamped it, instructed me to choose four or five poems, put them in with four lines of biography which she dictated, and ordered me to post them. They were the first poems I ever submitted to a national newspaper, and they were published. I thought this was very generous of them, but was bound to be a flash in the pan, but they were shortlisted for a Hennessy Award. I was published again the following year, and won. I still thank Ciaran Carty for giving me the confidence to put a manuscript together for my first book, *A Consideration of Silk*. Without him, I wouldn't have done it for years, if at all.

The other national publication I submitted to at that time was the *Poetry Ireland Review*. Both were started by David Marcus. I was vaguely aware that he was Jewish, a bit of an outsider. I trusted that sense. How lucky we were as writers to have had him for so long, that brilliant, dedicated man.

II

Tim Pat Coogan

David and *The Irish Press*

Interviewed by Paul Delaney in Dublin on 29 February 2024

Paul Delaney: *Can you tell me about the background to the 'New Irish Writing' page in* The Irish Press, *and how you first came to meet David Marcus?*

Tim Pat Coogan: Well, I wasn't long editor of *The Irish Press*, having been appointed earlier in 1968. I was trying to reform the paper, which had fallen on very evil days, and I was getting in any new people I could within the limits of the budget. Sean McCann was a vital link. Sean was literary editor of *The Evening Press* and had been seconded to *The Irish Press* to help me relaunch the paper. He had a talent, you know—he was very good at picking young writers and contributors.

One day, Sean came in to see me with this unobtrusive figure with a moustache. I hadn't met David before but I knew him by reputation. What David proposed was that *The Irish Press* should give over a full page once a week, every week, to some sample of new Irish writing. I thought this was an excellent idea, if I could get it past Vivion de Valera, who was managing director of the *Press*. Vivion expressed a worry—a slight worry—as to what John would make of it. David being a Jew and John being John Charles McQuaid, Vivion's mentor at Blackrock and designer of his father's Constitution, and a man in whom he lived in dread of. So that was the only real problem, but in fairness to Vivion he agreed to the idea, and he let me have the page.

PD: *Was that the first time you had come across David?*

TPC: Not quite. I was aware of David's earlier magazine, *Irish Writing*. Sean White, a friend of mine, had edited it for a while, after David had stepped down from it in the mid-1950s. I also knew him by repute because I was friendly with his uncle, the great Gerald Goldberg, the first Jewish Lord Mayor of Cork city. Gerald was a charming man, a patron of the arts, and a good spokesperson for the Jewish community. He was a broadminded man and was well respected. And I also knew David's younger brother, slightly—Louis Marcus, the filmmaker. So David couldn't have come better recommended, he had credentials. His relatives were good, solid people, very well respected. I'd heard that David had given up a job in insurance in England to come back to Ireland. So I knew he was sincere. And he was.

PD: *How did you find working with David?*

TPC: From the start, I was very taken with him. He was a moral man, he had a code. And I think his character, as it evolved over the years, was best summed up by an anecdote that his daughter, Sarah, gave when she was eulogising her father at his funeral. She described how she'd be lying there in the morning, dying with a hangover. And her father would come in and say, 'Oh, you were drinking too much!' But at the same time he'd have an Alka-Seltzer for her. So I thought that was David, you know!

I didn't see very much of him after he started in the paper because he was so efficient, he just went to work and did his thing. He was upstairs, in a little office on his own. He was an unobtrusive but a very popular figure in the Press—with the printers as well as the journalists. You wouldn't see much of him because he was out of the hurly-burly of daily newsgathering. But people liked him and he was very human. Sometimes you'd see him slipping quietly, but determinedly, down the backstairs and out to the bookies. David liked a flutter!

PD: *Were there ever any concerns about the 'New Irish Writing' page? And what did Vivion de Valera think about the idea?*

TPC: From time to time there'd be some grumble about the amount of newsprint given over to the page. And sometimes Vivion would ask could David not use that white space he was leaving at the top of the page, or get some material in it at the bottom of the page to justify the cost of the newsprint. That kind of thing—but it was only occasional and technical. There was no real objection, and you'd have to say there was support. I suppose that might be because there was a literary tradition in the *Press*. Practically all of the better journalists wrote for it at some stage or another, and there were contemporary writers of the 1950s and 1960s—as there had been in the 1930s and 1940s—who would write reviews or the odd article. Brendan Behan and Patrick Kavanagh had written for the *Press*, for instance, and Francis McManus had been the literary editor. There was a good tradition in the *Press* of that.

PD: *Were there ever any objections about what David wanted to include in 'New Irish Writing'? I'm thinking about his inclusion of work by Edna O'Brien, for instance, or by John McGahern—both of whom had had work banned in the 1960s?*

TPC: I think Edna was included in the fourth week of the page. David wanted to begin 'New Irish Writing' with her but I thought it might not be advisable in the first issue. So John McGahern ended up in the first week instead. But neither John nor Edna caused any trouble, and there was no backlash. I remember David saying to me, we'll have no four-letter words. He took precautions to avoid that kind of thing. I mean, if you'd had a couple of fucks in it, that would have brought down the whole page. As it was, I got very few objections. I'd have to say, David understood what he could do with the paper, and he tempered his page accordingly.

PD: *Over David's time with 'New Irish Writing', many writers must have visited the offices of* The Irish Press. *Did you meet many of them in Burgh Quay, and do you have specific memories of any of them?*

TPC: David was a good man for spotting talent, and for knowing who was who and what was going on. I remember one pretty young woman coming in, though, because she seemed to be around a bit. And I remember saying to David, 'You seem to be giving her a lot of encouragement. Is she a contributor?' or something like that. 'Oh yes, I'm helping her. I think she could make a very good writer.' And as we know… events, dear boy, events! And I thought that, as with the writers, he had a very good eye. He chose well when he chose Ita.

PD: Having said that David was good at spotting talent, it is remarkable to consider the number of writers he nurtured and helped to bring to print. You'd struggle to think of many writers of that generation — or of several generations — who were not published by him.

TPC: Indeed, there weren't many. Not in Ireland, anyway. Because when you think of it, a weekly page running 52 weeks a year, for almost 20 years. That's a lot of pages! I remember people from all sorts of backgrounds who submitted material to be considered. Some famous, others less well known. For instance, I remember once—when I was working on my IRA book—I was in Belfast to interview Seamus Twomey, who was on the run, and who was Chief of Staff of the IRA. I didn't meet Seamus but I met his son who was doing two things at the time. He was studying, in Stranmillis, I think, to be a teacher, and he was hoping to get stories published by David Marcus in *The Irish Press*. Even then, in the midst of shot and shell! He would have had some difficulty concentrating I'd say with the raids, and not knowing if his father was going to turn up dead, or in prison, or whatever! They were some very bad, nasty years, when it was all about assassinations, and murders, and reprisals. It was a lousy time in the mid-1970s. But I remember that the lad's main interest at the time was writing, and I just remember that little spark and being amused to find that in the thick of everything the lad was concentrating on getting published by David. It's a beguiling thought.

PD: David served as literary editor of The Irish Press *for a time, while continuing to edit 'New Irish Writing'. Is that right?*

TPC: That's right, he did both. He used to farm out the books to be reviewed, and obviously anyone who got books to be reviewed thought a lot of him. And some people weren't so happy with the reviews their books received. David would pick people who knew what they were doing—people he thought would write good reviews, and who would help the book trade. He had good judgement, and the whole venture was very wholesome.

Talking about Sean McCann, I think his son, Colum McCann, must have been deeply influenced by him. Sean was always thinking up good ideas for books, and he'd get different people to write a chapter for a book. And you might get paid something that would be the equivalent of ten euro now for it! But people liked Sean, and they were good ideas. In the same way that David brought people on, the marriage between Sean and David for a while was very good—they were both enabling men. I suspect Colum got a lot of exposure to reading books and encouragement from his father, and it has certainly paid off. He is a first-class writer, and he deserves every credit he gets.

PD: In David's later years with The Irish Press, *how was the success of 'New Irish Writing' considered by other parts of the Press group of newspapers?*

TPC: It built up a lot of jealousy—internal jealousy—in the Press. *The Sunday Press* and *The Evening Press* made money, you see, and they resented *The Irish Press* being regarded as the flagship paper. I thought the same, and I made that fact known. Soon after I left the *Press* in 1987, one of the first things they got rid of was 'New

Irish Writing'. There was that internal office rivalry between the different papers, and it was described as a cost-cutting exercise. But it was a disastrously wrong thing to do. If *The Irish Press* could have risen to having half a dozen David Marcuses, I think it would still be there. But that's another story.

PD: Do you know why David decided to finish up with 'New Irish Writing' in 1986?

TPC: I don't quite know why David packed it in. I think by then he had switched a lot of his energies to Poolbeg Press, though. And that was a really good thing too. Indeed, that should be recognised as the extension of the 'New Irish Writing' page, which springboarded into a full-scale publishing house. And it did very good work.

PD: It is striking how many writers who were included in 'New Irish Writing' went on to have books published by Poolbeg—especially books of short stories.

TPC: Absolutely. Well David, of course, knew who was who, and who was any good. If it was a question of commissioning a book, he knew exactly who to go to. And if someone contacted him with an idea for a book, he could tell (a) whether they'd have the stamina to stay the course and finish it, and (b) whether what they produced would be worth it. So in all those other activities he showed the talent and initiative that he brought to *The Irish Press*.

PD: How would you characterise David's work and his legacy?

TPC: Above all, David was a literary editor. That's what he was, and a good one. I don't know how history will judge his writing—his novels, and that. But I think of him as a man who cast a long and benign shadow, and 'New Irish Writing' was his most important legacy. He was that extremely valuable figure, an enabling man.

Gerard Smyth

A Golden Age

It is very tempting to call it a golden age of Dublin journalism and many of us who experienced it would do so. It was an era of much crossover between the literary and journalistic in the city's newspapers. Central to that memory is the role of David Marcus in *The Irish Press*—first as begetter of the weekly 'New Irish Writing' page and then adding literary editor to his responsibilities on Burgh Quay.

The page, distinctively branded between news and sport, was a much-anticipated weekly read, with contributions from both established and emerging short story writers and poets. His prediction in a letter to his parents in April 1968 that it would 'quickly establish itself as something people will look forward to every Saturday' was realised in the first weeks of its appearance. While the concept was something of a revival of the *Irish Writing* periodical David had founded in Cork in 1946, the 'crazy idea', as he called it, of a creative writing page in a daily newspaper was radical and brave.

My own first memory of 'New Irish Writing' was the discovery of a writer who became one of my gold standards in Irish fiction: John McGahern. His short story, 'Strandhill, the Sea', inaugurated the page. It would be no exaggeration to suggest that many of the poets and short story writers of my own generation who began publishing in late 1960s and 1970s had their first, or one of their first, outings in 'New Irish Writing'.

Having been a schoolboy reader of the page through the

summer of 1968—the summer I first 'dabbled in verse'—I decided, with the bravado and naivety of youth, to submit some of my apprenticeship efforts to the 'New Irish Writing' editor in October of that year. A cautiously worded response came from David in November, saying he wished to see more 'before coming to any kind of decision'. The request was for 'ten or twelve' poems—he was not taking any chances on the novice.

In time for Christmas I received back word that he was keeping five of the poems to publish, 'not all at the same time'. In fact all five appeared together, with a story by Elizabeth Bowen, the following month (18 January 1969). The two-guinea fee for each poem was a bonus—but seeing my work stand alongside a writer of Bowen's stature was the real thrill.

It could be said that the seeds of my own future, and my future relationship with another newspaper with literary credentials, were sown in the 'New Irish Writing' page that Saturday. Encouraged by my publication in 'New Irish Writing', I continued to have success placing poems here and there in magazines and journals. In the summer of 1970 I needed a job. My then short career as a published poet, initiated by David Marcus, brought me into contact with the architect and poet Niall Montgomery. That man of many gifts arranged for me to meet the editor of *The Irish Times*, Douglas Gageby. Montgomery had been a close friend of the author of the paper's iconoclastic 'Cruiskeen Lawn' column, Flann O'Brien (writing as Myles na gCopaleen). Gageby initially announced to me that 'the last thing this newspaper needs is another—expletive—poet', triggering a moment when my life might have taken a different direction. But he then introduced me to the chief sub-editor, Noel Fee, to whom I wisely said nothing about being 'a poet', though it soon became clear that the essential possessions of the sub-editor were the same as those of the poet—a good dictionary and a well-stocked mind.

The irony in this is that I was successful in gaining a foothold, as a trainee sub-editor, in a newspaper that had been advertising itself as 'the most-widely-read setting for contemporary Irish poetry', while David's attempt to find a home there for his 'New Irish Writing' project was unsuccessful. When he called in 'unannounced', as he writes in his memoir, to sell the idea of a new writing section, it seems he was doing so at a time of day when no one with the authority to hear his proposal was available to meet him. A stroke of good luck for a competitor newspaper, *The Irish Press*, and, I believe, a lost opportunity for the newspaper that was to become my habitat for the next forty years. David, however, found a home in a newspaper that had already been host to eminent literary men—the novelist Benedict Kiely had been its literary editor and Brendan Behan, before fame as a dramatist, author of a column now regarded as a treasury of that period in Irish life. The *Press* had also given the untameable Patrick Kavanagh a column under the pseudonym Piers Ploughman.

Cross-fertilisation between the literary and journalistic worlds was part of the everyday in the newspaper office and on the pages. *The Irish Times* into which I stepped still retained more than a vestige of what its then deputy editor, poet Bruce Williamson, called its 'enclave of magnificent Bohemianism'. Voices from the literary world were to be found not only on the books pages: Irish language poet Seán O Ríordáin, wrote a column for the paper as did Anthony Cronin whose weekly 'Viewpoint' was regarded by one young reader, Dermot Bolger, as 'a ray of subversive light'. The Belfast playwright Stewart Parker became the paper's first rock columnist, reviewing the latest album releases in his 'High Pop' column, which in later years was praised by poet Gerald Dawe as 'a kind of mini-history, a fascinating overview of popular music before business took over the music'. Perhaps the most authentic Bohemian in the office was George Hodnett (Hoddy) who reviewed live music events. Hoddy was the composer of the ballad, 'Monto', recorded by The Dubliners, but probably best known for his association with the innovative Pike Theatre whose co-founder Carolyn Swift was the paper's dance critic.

When the *Press* went into terminal decline in the 1990s and *The Irish Times* was fortunate in gaining several of its staff, it was a revelation to discover how many literary men and women had been attending to the daily and nightly production of the *Press* titles: John Banville, who had been chief-sub and later became *Irish Times* literary editor, the Joycean scholar, Terence Killeen and Mary Morrissy, now one of our finest novelists and short story writers. The *Press* subs desk also had its poets—including John Boland, Hugh McFadden and Brian Lynch.

David's experiences as an editor working closely on the production of his pages, as recorded in *Oughtobiography*, resonate with my own in *The Irish Times*. 'What I found most enjoyable,' he wrote, 'was that I spent a lot of time in the caseroom, where I soon formed warm friendships with the overseers, linotype operators and the men of the stone'. The stone and caseroom as well as the creed room, a kind of nerve centre with its machines dispensing news from around the world, were each subdivisions of that bygone newspaper office, each domain a law unto itself in those highly unionised days. Those of us from the editorial side had to watch our step but yet there was a bond of pride, as David discovered, in the nightly miracle.

The multiple responsibilities of the literary editor—choosing which books to review, finding appropriate reviewers, assessing, editing and then proof-reading reviews, and, no doubt, after some reviews appeared in print, dealing with irate authors—did not prevent David from giving time to the nurturing of young writers. Many can testify to the care he took with his responses to their work, responses that were a measure of his dedication to encouraging nascent talent. Despite what must have been a considerable inflow of correspondence to his desk, he often took the trouble to provide considered and sometimes lengthy responses, particularly to those whose writing careers he kick-started and whose development he closely followed. It turned out my 'New Irish Writing' debut, and his enthusiastic reaction to my poems, did not guarantee future easy entry onto his page. In a long letter to me two years after my inaugural five poems appeared, he was forthright and intuitive in expressing how he saw the poems I was then writing:

> You are, as it were, trying to take on a different sort of poet on his ground instead of working outward from your own base. You had a voice that was yours alone and that voice was your individuality. No one else could have written your earlier poems—almost anyone could have written this group.

I doubt if ever again I had so good and attentive a reader and been the beneficiary of such astute and meaningful guidance.

Meanwhile, in *The Irish Times*, 'that warm, indescribably dusty burrow', as another office Bohemian, Elgy Gillespie, so accurately described it, I was beginning to understand Gageby's comment that the last thing the paper needed was another poet. His legendary and unconventional predecessor, R. M. Smyllie, had, of course, established strong links between the paper and Dublin's artistic circles, especially the poets Yeats, F. R. Higgins and Austin Clarke. In ensuring a literary presence in a newspaper setting, Smyllie and Marcus were kindred spirits. Smyllie's pride in the paper's continuous publication of a weekly poem (which has continued for over a hundred years to the present day) is evident in his introduction to an *Irish Times* anthology published in 1948: '[T]he Irish Times can claim a unique war-time record in respect of its weekly literary page. An original poem has appeared on this page virtually every week throughout the war.'

The Irish Times of the early 1970s, like *The Irish Press*, continued to have its coterie of established and aspiring literati, its dabblers in verse. Gageby's deputy, the Belfast-born Bruce Williamson, was, as my colleague Conor O'Clery once described him, 'the sedentary poet and much-loved wordsmith'. Terence de Vere White, who had a notable reputation as a novelist and biographer, was the refined and dapper literary editor never without an open book in his hands as he ambled through the office. A solicitor by profession, he stood out as the only man in the office to wear a bow tie. There were others with literary pedigrees of one kind or another. The erudite features editor and visual arts critic, Brian Fallon, a writer with an encyclopaedic knowledge of both the literary and visual arts worlds, was son of the poet Padraic Fallon. His sidekick in the arts and features office, Fergus Linehan, had a run of theatrical successes. My chief mentor, who taught me the sub-editor's craft, was Peter Tynan-O'Mahony, a nephew of the poet Katharine Tynan and proud custodian of her literary legacy. Although the young poet, Eavan Boland, was not on staff, she was a regular contributor and presence in the office, brilliantly combining the dual occupations of poet and literary journalist.

In future years others appeared in various journalistic guises who would later make the transition from newsprint to literary acclaim: Nuala O'Faolain, who turned memoirist and novelist, and also the poet, Katie Donovan. Probably the most significant addition to the paper's literary ranks was Caroline Walsh, who began her career as a reporter. Not only would she go on to become one of the paper's finest literary editors, but she also encouraged the publication of short stories and established a place for them in the Features pages. It was no great surprise that she knew this art form intimately and with an instinctive love of the genre—her mother, Mary Lavin, was one of its supreme practitioners. Caroline's former teacher, Maeve Binchy, appointed women's editor in 1970, was soon on course to become an internationally popular fiction writer. A young Roddy Doyle spent the summers of 1975 and 1976 as a copy boy in the newsroom and sports department.

David's legacy lives on not only in the generation of fiction writers he brought into the light but also in the *Poetry Ireland Review*, a successor to the original *Poetry Ireland* which he established as an offshoot of *Irish Writing* in the 1940s. It should not be forgotten, as George O'Brien reminds us in his introduction to David's poetry volume, *Lost and Found*, that 'as well as his many other literary accomplishments David Marcus is also a poet'. It was as a poet he had his first engagement with *The Irish Times* and debut publication when his translation of 'The Yellow Bittern' was published in the literary pages in 1945.

His unfruitful visit to the paper in 1968 was not the end of his attempts to bring 'New Irish Writing' into the pages of the newspaper. In *Buried Memories*, his second memoir, he recounts a further attempt in 1990, in the wake of the demise of *The Irish Press*, to convince *The Irish Times* to take on publication of a weekly short story. David's persistence has to be admired: his correspondence on the subject with Gageby's successor as editor, Conor Brady, continued until 1998. Nor does *The Irish Times* connection end there. In 2015, forty-seven years after David was 'diverted' from *The Irish Times* to *The Irish Press* with his 'crazy idea', 'New Irish Writing' finally landed as a monthly section of *The Irish Times*. Alas David had not lived to see his great contribution to Irish literary life in the home he'd originally envisaged for it.

Ita Daly
A Meeting in Spring

from I'll Drop You a Line

I met David in 1969 when I submitted a short story to the 'New Irish Writing' page which he had not long before established in *The Irish Press*. I had never had anything published and I was delighted when, about three weeks after I sent in my story, I had a letter from David asking me to come in to discuss it.

The Irish Press was going through a golden era under the editorship of Tim Pat Coogan, who had set about transforming a dullish, partisan news sheet into a vibrant, intelligent newspaper, hiring young journalists like Mary Kenny and making room for one whole page every week to be devoted to Irish writing—poetry and fiction—without any advertisements.

'New Irish Writing' was a phenomenon that changed the face of contemporary writing in Ireland and it came about because of David's courage and devotion. In his career path we can see a consistency: he took chances and welcomed change.

I had been writing since I was twelve, stories and longer pieces, all abandoned before they were finished. I had even gone to a creative writing course—although it wasn't called that—when I answered a small advertisement in *The Evening Press*. It was one of the strangest experiences of my life.

At this time creative writing courses really took place only in American universities and maybe that is where our mentor got his idea. He was a chain smoker in his fifties and held the classes in his dank flat on Adelaide Road. There were four of us aspiring writers—me, an elderly Anglo-Irish woman and two men in their twenties, one of whom was writing a particularly bloody thriller which he insisted on reading to us with glee.

I think our tutor was English and he may have had something published in the 1930s but that is all any of us knew about him. He didn't talk very much, merely nodding now and then as he puffed on his roll-ups. He appeared to me to be deeply depressed and this, combined with the dankness of the room in which we gathered, seemed to give an air of authenticity to the proceedings. Occasionally, our mentor did utter an arcane comment but mainly it was a battle of egos among the writers to have their work heard.

The thriller writer was hard to shut up and the other young man spent most of his time staring at his boots, every now and again querulously squeaking a comment. The Anglo-Irish woman, timid but persistent, wanted to write about what she described as 'sadly, a dying world', and I didn't know what I wanted to write about.

I went to the class two or three times and found its usefulness lay in getting me motivated. Listening to the others gave me the impetus to get down to work and soon, although I stopped going to the class, I finished a short story.

But I was young and fickle, with many other things on my mind. I put the story in a drawer and forgot all about it. Then I met a man and fell in love and was duly dumped. When I had recovered from my broken heart, true to the cliché, I sought revenge—a literary revenge: I would write a story about what had happened but in the story I would do the dumping.

That story wrote itself and I wanted it to be published. Try 'New Irish Writing', someone suggested. We didn't subscribe to *The Irish Press* at home so I had never seen the page but when I got a copy I discovered that there was an invitation from the editor for writers to send in a story or poem. You didn't need to have been published; all you had to do was send a stamped addressed envelope with your submission and the editor would read your story and consider it for publication.

The page, I was later to learn, also published stories by established, even famous Irish authors. Writers like William Trevor and Edna O'Brien appeared there. Their story would not be an unpublished one, of course—*The Irish Press* couldn't have afforded such fees—but earlier publication in *The New Yorker* or some other American or English literary magazine meant that, in reality, the story was new for most Irish readers. The big names added lustre to the page and David's way of getting them was an example of his clever, dextrous thinking. He never worried about problems; he solved them.

I read my letter from David Marcus three times, then rang up and made an appointment to come in and see him, as I had been invited to do.

I arrived into the front office, all dressed up in my fun fur, and waited at the desk for David to descend from his eyrie, a small room right at the top of the building. I was already nervous and I was further intimidated by the formality of his greeting. As a friend said at his funeral, David had the manners of an Edwardian gentleman. After we shook hands he suggested that we go around the corner to the Silver Swan to talk about the story or, as he put it, 'to discuss your work'.

This phrase made me feel like a real writer but an increasingly nervous one and when David asked me what I would like—meaning tea or coffee—I looked around the almost empty pub and wondered how I could get through the next half-hour. I would be discovered. I wouldn't be able to talk about literature or say anything intelligent.

In desperation I said, 'I'll have a double Jameson.' Writers were serious hard-drinking people and, besides, I needed some Dutch courage. It was eleven in the morning but I was a writer.

To give him his due, my future husband didn't flinch.

David's love affair with the short story had begun long before we met and continued throughout our married life and until the day he died. In his late teens he had read William Saroyan's collection, *The Daring Young Man on the Flying Trapeze*, and fallen in love with the form. He read short stories, he wrote them and eventually he devoted his life to helping thousands of them, conceived by other writers, through the birth canal. His tiny office on Burgh Quay was the maternity ward where he combined the roles of obstetrician and midwife, reading every manuscript that came into him, working on it with the author, seeing talent in imperfect stories where other editors might have seen only flaws.

David told me straight away that the story I had submitted was not going to be published but that he thought I had talent. He suggested that I go home and write another story and send it to him. He told me to put the original story away and come back to it later on as it might be easier at this stage to embark on something new.

Any disappointment I felt was outweighed by my excitement. I had talent: what more can any young writer hope to hear? I also learned from that first meeting that writing is hard work. David explained that by a fluke a story, often a first story, will write itself but this seldom happens and if one wants to become a professional writer one must be prepared for the everyday dullness that goes with any job. There was no point in hanging around waiting for inspiration to strike because one might wait for ever. The thing to do was to sit down at a particular hour every day and try to produce something. You might sit there for a week and nothing will emerge but something will eventually happen provided you put in the work.

Now that creative writing courses have become commonplace, I imagine every young writer knows this but when David started his 'New Irish Writing' page, this sort of advice and encouragement was not readily available. You sent a story to one or other of the magazines that published short stories and if you were lucky you got a rejection slip. More often, the story disappeared into the ether and was never seen again. I sympathise with the editors of these magazines. We are a nation of writers and would-be writers; everyone has a book in them or, at the very least, a story. Most magazine editors soon found themselves fighting for breath under an ever-growing heap of submissions.

The reason David could cope so well was that his was an exclusive devotion. He had few distractions. Principally, as a non-drinker he didn't spend time in pubs, which in the 1970s played a large part in most people's lives. In those days you could divide people into the drinkers and dreamers who whiled away the hours in pubs and lounges and the doers who were usually teetotal and organised and ran amateur Ireland, from the dramatic and musical societies to the GAA. David established the 'New Irish Writing' page, breathing life into the short story and giving a platform to a whole generation of new writers. There was nothing amateur about his undertaking but being wifeless, childless and almost friendless as well as a non-drinker he had the necessary time to become something unique: an editor who read your story with care and gave you a considered answer promptly.

When I met him he was devoting his life to this project. He was a man of few needs and little ego. He was indifferent to or, more accurately, unaware of public opinion. He had come back from London to live in Dublin, a bachelor in his mid-forties and set in his ways, knowing nobody except his brother. I think he might have remained thus, contented and solitary, if I hadn't wandered into his life that spring morning.

I say contented rather than happy. He was glad to be back in Ireland, really glad to be doing work that mattered so much to him but, apart from that, his life was pretty bleak. Every evening he returned from work, his briefcase heavy with manuscripts. En route he would stop off at the supermarket to buy a tin of salmon or half a dozen eggs, ingredients for a simple evening meal that he would cook in his tiny kitchenette. He would read the stories and poems that he had brought home and, later on, listen to music until it was bedtime.

On Friday he would visit his brother, Louis, and his sister-in-law, Chookie, for Shabbat supper; otherwise he rarely went out. He was isolated, even more than he had been in London, but he was stoical and when I got a glimpse into this life for the first time I know that it upset me far more than it seemed to be upsetting him. He had learned acceptance.

His greatest passion, even maybe surpassing his love of the short story, was for music. He had a large collection of tapes which he listened to every day as well as listening to BBC Radio 3. He played the piano but, believing himself to be no good, never played in front of anyone. If someone came into the room he immediately stopped. However, after we were married the sound of his playing behind a closed door became the musical accompaniment of my life. He only ever played the same Mozart concerto, not in its entirety, just the first few bars. These he went over again and again, starting at the beginning each time he played a wrong note. I don't know if he could play anything else or why he never tried; I just accepted it as a quirk. Looking back now, it seems very strange, an indication, perhaps, of his intolerance of the mediocre. 'Ah sure it'll be grand' was not an approach that David entertained.

His most singular characteristic and the thing I envied most was the fact that he was always himself, no matter in whose company or whatever the circumstances. This is something that can be said about very few people and I see it as a sort of gift.

These are things I learned about David in the course of our life together. That we got together at all was due to David's persistence and confidence for, although he was diffident, if he really wanted something he went after it and didn't give up.

After that first meeting and I had had a story accepted we started going out together. Initially, I didn't see it in this light for I really only saw him in relation to my work. With his praise I began to think that maybe I could write and I started taking the whole thing seriously. When David asked me out to dinner, he may have seen it as a date but I saw it more as a workshop. We talked about writing and I listened, eager for any advice he could offer. I wasn't looking for romance: I had left that behind with my broken heart.

But romance developed—and quite quickly. I think that he had fallen in love with me straight away and after a few meetings, although slow on the uptake, I began to notice this. I saw how he looked at me and I knew that it wasn't just as one of his writers; this, inevitably, led to my viewing him in a different light. I saw that this mentor, this man, was very attractive—diffident but at the same time sure of what he wanted.

So our meetings became dates for me too and soon, without pretence on either side, we were going to the theatre regularly or out to dinner in the old Unicorn Restaurant on Merrion Row or the Trocadero, a very different restaurant then from what it later became.

As a suitor David had a lot going for him. For a start he liked women, something that is not at all a given. Then he had such delightful, old-fashioned manners that sort of wrapped around me, making me feel special and cherished. I know it goes against everything liberated young women are expected to feel but I liked the fact that, in restaurants, after we had chosen what we wanted to eat, he did the ordering. I liked the fact that he stood up when I came into a room and that he always walked on the outside on a pavement. I felt that I was protected but never for a moment did I feel that I wasn't David's equal and neither did he. This was why I could enjoy the old-fashioned courtesy: there was nothing condescending about it.

Frank McGuinness

Plum Soup

To make dessert,
I soak plums in
alcohol, oranges
juiced, sugared,
and vanilla.

These plums I toast
in ovens like
a furnace perfumed,
scenting the clean,
the cold kitchen.

Love eats and drinks
the purple plums,
discarding stones,
swallowing skin, sweet
himself, breathing.

Father Quigley And The Elephants

Father Quigley's troop of elephants,
they landed with him from Kenya,
carved from ebony with ivory tusks,
packed safely in his well-travelled valise
come to streets in dearest, darkest Donegal
to sit on our placid winged side boards.
Over the whole of Cluain Mhuire,
the steep Mill Brae, scary hairy Castle Park,
Father Quigley raised his benediction gold,
shielded by his army of elephants
who stood at peace to drink deep from
the holy well of Mc Daids' mineral waters.

Did Father Quigley lift from Africa
its forests and dainty orchards
of the pineapples, oranges, bananas
that squashed sweetness into Mc Daids?
Did he cart them northward on elephants,
the Hannibal of the Barnesmore Gap,
bringing ice cream soda from Carthage ?
Was it the harder stuff let us witness
elephants pink and assorted colours
dance a medley of old time waltzes,
military two-steps, foxtrots, valetas?
One woman, blinded by bad poitín,
swore these miracles were the last she saw.

Where are they now, Father Quigley's elephants?
Buried in sideboards, broken in black bits,
longing for the plains of lost continents,
having mastered long ago their names in Gaelic,
not that this mattered in our part of Ireland,
English speaking before the Great Famine.
No work could be found, manual, clerical,
forms necessitating sign your X,
a swipe of the trunk would also suffice.
Children held out hands, able to read palms,
hoping to find some strain of elephants
now long gone, despatched into graveyards
where he himself lies, gentle Father Quigley.
That poitín woman, blaming church and state,
asked never to let her near Africa.

— — —

David Marcus in 'New Irish Writing' in the mid-1970s had no fear of publishing gay poetry and fiction. He, and the editors of *Cyphers*, took that risk happily, and I celebrate them for that recognition. 'Plum Soup' draws intensively on William Carlos Williams, my hero at that time while I was studying English in UCD, especially his beautiful, brief 'This Is Just To Say', centred on plums in the fridge, so sweet and so cold. Delicious. 'Father Quigley And The Elephants' came from my Buncrana past, and David encouraged me to explore the many high ways and byways its legacy drew for me, seeing signs of all the earth in County Donegal.

Michael Harding
Dining on Dreams

I was fifteen when I first posted a poem to David Marcus at *The Irish Press*. I was sixteen when I received a letter of reply. It sat on the dining-room table all day while I was at school. I came home on the bus, worrying about Leaving Cert Honours Maths classes, which I had recently begun. I had completed the Inter Cert and was being forced to do Honours Maths against my will.

I loved History and English but Maths frightened me. I feared the following two years might likely shatter my self-confidence and destroy any sense of worth I was developing. Instead of allowing me to do subjects I loved and write poetry, I was informed that my future was in numbers which I hadn't any possibility of comprehending.

In those days I studied in an empty dining room, at a sombre mahogany table, on which the letter had been left by my father unopened.

The table was bought in a swanky store in Dublin where my father had once worked as a child, packing boxes. While at national school, he was obliged to sell newspapers on the streets every afternoon, to help support his impoverished family. He missed the end of each school day and it so happened that the final lesson in those days was Algebra. So, like other poor children, he never got beyond adding and subtracting.

Being cheated out of what he loved, the magic of numbers, he resolved to make them a part of his adult life. So when he lost his job packing boxes at Pim Brothers on George's Street, in his early twenties, due to the onset of an economic depression, he decided to change his life and begin night classes; and there began the long ordeal of menial jobs by day and correspondence courses by night, from Rathmines to the University of Glasgow, until he eventually reached the dizzy heights of a profession, and became County Accountant for Cavan.

Married in his fifties, he went back to an old friend who had packed boxes with him as a child and bought a sideboard, four chairs and the dining-room table at which I did my homework.

I loved that table. I saw it as a kind of symbol of my father's journey and struggle, and so when my parents were long dead and the old house was being sold, I made sure to take the table with me to Leitrim where I intended it to function as a temporary addition to our humble abode until we got some furniture of our own. But it lasted the length of my own child's childhood, and I would come home sometimes and smile to find her sitting there in the evenings attending to whatever absorbed her on the screen of her laptop.

The letter that lay unopened in my youth was addressed to me in bold type, which indicated that it must be from an adult. And there was only one adult who might be writing to me in such an officious tone, using a white business-class envelope and affixing the title Esquire to the end of my name.

I didn't open it instantly. I needed to get my Maths homework out of the way. If I opened the envelope and read a letter of rejection before I opened my Maths books, I wouldn't have been able to finish any homework. So I slipped the letter between the pages of Patrick Kavanagh's *Collected Works* which had been published about a year earlier and which was to me a sacred text during those days.

Eventually before bedtime I opened and read the letter, written and signed by David Marcus.

It was like reading something from Moses. Like listening to the verdict of a remote judge. The editor in chief of the most important poetry platform in the nation was addressing me. And he liked the poems. And he wanted to publish them.

In those days I used to get the bus to school, but I might as well have been a ghost. Neither the Loretto girls in their burgundy skirts nor the demure daughters of the Royal School ever bothered with me. I didn't play football, didn't have long hair and was never in trouble with the police; so I was a complete non-entity.

Getting in trouble with various police forces would have been easy in those days even if I was only sixteen. In Enniskillen, where we went regularly as a family to buy butter, there were always RUC men patrolling the street outside Wellworths and Woolworths, fingering their pistols as they glared at young boys like me, and I'm sure the slightest impudence would have brought their ire down upon me as I brushed past them in search of Milky Way bars that were not available in the Free State. Non-entities like me dreamed of such drama. How wonderful it would have been if the story got out in Loretto that I was in trouble with the RUC.

It never happened. Although it wasn't the RUC that I feared. It was my mother who policed my adolescence as if I were a medieval prince. She marked out the social boundaries I dared not cross. And being rude with uniformed officers in Enniskillen was the gravest of boundaries; particularly since our car was stuffed with so much butter on the way home.

And besides, I was so incompetent at everything that I couldn't even get arrested for not having a light on my bicycle.

And I did try regularly, but without success. There was a guard in Cavan at the time who was zealous about the law regarding bicycle lamps. He would wait in the bushes or behind a low wall of suburbia, watching for college students cycling home after official study hours at night, hoping to catch someone who wasn't adequately illuminated. Even my mother thought he was an ignoramus, so it was a notoriety I could have aspired to, without fearing her wrath if I had ended up in court. I regularly cycled out in front of the pack, alone and as visible as a black cat in a coal shed, but I was never fortunate enough to do it on a night when the guard was on duty.

It would have been an heroic narrative had I been caught, and might have secured me more attention on the school bus, but at sixteen I had resigned myself to a life of invisibility.

Then the poems were published and my life changed. The Beatles had recorded a few LPs and Bob Dylan whined and wailed on transistor radio sets beneath the pillows of a thousand young girls all over the country, and some of them sat by day on my school bus, and up until then, if ever I brushed past their shoulders they remained as detached as zen monks.

But being a poet trumped even playing football. The heroic poet, solitary and melancholic, languishing in an attic and writing love poems, would have been a matchless prize for any girl in burgundy or green. And sure enough, the moment I stepped onto the dance floor in Cavan after that first publication I realised I had become a different person. At teenage dances, or 'Hops' as we used to call them, I slung my coat over my shoulders like it were a Yeatsian cloak and for eighteen more months I strode along the aisle of the school bus like a great colossus of wounded grace.

I never mentioned this aspect of my good fortune to David Marcus when I met him for the first time some years later in his home in Dublin. Even then I was terrified of adults who had achieved so much in life.

But I remember him being curious about my life as a writer and so I mumbled to him something about a book I was working on and how I hoped it would be published.

'Oh it will,' he said with assurance, 'it will.' And then he added: 'The first of many, I hope.'

For me that moment was as life-altering as the first letter, though it was just a casual remark. In that one supportive phrase, my self-image was reframed again. He was graciously presuming that I might be on a pathway as a writer for the long term.

David Marcus influenced the shape of my life in both those

moments. Brief and terse and casual, but yet transformative for me. I felt his presence constantly as a mentor and teacher to whom I remained deeply indebted.

There were further letters from Mr Marcus, and further poems by me in *The Irish Press*. There were short stories too and some years later I received a Hennessy Award, which was another milestone on the way towards life as a full-time writer.

It was David Marcus who advised me to use the title Michael P. Harding on my first book, since my father was already known as Michael Harding from his regular book reviews in the same newspaper.

All my opportunities for writing and publishing were direct or indirect consequences of that first letter, and of David Marcus's confidence in my writing, and the generosity with which he treated me as a writer; as if he were sure that I had a future.

And my father was quietly proud. Even though I may have written an occasional disparaging line about my childhood or my relationship with him, he never flinched in the face of poetry. Whenever he saw me at that old table in the dining room opening other letters or reading anything other than schoolbooks, he would say, 'I won't interrupt you, you're at your work.'

My father died only six years after those first poems were published and the table outlasted him by almost fifty years. Then one leg collapsed and the table top was recycled as a work bench in the garden shed. That happened last year. So, in fact, it even outlasted David Marcus by almost fifteen years.

There is a way in which I believe that our loved ones are forever with us and in us. So my father's ghost is still a real presence in my life. He shapes my determination to live well. And for an accountant in his later years, he got enormous pleasure from reading books and composing sentences and writing book reviews. Because David Marcus was the mentor who showed confidence in him too, in that long-ago time of my childhood when I dined on dreams.

Neil Jordan

Sand

I entered the premises on Burgh Quay, through a kind of library of bound newspapers, and was led upstairs to an office overlooking the river. David Marcus sat there, behind a large wooden desk, in a pinstriped suit, briliantined hair combed back. He rose, shook my hand and thanked me for the story I had submitted to 'New Irish Writing'. There was a problem, though, with one particular word, which was why he had asked to meet.

So this is what literature is like, I thought, this elegant, courtly man with inquisitive brown eyes, who would request a meeting in person to discuss a particular word. He had the printed story on the desk beside him, about a brother and a sister and a donkey on a beach. The word referred to the donkey's member, which swung suggestively beneath his haunches on the dunes. And rather than mention the word, David pointed at it, with his fountain pen.

Would the story survive without it, he wondered? It would be a pity to lose it, I said. Indeed, he replied, but he had to answer to sensibilities other than his own. This was *The Irish Press*, after all, founded by Éamon de Valera, mouthpiece of the Fianna Fáil party. The fact that he was allowed a page, every Saturday, devoted to new Irish writing was a kind of miracle in itself. And it would be a greater pity if the story wasn't published.

So I agreed. The story would survive without it. But I'm not sure that Irish writing, at the time, would have survived without him.

Desmond Hogan
The Mourning Thief

Coming through the black night he wondered what lay before him: a father lying dying; Christmas, midnight ceremonies in a church which stood up like a gravestone; floods about his home.

With him were his wife and his friend Gerard. They needn't have come by boat but something purgatorial demanded it of Liam, the gulls that shot over like stars, the roxy music in the jukebox, the occasional Irish ballad rising in cherished defiance of the sea.

The night was soft, breezes intruded, plucking hairs, threads lying loose in many coloured jerseys. Susan fell asleep once while Liam looked at Gerard. It was Gerard's first time in Ireland; Gerard's eyes were chestnut. His dark hair cropped like a monk's on a bottle of English brandy. With his wife sleeping Liam could acknowledge the physical relationship that lay between them. It wasn't that Susan didn't know but despite the truism of promiscuity in the school where they worked there still abided laws like the Old Testament God's, reserving carnality for smiles after dark.

A train to Galway, the Midlands frozen in.

Susan looked out like a Botticelli Venus, a little worried, often just vacuous. She was a music teacher, thus her mind was penetrated by the vibrations of Bach whether in a public lavatory or a Lyon's Café.

The red house at the end of the street; it looked cold, pushed away from the other houses. A river in flood lay behind. A woman, his mother, greeted him. He an only child, she soon to be a widow. But something disturbed Liam with excitement. Christmas candles still burned in this town.

His father lay in bed, still magically alive, white hair smeared on him like a dummy, that hard face that never forgave an enemy in the police force still on him. He was delighted to see Liam. At eighty-three he was a most ancient father, marrying late, begetting late, his wife fifteen years younger.

A train brushed the distance outside. Adolescence returned with a sudden start: the gold flurry of snow as the train in which he was travelling sped towards Dublin, the films about Russian winters. Irish winters became Russian winters in turn, and half Liam's memories of adolescence were of the fantasised presence of Russia. Irons, candles, streets agleam with snow.

'Still painting?'

'Still painting.' As though he could ever give it up. His father smiled as though he were about to grin. 'Well we never made a policeman out of you.'

At ten, the day before he was to be inaugurated as a boy scout, Liam handed in his uniform. He always hated the colours of the Irish flag, mixing like the yolk in a bad egg.

It hadn't disappointed his father that he hadn't turned into a military man, but his father still preferred to hold on to a shred of prejudice against Liam's chosen profession, leaving momentarily aside one of his most cherished memories, visiting the National Gallery in Dublin once with his son, encountering the curator by accident, and having the curator show them around, an old man who had since died, leaving behind a batch of poems and a highly publicised relationship with an international writer. But the sorest point, the point now neither would mention, was arguments about violence. At seventeen Liam walked to the local hurling pitch with petitions against the war in Vietnam.

Liam's father's fame, apart from being a police inspector of note, was fighting in the GPO in 1916 and subsequently being arrested on the republican side in the civil war. Liam was against violence, pure and simple. Nothing could convince him that 1916 was right. Nothing could convince him it was different now, old women, young children, being blown to bits in Belfast.

Statues abounded in this house; in every nook and cranny was a statue, a statue of Mary, a statue of Joseph, an emblem perhaps of some saint Mrs Fogarthy had sweetly long forgotten. This was the first thing Gerard noticed and Susan, who had seen this menagerie before, was still surprised. 'It's like a holy statue farm.'

Gerard said it was like a holy statue museum. They were sitting by the fire, two days before Christmas. Mrs Fogarthy had gone to bed.

'It is a museum,' Liam said, 'all kinds of memories, curious sensations here, ghosts. The ghosts of Irish Republicans, of policemen, military men, priests, the ghosts of Ireland.'

'Why ghosts?' Gerard asked.

'Because Ireland is dying,' Liam said.

Just then they heard his father cough.

Mr Fogarthy was slowly dying, cancer welling up in him. He was dying painfully and yet peacefully because he had a dedicated wife to look after him, and a river in flood all around, somehow calling Christ to mind, calling penance to mind, instilling a sense of winter in him that went back a long time, a river in flood around a limestone town.

Liam offered to cook the Christmas dinner but his mother scoffed him. He was a good cook Susan vouched. Once Liam had cooked and his father had said he wouldn't give it to the dogs.

They walked, Liam, Susan, Gerard, in a town where women were hugged into coats like brown paper accidentally blown about them. They walked in the grounds of Liam's former school, once a former estate, now beautiful, elegant still in the east Galway winter solstice.

There were tinkers to be seen in the town and English hippies behaving like tinkers. Many turkeys were displayed, fatter than ever, festooned by holly. Altogether one would notice prosperity everywhere, cars, shining clothes, modern fronts replacing the antique ones Liam recalled and pieced together from childhood.

But he would not forfeit England for this dull patch of Ireland, southern England where he'd lived since he was twenty-two; Sussex, the trees plump as ripe pears, the rolling verdure, the odd delight of an English cottage.

He taught with Susan, with Gerard, in a free school. He taught children to paint. Susan taught them to play musical instruments. Gerard looked after younger children though he himself played a musical instrument, a cello.

Once Liam and Susan had journeyed to London to hear him play at St-Martin-in-the-Fields, entertaining ladies who wore poppies on their lapels, as his recital coincided with Remembrance Sunday and paper poppies generated an explosion of remembrance.

Susan went to bed early now, complaining of fatigue, and Gerard and Liam were left with one another. Though both were obviously male they were lovers, lovers in a tentative kind of way, occasionally sleeping with one another. It was still an experiment, but for Liam held a matrix of adolescent fantasy. Though he married at twenty-two, his sexual fantasy from adolescence was always homosexual. Susan could not complain. In fact it rather charmed her. She'd had more lovers since they'd married than fingers could count; Liam would always accost her with questions about their physicality, were they more satisfying than him? But he knew he could count on her; tenderness between them had lasted six years now.

She was English, very much English. Gerard was English. Liam was left with this odd quarrel of Irishness. Memories of adolescence at boarding school, waking from horrific dreams nightly when he went to the window to throw himself out but couldn't because the window frames were jammed. His father had placed him at boarding school, to toughen him like meat. Liam had not been toughened, chastened, ran away once or twice. At eighteen he left altogether, went to England, worked on a building site, put himself through college. He'd ended up in Sussex, losing a major part of his Irishness but retaining this: a knowledge when the weather was going to change, a premonition of all kinds of disasters and, ironically, an acceptance of the worst disasters of all, death, estrangement.

Now that his father was near death old teachers, soldiers, policemen called, downing sherries, laughing rhetorically, sitting beside the bed covered by a quilt that looked like twenty inflated balloons. Sometimes Liam, Susan, Gerard sat with these people, exchanging remarks about the weather, the fringe of politics or the world economic state generally.

Mrs Fogarthy swept up a lot. She dusted and danced around with a cloth as though she'd been doing this all her life, fretting and fiddling with the house.

Cars went by. Geese went by, clanking terribly. Rain came and church bells sounded from a disparate steeple.

Liam's father reminisced about 1916, recalling little incidents, fights with British soldiers, comrades dying in his arms, ladies fainting from hunger, escape to Mayo, later imprisonment in the Curragh during the civil war. Liam said: 'Do you ever connect it with now, men, women, children being blown up, the La Mon hotel bombing, Bessbrook killings, Birmingham, Bloody Friday? Do you ever think that the legends and the brilliance built from your revolution created this, death justified for death's sake, the stories in the classroom, the priests's stories, this language, this celebration of blood?'

Although Liam's father fought himself once he belonged to those who deplored the present violence, seeing no connection. Liam saw the connection but disavowed both.

'Hooligans. Murderers,' Liam's father said.

'Liam said, 'You were once a hooligan then.'

'We fought to set a majority free.'

'And created the spirit of violence in the new state. We were weaned on the violence, me and others of my age. Not actual violence but always with a reference to violence. Violence was right we were told in class. How can we blame those now who go out and plant bombs to kill old women when they were once told this was right?'

The dying man became angry. He didn't look at Liam, looked beyond him to the street.

'The men who fought in 1916 were heroes. Those who lay bombs in cafés are scum.'

Betrayed he was silent then, silent because his son accused him on his deathbed of unjustifiably resorting to bloodshed once. Now guns went off daily in the far north. Where was the line between right and wrong? Who could say? An old man on his death bed prayed that the guns he's fired in 1916 had been for a right cause and, in the words of his leader Patrick Pearse, had not caused undue bloodshed.

On Christmas Eve the three young people and Mrs Fogarthy went to midnight mass in the local church. In fact it wasn't to the main church but a smaller one, situated on the outskirts of the town, protruding like a headstone. A bald middle-aged priest greeted a packed congregation. The cemetery lay nearby but one was unaware of it. Christmas candles and Christmas trees glowed in bungalows.

'Come all ye faithful' a choir of matchstick boys sang. Their dress was scarlet, scarlet of joy.

Afterwards Mrs Fogarthy penetrated the crib with a whisper of prayer.

Christmas morning, clean, spare, Liam was aware of estrangement from his father, that his father was ruminating on his words about violence, wondering were he and his ilk, the teachers, police, clergy of Ireland responsible for what was happening now, in the first place by nurturing the cult of violence, contributing to the actuality of it as expressed by young men in Belfast and London.

Sitting up on Christmas morning Mr Fogarthy stared ahead. There was a curiosity about his forehead. Was he guilty? Were those in high places guilty as his son said?

Christmas dinner; Gerard joked, Susan smiled, Mrs Fogarthy had a sheaf of joy. Liam tidied and somehow sherry elicited a chuckle and a song from Mrs Fogarthy. 'I have seen the lark soar high at morn.'

The song rose to the bedroom where her husband who'd had dinner in bed heard it.

The street outside was bare.

Gerard fetched a guitar and brought all to completion, Christmas, birth, festive eating, by a rendition of Bach's 'Jesu, Joy of Man's Desiring.'

Liam brought tea to his father. His father looked at him.

''Twas lovely music,' his father said with a sudden brogue. 'There was a Miss Hanratty who lived here before you were born who studied music in Heidelberg and could play Schumann in such a way as to bring tears to the cat's eyes. Poor soul, she died young, a member of the ladies' confraternity. Schumann was her favourite and Mendelssohn came after that. She played Mozart and afterwards in the hotel sang a song, what was it? O yes, "The Star of the County Down".

'Such a sweetness she had in her voice too. But she was a bit of a loner and a bit lost here. Never too well really, she died maybe when you were a young lad.'

Reminiscences, names from the past, Catholic names, Protestant names, the names of boys in the rugby club, in the golf club, Protestant girls he's danced with, nights at the October fair. They came easily now, a simple jargon.

Sometimes though the old man visibly stopped to consider his child's rebuke.

Liam gauged the sadness, wished he hadn't said anything, wanted to simplify it but knew it possessed all the simplicity it could have, a man on his deathbed in dreadful doubt.

Christmas night they visited the convent crib, Liam, Susan Gerard, Mrs Fogarthy, a place glowing with a red lamp. Outside trees stood in silence, a mist thinking of enveloping them. The town lay in silence. At odd intervals one heard the gurgle of television but otherwise it could have been childhood, the fair Green, space, emptiness, the rhythm, the dance of one's childhood dreams.

Liam spoke to his father that evening. 'Where I work we try to educate children differently from other places, teach them to develop and row from within, try to direct them from the most natural point within them. There are many such schools now but ours, ours I think is special, run as a co-operative, we try to take children from all class backgrounds and begin at the beginning to redefine education.'

'And do you honestly think that they'll be better educated children than you were, that the way we educated you was wrong?'

Liam paused.

'Well it's an alternative.'

His father didn't respond, thinking of nationalistic comradely Irish schoolteachers long ago. Nothing could convince him that the discipline of the old style of education wasn't better, grounding children in basic skills. Silence somehow interrupted a conversation, darkness deep around them, the water of the floods shining, reflecting stars.

Liam said goodnight. His father grunted. Susan already lay in bed. Liam got in beside her. They heard a bird let out a scream in the sky like a baby and they went to sleep.

Gerard woke them in the morning, strumming a guitar.

Saint Stephen's day; mummers stalked the street, children with blackened faces in a regalia of rags collecting for the wren. Music of a tin whistle came from a pub, the town coming to life. The river shone with sun.

Susan divined a child dressed like old King Cole, a crown on her head and her face blackened. Gerard was intrigued. They walked the town. Mrs Fogarthy had lunch ready. But Liam was worried, deeply worried. His father lay above, immersed in the past.

Liam had his past too, always anxious in adolescence, running away to Dublin, eventually running away to England. The first times home had been odd; he noticed the solitariness of his parents. They'd needed him like they needed an ill-tended dog. Susan and he had married in the local church. There'd been a contagion of aunts and uncles at the wedding. Mrs Fogarthy had prepared a meal. Salad and cake. The river had not been in flood then.

In England he worked hard. Ireland could so easily be forgotten with the imprint of things creative, children's drawings, oak trees in blossom, Tudor cottages where young women in pinafores served tea and cakes, home-made and juiced with icing.

He'd had no children. But Gerard was now both a twin, a child, a lover to him. There were all kinds of possibilities. Experiment was only beginning. Yet Ireland, Christmas, returned him to something, least of all the presence of death, more a proximity to the prom, empty laburnum pods and hawthorn trees naked and crouched with winter. Here he was at home with thoughts, thoughts of himself, of adolescence. Here he made his own being like a doll on a miniature globe. He knew whence he came and if he wasn't sure where he was going at least he wasn't distraught about it.

They walked with his mother that afternoon. Later an aunt came, preened for Christmas and the imminence of death. She enjoyed the tea, the knowledgeable silences, looked at Susan as though she was not from England but a far off country, an Eastern country hidden in the mountains. Liam's father spoke to her not of 1916 but of policemen they'd known, irascible characters, forgetting that he had been the most irascible of all, a domineering man with a wizened face ordering his inferiors around.

He'd brought law, he'd brought order to the town. But he'd failed to bring trust. Maybe that's why his son had left. Maybe that's why he was pondering the fate of the Irish revolution now, men with high foreheads who'd shaped the fate of the Irish Republic. His thoughts brought him to killings now being done in the name of Ireland. There his thoughts floundered.

From where arose this language of violence for the sake and convenience of violence?

Liam strode by the prom that evening, locked in a donkey jacket. There were rings of light around distant electric poles. He knew his father to be sitting up in bed; the policemen he'd been talking about earlier gone from his mind and his thoughts on 1916, on guns and blazes, and rumination in prison cells long ago. And long after that thoughts on the glorification of acts of violence, the minds of children caressed with deeds of violence. He'd be thinking of his son who fled and left the country.

His son was now thinking of the times he'd run away to Dublin, to the neon lights slitting the night, of the time he went to the river to throw himself in and didn't, of his final flight from Ireland. He wanted to say something, urge a statement to birth that would unite father and son but couldn't think of anything to say. He stopped by a tree and looked to the river. An odd car went by towards Dublin.

Why this need to run? Even as he was thinking that a saying of his father returned, 'Idleness is the thief of time.' That statement had been flayed upon him as a child, but with time, as he lived in England among fields of oak trees, that statement had changed; time itself had become the culprit, the thief. And the image of time as a thief was for ever embroiled in a particular ikon of his father's, that of a pacifist who ran through Dublin helping the wounded in 1916, was arrested, shot dead with a deaf and dumb youth. And that man, more than anybody, was Liam's hero, an Irish pacifist, a pacifist born of his father's revolution, a pacifist born of his father's state.

He returned home quickly, drew the door on his father. He sat down.

'Remember, Daddy, the story you told me about the pacifist

shot dead in 1916 with a deaf and dumb youth, the man whose wife was a feminist.'

'Yes.'

'Well, I was just thinking that he's the sort of man we need now, one who comes from a revolution but understands it in a different way, a creative way, who understands that change isn't born from violence but intense and self-sacrificing acts.' His father understood what he was saying, that there was a remnant of 1916 that was relevant and urgent now, that there had been at least one man among the men of 1916 who could speak to the present generation and show them that guns were not diamonds, that blood was precious, that birth most poignantly issues from restraint.

Liam went to bed. In the middle of the night he woke muttering to himself 'May God have mercy on your soul,' although his father was not yet dead, but he wasn't asking God to have mercy on his father's soul but on the soul of Ireland, the many souls born out of his father's statelet, the women never pregnant, the cruel and violent priests, the young exiles, the old exiles, those who could never come back.

He got up, walked down the stairs, opened the door on his father's room. Inside his father lay. He wanted to see this with his own eyes, hope even in the persuasion of death.

He returned to bed.

His wife turned away from him but curiously that did not hurt him because he was thinking of the water rising, the moon on the water and as he thought of these things geese clanked over, throwing their reflections onto the water grazed with moon which rimmed this town, the church towers, the slate roofs, those that slept now, those who didn't remember.

Mary Leland
We Are What We Give

Never go back. In response to the invitation to contribute to this miscellany, I went back, and found myself a stranger. Had this been me? Yes, that was me, answering that telephone call, reading that letter on blue writing paper, introduced to that distinguished typewriter and to the almost medieval flourish of the signature which was to become so warmly potent. And those are my words over which David Marcus threw a blessing of acceptance, allowing them the status of a readable short story, a work that would be published.

But memory is both random and imprecise; so much is true, but the writing paper, if it ever was the blue I recall, has mellowed to grey, although the indissoluble words, the font and signature, remain accurate. The first of these letters was a response to a short story, 'Windfalls', also a first. Writing now, after a gale of apples, I recall the stress of bounty, of another kind of dependant, changing painfully into something close to a gift of transformation. That was an autumn in which a known life was turning its face to the wall yet the harvest of fruit had to be gathered, wrapped and shelved in the old garage at the end of the garden. It was a ritual, a compulsion of storage laying questions in the dusty sunlight of a shed.

There is no evidence that I know of that David Marcus understood the personal impact of his response to 'Windfalls', although a subsequent letter detected a theme which, while unique in my self-absorption, he found of wider relevance. That initial letter from his desk at *The Irish Press* in 1978 also was unique to me but was not rare, by any account, in his publishing career. It carried with it an implication of entitlement, a condition that has to be earned, but that also allows the hope (and then the conviction, however hazardous) that a singularity was implied. That one was somehow singled out, or invited in, or at least accepted as a postulant member of a community almost borderless in its dimensions and scope.

What was liberating about such exchanges was the sense of one professional communicating with another although of unequal weight. Such acceptance opened a landscape familiar but not exclusive to writers: a territory of facts moulded or melted into a narrative which might be read by someone else. I grasped, and gladly, that writing about a personal trauma might make the damage emotionally legible as a story of someone else, so that what seemed intensely specific seeded on to common ground. It assumed the distance of the useful normality of experience. I had not yet read the warning from Flaubert, quoted in *The Writer's Voice* (2005) by Al Alvarez: 'Do not imagine you can exorcise what oppresses you in life by giving vent to it in art.'

I did imagine that. My attitude was emboldened by the notion that I must write to find myself. Weren't we all finding ourselves, only to wonder what to do with the self emerging from what kindly might be called a work in progress. But work anyway, and balanced by David's best advice: write what you know. There was no requirement to 'tell it slant' that I remember. The emphasis instead was on accuracy, detail, emotional candour.

Working, as so many writers do purposely or by necessity from the dubious comfort of our own home, I once complained to him of the interruptions of casual visits by family or friends, who seemed not to take seriously a writer's need for undistracted hours. 'They'll take it seriously when you do,' he said. His tone was unusually crisp; he did not accept an excuse which denied the discipline he knew to be crucial to a writer's work.

That phrase, easy to admire, difficult to emulate, has remained a wistful dictum. It has lodged here although journalism permits a flexibility, the results being quick and obvious, the commissions can be talked about. Creative, self-impelled and solitary work has hope, but no promises to meet the urgencies of a life which anyway is gathering pace and other responsibilities. Also, it must be admitted, other gratifications. With writing, conversation disseminates a project; a phrase once spoken seems fixed, no need to write it down; solitariness a self-inflicted exile.

That blue letter signifying approval and acceptance was a crucial motivation. Not that David did not criticise or indicate disapproval and that, once, quite vehemently. I still wonder as I write what he might have thought of this, or that, and dare I assault what in his case was not merely taste, but standards. His opinion has such retrospective compulsion that sometimes I hesitate over a word, a sentence, a paragraph, even an idea. Commonplace language has assumed or has been invested with a vulgar aggression, more Mailer than Heaney. I don't think David repudiated shock or extremes, no one who translated *The Midnight Court* could be averse to either; but I believe now that he looked for grace.

While I understood that David's gift of empathy was that of a fellow practitioner and never implied competition, there was a more personal, if coincidental, linkage in that we were both Corkonians. This had no literary significance or even reference in our dealings except that my acquaintance with Gerald and Sheila Goldberg occasionally revealed aspects of that boyhood lived in Cork and evoked in David's first novel *To Next Year in Jerusalem* (1954). Gerald Goldberg, self-described as 'a traditional Jew' who became Lord Mayor of Cork, was David's maternal uncle and, like David and his brother Louis, had himself grown up in Cork city. As a solicitor Gerald led a complex, occasionally combative life; in private this was supplemented by the richly artistic and charitable sponsorships and engagements he shared with Sheila. His academic passions included Joyce and Shakespeare, Shylock sometimes soothing a fret with the reminder that sufferance was the badge of all his tribe.

A discriminating crow flying northwards from Ben Truda, the Goldberg home on the Rochestown Road, might perch on the railings of Wellesley Terrace. There my close friend Maighread Murphy was visited frequently by David's brother Louis Marcus, filmmaker and supporter of Maighread's husband, the sculptor Seamus Murphy. With Maighread and with Gerald and Sheila, my relationships originated in journalism as both locations were dense with associations, personalities and events. It is some evidence of the cultural symbiosis of both households that it was Seamus who cut into the façade of Ben Truda the lines from Sean O'Faoláin: 'I looked at the climbing stairways of roofs upon roofs up to the great bell tower of Shandon the clouds fell down into the water's stillness the bells sank into the water and were drowned.'

Reminiscence is seldom without some regrets, and I remember with self-justifying shame that I disappointed David. At some point I had submitted a short story which he suggested should be worked on as a novel. It was, and it became *The Killeen* (1985), but I had ambition now and wanted to try for a wider audience and found a London agent and publisher. It was not that Poolbeg Press was offering a contract or was even in discussion, but I discovered that David had expected me to bring the book to him. It might have seemed that I had turned my back on all he had done for me, but I thought I was advancing and forgot that there might be a cost. As there was, but not from David. If he was angry I never heard or felt it, I remained in his steadfast and judicious sights. In one short story competition judged by him I came second, in another I came first; I was included in six anthologies for which he was editor. In 1992 'Windfalls' appeared in *State of the Art: Short Stories by the New Irish Writers*. In 2007 I joined, among others, John Banville, Emma Donoghue, Éilís Ní Dhuibhne, Patrick McCabe, Anne Enright, Mary Dorcey,

Frank McGuinness, Eoin McNamee, Sebastian Barry and Joseph O'Connor, in David's last anthology, *The Faber Book of Best New Irish Short Stories 2006–7*.

Such prophetic listings endorse the resonant truth of William Wall's comment to the Irish PEN conference in 2008, that it was David Marcus who 'helped shape how Ireland thinks of itself'. That internal geography was mapped by another Marcus characteristic: in that earlier era of Irish publishing he was a rarity. Those were the days when the late lamented Lar Cassidy could bring an Arts Council cheque down to Cork in his breast pocket and hand it over on the street. There was an accepted but crippling habit of informality, as if writers, perhaps all Irish artists, were amateurs at heart. It was an atmosphere, an almost humorous air breathed in a fellowship of want.

The fact that this has changed so dramatically and bureaucratically must be put to the credit of several canny activists, David not the least of them. With David, the payment or the advance came when promised. Such developments, as if in a continuing recompense, must be a crucial factor in the endurance, resilience, promotion and fame of newer Irish authors today. Newer, that is, rather than younger, the young have plenty going for them already, while those who have outlived their youth and its promise continue to work not in hope so much as because they just can't help it. I believe that this above all was David's editorial credo: to keep alive in his writers the compulsion to create as it was so strongly alive in him, as alive as his faith in the infinity of books.

There was something else, a conviction, I think, stronger even than a commitment. In September 2023 Chief Rabbi Sir Ephraim Mirvis spoke in the BBC Radio 4 slot 'Thought for the Day'. In the Jewish tradition, he said, the sum of one's merit is reckoned by what is done for others. 'We are what we give,' he said. I remembered the Goldbergs as I listened, and thought of David and all that he gave.

When I sent my first story to David Marcus I had not read Alvarez and, indeed, not very much of Flaubert. But I had read Elbert Hubbard's advice, that when life gives you lemons you should make lemonade. Life had given me apples, and I made fiction.

Sebastian Barry

When I was twenty-three, and living in a tiny room in Paris, I was writing stories fiercely. I was so young and so full of belief. But there is an edge to that belief, a border, a boundary. You begin to think that you're just a broken old radio set which doesn't have a wire leading into it. That the things you are broadcasting are just words falling on the ground. I'd been working on a story, 'The Beast', for four months without any guarantee it was any damn good. I sent it off to David Marcus at 'New Irish Writing' and a letter came back in his small black handwriting, telling me he was accepting it.

I suppose even if you're not a writer you can suspect what that might mean to a young fellow living off vegetables in Paris. It caused enormous difficulty for us. I thought I had to get my hair cut because a photograph was required. This was going to ruin us financially for two weeks. My girlfriend at the time gave me a sort of pudding-bowl cut. I went to collect the photograph, and it was incredibly expensive for us. I think we didn't eat for a few days. But that transition from you alone in a room and alone in the very early days of writing and for someone to raise a flag of approbation, it was immense. I walked around Paris in my poor shoes with a special warmth. I've certainly never forgotten it.

David was a sort of prophet, Old Testament-style, of good writing. Such people are rare, looking out over the sea for the skiff of the good poem and the small craft of the good short story.

— — —

The Beast

It seemed possible I was up before the hens were at last. The air in the farmyard was thin, and the sunlight cold. The rooks were quiet in the lane. With my breath held painfully, I crept to the hen-coop. A small cluck cluck sounded from the roost. The morning had fooled me.

I opened the hatch and let the birds out to wander. The best hen, Aunt Anne's favourite, went off quickly to its patch in the hay-barn.

'Hurry in from the yard!' Aunt Anne called. 'Or I'll give the brown egg to Mairead.'

My sister didn't like brown eggs, but I ran in anyway.

Sarah—who shared the farm with Aunt Anne—crossed the stone floor in front of me.

'They're all out,' I said.

'I'll go to my sisters',' Aunt Anne was saying to Sarah, 'and be back before eleven. The children can come with me.'

'That's fine,' Sarah said.

'But if Billy comes by, don't sit in the house with him.'

'You'd meet him on the road,' Sarah said, 'if he was coming here. There's one way only from your sisters'. You'd meet him on the road.'

'Not if he saw me first,' Aunt Anne said.

The brown egg made me sleepy. I stumbled along beside Aunt Anne for half an hour, listening to the mumble of Mairead on the other side, till we reached a ragged boundary. We came in through a stile from the shaded road, and the sudden lack of trees made the farm look flat and bright. They had an old house, the three sisters, and a broad dry field around it. Aunt Anne said that Billy—who did most of the farmwork—wasn't a brother, but a friend. And when she emphasised a word like that, I knew she was only telling me as much as she wanted.

It looked a strange house to enter at the age of seven. I held Aunt Anne's hand the length of the drive. She saw I was wary, and smiled down.

'The birds aren't up yet, Nessie,' she said. 'That's why it's quiet here.'

The birds were up alright, I thought—but they were keeping out of sight. There was a dark patch of copsewood across the field. The birds were in there, with the bogey-men.

'You're as pretty as your mother,' one of the sisters said to Mairead as we came in.

They scowled at me. They didn't trust boys in Wicklow. I didn't like the look of them either, and struggled to accept them as actual aunts of my father. They were wild and creased in their faces, and seemed unable to smile at anything. Their gentleness—reserved for my sister—lay in glances of sad concern, which feathered from a height. I was glad of their disinterest in me. I sat on a wooden trunk under a window and kept my mouth tight.

'We've a piece of lettuce for the children,' another said, perhaps Maggie. 'But meat for you, Annie, after your long walk. Billy's away up in the back field, but he said to give meat to his favourite visitor.'

'Oh no,' Aunt Anne said, 'I'm not having meat. Give me a slice of bread, and put your butter on it. I'd start growling like a wolf if I'd meat this early.'

It was better to be over by the window, with talk of wolves going on. Mairead was being made a fuss of, with her blue summer dress our mother had sent from London. I thought her too big and bad-tempered for so much attention.

'And the little boy,' Maggie ventured, 'is he a good little man?'

'He's good when it suits him,' Aunt Anne said. 'He's not too bad. He'd surprise you sometimes.'

There was a rustle of interest. One of the sisters thought it as well to examine me. I leaned back against the glass, and raised up my legs out of her reach. It was little use. Her hand came out of her cardigan for me, and there was nothing to do but hope she had no claws.

She didn't have anything except a hand, but a congealing wound crossed the back of it. There was a black and red scab. It didn't appeal to me, and she was quick to see my disgust.

'Ah go on with yourself, it's just a cut! It's just a slit I got off the plough!'

'Oh,' I said, in a froth between being relieved and unconvinced. 'You plough here, do you, cousin?'

'Cousin!' she squealed, in delight of a kind. 'Did you hear that, Annie? Cousin! What's he thinking of? Oh little boys!'

'He has a quaint side too,' Aunt Anne said, and she looked at me from across the room to make sure I was bearing up.

Their attention troubled me. It seemed time to state my position.

'And I hate lettuce,' I said.

The three sisters glanced at each other, reddened by the triumph of their original distrust. I was normal after all.

'He's a real boy, your brother,' said Maggie to Mairead.

'The attention went straight to his head,' said another.

Aunt Anne shared her disappointment with the view beyond the window.

It was still bright clear morning when we left the farmhouse. What Aunt Anne was doing there so early I wasn't sure. I did a lot of not being sure in those days. Some complaint about Billy was the usual thing though. She never liked Billy.

Mairead ran on down the drive, and I chased after her, frightened of Aunt Anne's disfavour. But she called me back—her voice very small across the open space of air—and gave me her purse to carry home. It was a recognised way of being returned to grace.

On the walk back to our farm—though we only stayed with Aunt Anne half a year, the farm did feel like 'our' farm—we had to pass the few fields of the Hacketts' place. It should have been called Mrs Hackett's place, because her husband and sons were dead. To me Mrs Hackett was a witch, at a time when most old and crinkled women were of that sorority.

The road past her farm was straight and broad, for one that sallied across a back hill. My feet had trouble with the black mud, and the dry white stones that poked up out of it to trip me. Along the road was a ditch, and across the ditch a bank of grass and bell-flowers. I was fond of popping the buds of bell-flowers. When I spotted a good plant, I leapt over the ditch, and dropped Aunt Anne's purse into the murk below. She had a splatter of green mud up to the elbow of her dress after she had fished it out, and two dark green knees. She took Mairead's hand gently, and whipped mine up from my side. But my memory was bad—a few yards on I could hardly remember why Aunt Anne was silent.

Through the tangle of a hedge I saw Mrs Hackett crossing an old field to her cow. I climbed on the bar of a gate to see her better. She had a tight bow of a back, and wore the same blue-spotted dress that Aunt Anne did. So at the same time, there was something familiar about the bent woman, and something uncomfortably alien.

'Better get off the gate, Nessie,' Aunt Anne said behind me, breaking her silence, 'and hold on to my hand like your sister.'

'But Auntie Anne, she's going to milk her cow. I'd like to see her.'

'It'll frighten you,' she said. 'Blood milk frightens little boys. Come off the gate, Annesley, when I say to.'

'Blood milk?' my sister said. 'What's that, Auntie?'

'The cow has a kind of bleeding inside it, a continuous flow. It should be slaughtered, but Mrs. Hackett won't have it. She says the blood's keeping her alive. And maybe it is, because something's doing it. Anyway, Nessie, if you want to see pink milk coming out of that cow, you can stay there on the gate. Else take my hand. I won't tell you again.

Pink like the bell-flowers! I got down off the gate. She was probably only trying to get me to come along, because the cow was too far away to see the colour of its milk, but I got down anyway.

As we went up the track I asked:

'Is she the one who muddies the well, Auntie?'

'We all muddy the well when we use it, Nessie. But she's the one who uses our well.'

'But she doesn't clean anything in it?'

'I hope not.'

'But you should tell us if she does or not. Maybe she cleans out her milk-bucket there. Maybe she washes her hands.'

'If you could learn to ask questions without being rude,' Aunt Anne said.

'Yes, but maybe she'll poison us!'

'I don't think so, Nessie. She washes her bucket in the yard with rain-water, where buckets should be washed.'

'In a tub like yours?'

'In a tub like ours, a big wooden tub, like every other tub in Wicklow.'

'I suppose it's living in that little black cottage has her the way she is,' I said, giving the matter up. The road had taken us past her. My thought was quick to follow the road.

'I wish we had the pony and trap still,' said Mairead near the farm. 'I did love the pony and trap.'

'A dangerous creature,' said Aunt Anne. 'He's better off…'

'Better off what, Auntie?' I asked.

Because after the pony threw Aunt Anne and Sarah, and put them with a shock on the muddy road, they locked him up in his stall a long time before deciding what to do with him. The pony got fat in his stable, and when the time came to bring him out to give to Billy, his sides were so thick the door couldn't manage him. Billy knocked down a side-wall of the lean-to, and let the pony out that way. He never built up the wall again though. Aunt Anne said he should have widened the door, and that there had been no call to make her farmyard ugly.

'Better off what?' I repeated. I was anxious about unfinished sentences. I thought something unpleasant had just been left unsaid. I suspected she meant to say 'Better off dead'. It was a phrase they used sometimes in the kitchen, she and her friend Sarah—not about horses, but about people who died.

'Better off with Billy,' said Aunt Anne.

We turned up the lane. There was no dog anymore to greet us at the gate, because Aunt Anne gave her collie to Billy when it bit my cheek. Billy shot it. But she whistled on the lane out of habit, a short quiet whistle that stopped before it was half done. I was sorry again to have teased the collie's tail.

'The dot of eleven,' said Sarah when we entered the kitchen. 'And you can take that look off you, Annie, because Billy wasn't by.'

After Aunt Anne had drunk a cup of tea with Sarah, and had settled the eternal fire—which was one of her particular duties—she brought us both up to the picnic field. We never did have a picnic there, but it had to be called something for our sakes. It was a big sloping field—I could forget that Aunt Anne was near if I wanted to.

I walked to the field's head and lay down. There was wood and scrub above me, and above that a heathery hill. Aunt Anne took us strolling there once. I didn't like the climbing. Instead of being brought again, the hill was turned into a realm of bogey-men. Aunt Anne never raised an arm to me. The power of the bogey men outmatched so slim and aging an arm as hers.

'Don't wander!' she called to me from the base of the field. 'Don't wander near the bogey-men, Nessie!'

I lifted my head briefly from the ground. I saw Aunt Anne

sitting far below. Mairead was distant too, but she was climbing the field towards me. I began to roll slowly to meet her.

The ground tipped beneath me, tossing me away. After some seconds it felt as steep as a standing wall. The hay bunched, clinging to the cloth of my clothes, and, as Aunt Anne shouted, made 'work for three hands!' The dust in the hay found my mouth and nose. I stopped in a sudden hollow, among Mairead's ankles.

'Clean yourself off, Nessie, clean it off!' called Aunt Anne below.

'He can't,' Mairead called back. 'He's dead.'

'I'm not,' I said, and dizzily stood up.

'Do not roll down the field, Annesley!' Aunt Anne shouted. 'Or I'll fetch the bogey-men!'

So I and my sister contented ourselves with the fighting game. The fighting game was not always purely for fun, it was for the feeding of one's malice too.

'Nessie, you beast, play nicely! Play nicely... or I'll tell Auntie!'

That was a frequent tune. It was an ordinary and usual one to have had in one's ears.

I got tired of Mairead, and slipped away from her down the field, and around Aunt Anne darning my socks near the first outhouses, and carefully into the yard.

I had a forbidden and favoured toy that I kept there. It was not forbidden in itself, but only in the use I liked to put it to. It was a large wooden fire-engine, with stout wheels for skating on. The skating was the forbidden part of it.

It was hard work along the cobbles, but I was managing satisfactorily when Aunt Anne came around the stable. She had my two blue socks in her hands, and a work-basket under her arm. She looked at me silently, and it was a look that reminded me of my father when he was disappointed and anxious too. I stood quietly, with one foot balanced on the red engine.

'Inside, Nessie, she said at last. 'You've surpassed yourself today. And that's the last you shall see of your red engine.'

I went to my bedroom and talked to myself silently. Mairead

saw Aunt Anne hiding my toy in the deep hill of dung behind the cows' shed, and came straight away and told me.

I thought of it rotting away there, with no one to save it. I imagined it thrown on the fields with the dung, and left to bury itself in the Wicklow earth. Mairead said it was better that, than cracking my head on the cobbles, and having our father and mother return from London to patch me up. But I didn't agree. And impatient of orders I returned out to the yard.

Aunt Anne's favourite hen—the best of the layers—was pecking about from spot to spot. A light breeze played along its back, raising a few small feathers. The bird seemed equal in my mind to the red engine, so I followed it around the yard. It was enough at first to prod the hen gently with a long switch. But then the dunghill, the wet grave of my engine, rose in front of me. The sorrow of Aunt Anne's crime overcame me, and I turned the hen towards a corner of the yard, where there was an old milking bucket with a little hole in it. When the bird was trapped in the corner, I put the bucket over it as deftly as I could—for the pail was awkward and rusty—and moved away.

I went into tea then since Sarah called me, and crowded into the fireside seat with Mairead. There was room enough for us both, and there would have been room to spare, had not we both had a fear of the crickets in the bricks of the chimney. Mairead kept pressed away from me too, because I was covered still in the hay of the field.

Sarah and Aunt Anne sat at a small table of their own. They seemed unusually apart from us, as if they weren't alive in the same world.

'He'll be over tonight,' Sarah was saying. 'Or he said he would be before dark, so there's a fair chance he'll stick to that.'

'He can do as he pleases, but we won't sell neither this night nor the next. And whatever the blackguard's hoping, you won't marry him.'

They were talking about Billy. With his taste for other people's possessions, he wanted our farm.

'Auntie, would the crickets go away ever?' Mairead asked. 'Could we sit here ever without the crickets?'

But I didn't care for once about the crickets. I was thinking of Aunt Anne's hen beneath the bucket.

I was arranging some cabbage on my plate, making designs with it, when we all heard someone enter the yard. You knew someone was coming by the noise of the gate. It always gave a clang as it hit its post again, because no one ever seemed to remember to put it back by hand. The reason it swung so was that the yard was on a slope, no doubt the same slope the hill was on. That is to say the house was built there at the base of the sloping field.

When the gate clanged, Sarah hurried to the window. She pushed a pot of geraniums to the corner of the ledge.

'You're an old fool,' Aunt Anne muttered. But Sarah signalled to be silent when she saw who it was.

'Gypsies,' she said.

There was a small tower of sun coming in through the glass. It lit up Sarah's hair. I could see plainly the outline of her skull.

Aunt Anne leaped to the half-door, banged shut the top—left open for air—and shot the bolt through. Mairead and I came away from the fire and peeped out through the other window of the room. There was a chair for us to stand on. Pale hot-looking light hung in the yard, and it seemed late to us both for people to be up begging.

'If we only had the collie still,' Mairead said, looking at me.

The gypsies started knocking on the door and shouting in through a crack in the middle:

'Sher jaysus crisht open here ye bitches!'

'The blackguards,' Aunt Anne said.

But they couldn't help cutting a dash for me with their brown and white horses, and the wild dirty hair they wore, man, woman, horse, and child.

One of them put his hand on the latch outside and began to

rattle it. Aunt Anne flashed her hand to it on our side, in case the bolt gave away, and a struggle started up for control of the latch. I ran up beside her and pressed my back against the door. My face smothered in her skirt and apron. I was choking in starch, but I held firm. Sarah was looking worried and angry over at the window, shouting back things at the people outside.

'Get off! Get off! Get off!' she kept roaring, as if there were a bunch of hens in her way. She always said 'Get off!' to the hens when she was feeding them, and they ran in too close.

Then Sarah said Billy was coming up the road. She smiled.

The gypsies had a short talk with Billy at the gate, and went off down along the track to Mrs Hackett's place. There wasn't any loud exchange or argument, more an understanding.

'You see, Sarah,' said Aunt Anne, 'he's a true thief, and mixes with anyone.'

'It's true,' Sarah replied, 'he's agreeable to a fault.'

Agreeable or not, Billy came and went. He didn't like the look of Aunt Anne enough to linger.

Sarah retired to bed. She pulled the covers over her face to get a good sleep. I stood looking in through the open bedroom door.

'It's her way of taking it well,' Aunt Anne said behind me.

A little later I tried to slip out to the yard, but Aunt Anne, reading in a chair, made me sit by the chimney. The fire gleamed in the glass of her spectacles. She didn't know about her hen. I thought if she knew about her hen she wouldn't sit so still.

A donkey brayed out abruptly somewhere, pleased or troubled by the twilight. It left behind it an unsmiling silence.

'You look sick, Nessie,' she said, glancing down at me.

'You weren't eating grass again, were you?'

I couldn't reply.

'You'd better go to bed. It's probably nine. Mairead's gone a long time.'

'It's you,' I said, threatened by that. 'You didn't see me helping.'

'Helping, Nessie? Who did you help?'

'You on the door—when the gypsy was rattling.'

'Well I'm sorry. Thank you for helping, Nessie. I didn't see you, you're right.'

'You never see me,' I said, and suddenly felt pleasure.

'Maybe I don't,' she replied, 'but I'm sorry for it.'

I watched the flames walking on the last of the fire. If she was being so gentle, I thought, her bird would survive till morning. Somehow or other, she had improved the hen's position—that was how I saw the matter anyway. It made me sleepy. I didn't mind so much now about going to bed.

'Nessie?'

I looked up.

'Stay with me here by the fire,' she said.

My memory was bad. The hen stayed trapped for three summer days. When I did remember I brought Aunt Anne out into the yard, and silently pointed to the bucket. She turned it up and the hen walked to freedom. She hurried to the barn for grain. As much as she threw at its feet, it ate.

The bird laid its eggs in fields and ditches after that. From time to time, flapping vigorously across the half-door, it came into the kitchen, and climbed about the fireplace and the chairs. We never had much peace from it, especially Aunt Anne, who always remembered the worth it once possessed.

'It must have been the gypsies,' Sarah ventured.

Aunt Anne knew better. She was sure in her heart that Billy had done it for spite.

Mary Morrissy
The Art of Rejection

David Marcus lived at the top of the house, the house being the *Irish Press* building on Burgh Quay. On a higher level than even the editor of the paper whose office had a grand door with a highly polished brass letter box through which an inebriated *Irish Press* staffer once urinated—in a pungent protest at the paper's leadership. This was more dangerous than it might sound since the letter flap was extremely highly sprung and the gentleman in question could well have been cut off in his prime.

These were different times.

I was never in David's office even though I was a night sub on the paper, and also, as it happened, a closet writer. In those days you kept quiet about your literary ambitions among journos, particularly if you were a woman. It was enough of a challenge to hold your own in this very male world. In my job interview I was asked if I intended to get married, and how did I feel about men swearing on the desk. (I was tempted to answer with an expletive.) In this same world David Marcus lived, though by the time the swearing men arrived for their shifts, he was probably safely at home. He was my first literary editor. First to publish me and first to reject me.

Most people associate David with the 'New Irish Writing' page, but in fact my first story appeared in the 'Young Irish Writing' page in the mid-1970s. This was a much shorter-lived off-shoot that David edited for writers under twenty-one. The story, 'A Traveller's Paradise', features a couple, Stefan and Inge—German, or perhaps Swedish?—inter-railing around Europe. Stefan has an epiphany while talking to a sex worker in a darkened town square while Inge is off the page getting a traveller's cheque changed.

At this remove, I've no idea why I 'estranged' the couple. (Did I think it was more plausible that a foreigner would engage with a 'lady of the night'?) Although it was one of my earliest publications, it belongs firmly in the juvenilia file. But David liked it, and what's more, he published it, although I don't have the acceptance letter for this first literary triumph. (They say you can always paper the walls with your rejection slips, but acceptances are too few and far between to be of much use in the interior decoration department.)

It was eight years before another story of mine appeared in *The Irish Press*, this time in the 'New Irish Writing' page in 1984. I have kept that acceptance written on *Irish Press* headed notepaper. 'I enjoyed it tremendously,' David writes. 'It is different—and something different is always so welcome—and it is most stylishly written… Hope to see more from you as soon as you like.'

By this stage I was working for the paper, and out of fears there'd be accusations of nepotism if a staffer had a story published—from other writers, mainly—I used a pseudonym. But it was also because I was struggling with the dual identities of journalist and writer, and didn't have the confidence to 'own' my own work.

That modesty, shame, cowardice—call it what you will—had comic consequences. The story won a Hennessy Award that year and the morning after the awards ceremony my photo appeared in the paper at the reception holding the (incredibly heavy) award along with David and the aforementioned editor. When I went into work the next day someone said—'there's been a right f**k-up—your pic is in the paper but with the caption of some other dame underneath.'

My two worlds had collided. I had to fess up, come out, declare it wasn't a subbing error or a case of mistaken identity. This indeed was me.

The pseudonym was quietly dropped. David never mentioned it again. Neither did I. Over the next two years I sent him six more stories. One was accepted, but otherwise it was a flurry of rejections.

> 'I'm sorry—really sorry—to be sending this one back. I wish I could like it enough to accept. The writing is wonderful—individual and polished. But what the story... seems to be saying quite eludes me.'

> 'Mary: Sorry again. The writing is absolutely wonderful but I felt with such an off-putting central character you need much more of a story than you have given the reader. Bernard's bitterness is understandable, but I don't think it, and the accompanying outline of his life, are quite enough.'

> 'I read this a number of times but was never able to feel convinced that it really succeeds. It's beautifully written but for me the cliché scenario failed to come alive and the whiff of invention and character manipulation hung in the air. Many regrets.'

All of these rejections end with the exhortation to try again, to send more.

Reading back over these responses, several things strike me. Firstly, how considered they were. You knew the work had been read—not something you know from today's form rejections. David's notes were subjective, certainly. But he often ascribed faults in the story to his incapacity as a reader—was he missing something, maybe?—rather than the author not having made things clear enough.

Such subjectivity might be frowned on now, but it was what I valued about his responses. He was saying quite clearly—this is my take, just that.

This was the pre-technology era so all of David's rejections were handwritten, often on *Irish Press* compliments slips, so they were personal, not generated automatically and they were always fastidiously courteous. That's not to say he couldn't be stern.

I've written elsewhere of a rejection he sent which said that no amount of fine writing could disguise the fact that mine was a thoroughly nasty story. And indeed it was. It appeared in my first collection and concerned a pair of sisters who abandon an 'illegitimate' new-born in the crib of a department store to die over the Christmas holidays.

This was the 1980s, when contraceptive and reproductive rights were being battled over on the streets. In 1984, the year I won the Hennessy, schoolgirl Ann Lovett (15) and her baby, died in childbirth in front of a grotto in Granard, County Longford.

Nasty things were happening.

I comforted myself at the time with the idea that I was too edgy for David Marcus, that he was old and a man and how could he understand? But now I see that he too had his constraints. He was publishing fiction in a mass-market newspaper, not an elite literary magazine. His audience wasn't a small literary coterie, but a large religiously conservative cohort of society. (There was an apocryphal story told about a survey conducted in the 1960s to identify the typical *Irish Press* reader. Their conclusion was that more men with caps read the paper than any other.)

But this was the genius of the 'New Irish Writing' page. It brought literature to the heart of public life, but it came with its own caveats and prohibitions. If the public of Ireland weren't ready to read about infanticide in the news pages of the paper, would they take any more readily to it under the guise of fiction?

There must be hundreds of writers like me who were nurtured in the same way by David Marcus over the years. The relationship with him reminds me of that of patient/therapist where you know you're not the only one, but he made you feel as if you were. David offered a civilised, old-style introduction to the literary world, one that shaped me, and I'm glad of it, even if it wasn't always a preparation for more brutal experiences down the line.

I'm a working writer so I'm still sending fiction out to

competitions and literary editors. With some honourable exceptions, you're lucky these days to get any notification that your work has been rejected; usually, only the successful are informed. There are all sorts of formulas that are now used to be told no. I've received little diagrams, like those theorems we used to do at school, with five dots marked on them, each one representing key fictional points—plot, diction, punctuation, etc—and giving me a mark out of 10 for each one.

If you do get a text-based rejection, it'll be a round-robin, which will tell you how you fared in competition with other writers. You're supposed to draw comfort from the fact that you 'scored' highly, that you 'came so close', that they always have to turn away 'good work'. The emphasis here, like much of modern life, is on crude measurement, of ranking you while studiously avoiding considering the work critically.

In contrast, David had honed and refined the art of rejection. He recognised that all rejection was personal for the writer, so he made his side of the correspondence personal too. His notes read as one writer responding to another, because he, too, was a writer. This meant that he was conferring status and respect on you, even when he was saying no.

Eoin McNamee

Intensive Care

'Queenio, Queenio,
Who's got the ball?'

It reminded me of radar:
A dumbstruck
Ball of light
Hurled through silence.

'I haven't got it
In my pocket.'

A far cry
From the bow-swung
Plumbline
The Phoenician invented.

'Queenio, Queenio,
Who's got the ball?'

And a far cry
From your astonished face
When I came upon it
In a hospital bed.

'I haven't got it
In my pocket.'

A curious intentness
About you, as if you were taking
Deep soundings
From the heart monitor.

'Queenio, Queenio,
Who's got the ball?'

Its sonic blip
A tennis ball
You lobbed and retrieved
From the wall of your heart

'I haven't got it
In my pocket.'

While the nurse keeps half
An eye on the screen
For the one that bounces
Out of reach.

'Queenio, Queenio,
Who's got the ball?'

— — —

EOIN MCNAMEE

We were in Donegal and after a lot of searching I found *The Irish Press* containing this poem in a newsagents in Ardara. I can't remember if it was the first piece I had published. The first poem perhaps. It was dusk on New Year's Day when I found it. I remember the evening light distinct to the north west at that time of year, blackish, tarn-coloured, and I remember that we were young and a kind of yearning became us or at least we thought it did. The person in the poem attached to the heart monitor was my uncle Eugene who died in early middle age, a gentle, well-dressed man who fell away quietly from the light. When my father died decades later I found a damp bundle of the same edition of the paper in a back office, maybe forty of them, which he had I think bought to distribute to friends but hadn't done because if he had I would have heard of it. Sometimes intentions, even unfulfilled ones, are good enough. Sometimes they are all you have.

— — —

Éilís Ní Dhuibhne
David Marcus the feminist?

David Marcus's visionary editorship of the 'New Irish Writing' page in *The Irish Press* coincided with a period during which Ireland was becoming aware of the less than equal representation of the female voice in Irish literature, or in any other public sphere. 'New Irish Writing' was established in 1968, and Marcus was at the helm until 1986, when he retired from *The Irish Press* to concentrate on editing books for Poolbeg Press, which he had founded in partnership with Philip McDermott in 1976. During the 1970s and 1980s, for a variety of reasons, national and international, the feminist movement exerted a powerful influence on society and legislation in Ireland. There is no need to rehearse the changes which occurred then relating to the status of women. But highly significant was the 1973 abolition of the Marriage Bar, which obliged women to resign from public service jobs on marriage, and the Anti-Discrimination (Pay) Act of 1974, which outlawed pay discrimination on the basis of gender. While Ireland lagged behind much of Europe and the Western world in providing access to contraception, abortion, divorce, protection from domestic violence and abuse, the first steps towards gender equality were taken in the early 1970s.

Inevitably the mood of the times affected the publishing industry, which until then was dominated by men. In 1975 Catherine Rose set up the publishing house, Arlen House, devoted specifically to publishing work by women; in 1978 Irish Feminist Information was set up, and this evolved into Attic Press in 1984, another press devoted to publishing work by women. In the UK, Virago, with a similar mission, was established in 1973, and was hugely influential.

David Marcus, as editor and publisher, exercised his most powerful influence on Irish literature during the 1970s and 1980s. That is to say, Marcus's greatest influence coincided with the time when feminism became a force to be reckoned with in Ireland and when change was afoot. To what extent Marcus was influenced by the mood of the times, and to what extent he was an active pacesetter when it came to promoting writing by women and about women's lives, is hard to judge. His editorial commitment was to good writing, and to new writing. In April 1968 he wrote in *The Irish Press* that his ambition in founding 'New Irish Writing' was that 'the greatest possible number of Irish writers can place their work before the greatest possible number of readers'. The gender issue was not mentioned. He welcomed new work, sometimes by very young writers. My first story was published by him when I was only nineteen, in 1974. Deirdre Madden was also published when she was nineteen, in 1979; indeed, Deirdre had appeared on another Marcus page, 'Young Irish Writing', even earlier. He also published established writers on the page—a clever strategy which gave 'New Irish Writing' prestige, and which presumably attracted readers. It meant that one week he had a story by John McGahern or Edna O'Brien, the following week a story by an unknown writer just beginning their publishing career who benefited from being in good company.

My personal impression, partly based on the fact that he published several of my stories in the 1970s and 1980s, and partly because I associate certain female writers of those decades with 'New Irish Writing' and Poolbeg Press (Emma Cooke, Maeve Kelly, Ita Daly, Eithne Strong, Kate Cruise O'Brien), is that David Marcus was hugely important in encouraging women's writing.

But what do the statistics tell? Marcus edited, single handed, 'New Irish Writing' for almost twenty years. The page was published once a week, initially on Saturday, and, from 1982 on Friday, sometimes on Thursday. (Perhaps this switch, and the occasional appearance of 'New Irish Writing' on a Thursday, was an indication that its popularity was declining?) In 1983 Mary Butler, an MA student in UCD under the supervision of Augustine Martin (who, like Marcus, was a devotee of the short story), wrote her thesis on 'New Irish Writing 1968–1983'. In this invaluable work, sadly unpublished, which is available in the National Library of Ireland's Manuscript Collections, Butler provided a catalogue of all the writers who contributed to the page during those years, as well as a commentary and some statistics, including a gender breakdown, on the writers and their works.

Butler interviewed Marcus while researching her thesis. He told her that, on average, he received 60 stories and 200 poems each month. There is no information on the gender of those who submitted their work for consideration and whose work was not published—one can take it, though, that approximately 56 submitted stories were rejected monthly. A reader at the Abbey Theatre told me once that all Irish plays are submitted to the Abbey. (All are read, of course, but only a tiny handful are ever performed.) It looks as if every Irish writer submitted stories to 'New Irish Writing'—and anecdotal evidence bears this up. 'I sent him a few but he didn't take them', 'He sent me very nice rejection letters', is something I have heard from writers whom I know. Such was the popularity and the importance of the 'New Irish Writing' page as an outlet.

Between 1968 and 1983, 31.2 per cent of the stories published in 'New Irish Writing' were by women authors. Butler adds that of the 'new writers'—that is to say, the writers who were publishing their first story—that statistic rises to 36 per cent female. During that period, 550 stories by men and 249 stories by women were published in the page. Of the new writers who were published, 138 were men and 78 were women.

As a supplement to Butler's dissertation, I looked at 'New Irish Writing' between the years 1983 and 1986 in preparation for writing this essay. In 1984, the percentage of women writers who were published in 'New Irish Writing' was around 34 per cent.

In other words, although Butler felt there was an accelerated rate of development as far as the inclusion of women writers were concerned over the course of the 1970s and early 1980s (she points out that in 1976–1977 more women than men were published), the male–female ratio did not appear to change radically over the 18 years of Marcus's editorship. About one-third of the short stories he published in 'New Irish Writing' were by women. (I have not examined the situation regarding poems; he usually published one or two poems a week, alongside the featured short story.)

This is not a stunning statistic from the point of view of gender equality. But it is not bad. Women writers were much better represented in 'New Irish Writing' than in most other outlets of the period. As Sinéad Gleeson observes in her introduction to *The Long Gaze Back*, an anthology of short stories by Irish women which she edited in 2015:

> Pick up any anthology of Irish short stories published between 1950 and 1990, and there was a certain predictability when it came to what was included. [...] a reader would usually find there were rarely more than five stories by women. Many anthologies had none, others had just two female writers, and it was always the ubiquitous names, the female stalwarts of the form like Mary Lavin, Edna O'Brien, Somerville and Ross, and Elizabeth Bowen.

It is worth making the point, with respect to anthologies, that those edited by Marcus tended to buck this dismal trend. For instance, *The Faber Book of Best New Irish Short Stories 2006–7* (8 women, 16 men), the short story and poetry anthology, *An Irish Eros* (18 women, 42 men), *Phoenix Irish Short Stories 2003* (7 women, 7 men) are just a few of the many anthologies that he edited, which I happen have to hand on my shelves. Even still, male writers generally comprised the majority of contributors to Marcus's anthologies.

It is unlikely that Marcus had any forthright feminist agenda. If he had any ideological commitment, it was to the encouragement and promotion of Irish writers, and particularly young Irish writers. As his wife, the novelist Ita Daly, puts it in her memoir, *I'll Drop You a Line* (2016), what he had was a nose for literature:

> A nose for literature, just as rare as a nose for wine—that's what David had [...] [Frank] O'Connor spoke and wrote about 'the voice' which is the instrument of the writer as much as it is of the singer and which is the reason one writer thrills us and another interests us mildly. Great editors recognise the voice, even at the stage that it is struggling to emerge.

But if Marcus's motivation wasn't overtly political, without any doubt he nosed out and encouraged writing by women.

It was not only that he did not resist publishing women's work, nor that he discouraged writing on themes which could be described as 'female', but it is clear from 'New Irish Writing' that he encouraged women writers whom he believed in. Some names recur in the page. Among them are the 'new' writers, Helen Lucy Burke, Emma Cooke, Maeve Kelly, Eithne Strong, and Maura Treacy, as well as well-established figures like Edna O'Brien. Each of these writers published upward of eight stories between 1968 and 1983. Among those who published more than five during the same period were Kate Cruise O'Brien, Val Mulkerns, Ita Daly, Elizabeth Dean (i.e. Éilís Ní Dhuibhne), K. Arnold Price, and Evelyn Haran. (Only William Trevor, Desmond Hogan, and Vincent Lawrence published as many stories as Maeve Kelly and those in the first group.)

Some of these women had three or four stories published in a single year—Kelly, Strong and Burke, were particularly prolific. Several of them went on to have their first collections of stories published by Marcus in Poolbeg Press. Cooke, Kelly, Treacy, Strong, Daly, and Burke, all had books published in the late 1980s by Poolbeg, and these collections generally included stories which had been given a first outing in 'New Irish Writing'. In some respects, it looks as if Marcus almost founded Poolbeg to ensure that these writers' stories would be available in a form that was more durable than the ephemeral newspaper. (In those pre-internet days, the newspaper was much more ephemeral than it is now. *The Irish Press* was not even microfilmed until relatively recently—although it is now available in digitised form.)

There is a generational aspect to this. The writers who got most encouragement from Marcus in 'New Irish Writing', and especially in Poolbeg Press, were those who were born in the 1930s and 1940s. By the 1970s, the heyday of the page, as well as being talented writers, each of these women was mature enough to have something to say, and they had the discipline to write with regularity. I suppose when I look back at my own level of production during the 1970s and early 1980s (five stories over ten years), I feel ashamed. In a shorter span of years Maeve Kelly, Emma Cooke, and Juanita Casey each published about a dozen stories apiece. My excuse is that I was busy doing other things—working, academic research (I worked on an MPhil and a PhD), falling in and out of love, getting married, etc. ('All things can tempt me from this craft of verse.') Those older women valued their talent more, and perhaps appreciated the opportunity to be published more, although I certainly valued it and never abandoned my sense of myself as a writer. Nor did I ever feel in any way marginalised as a writer because I was a woman—this is entirely thanks to David Marcus. The younger generation, people like Claire Keegan, who was also spotted by Marcus, focused on writing from the word go—partly perhaps thanks to the professionalisation of creative writing programmes in universities.

So far I have done a lot of number crunching in this essay. But what about the themes of the stories that he published? If David Marcus had a nose for good literature, what sort of stories were these women writers giving him? Perhaps the answer to the question regarding his feminism lies there, as much as in the statistics.

Maeve Kelly was born in 1930 and published her first story in 'New Irish Writing' in 1971; she was a regular contributor to the page from then on. In 1976 her first collection, *A Life of Her Own*, was published by Poolbeg. Several of the thirteen stories in that volume had previously been published in 'New Irish Writing'.

The title alone, a nod to Virginia Woolf's famous essay on women writing, also suggests the theme of the stories—women's lives, women's independence. Kelly, from Ennis in County Clare, was particularly interested in the lives of rural women. Her opening story, 'Amnesty', focuses on a middle-aged woman who lives with her deaf mute brother on an island in the river—the Shannon, one guesses, although it is not named. They fish for a living and run a small farm on the island. Details regarding the fishing, and the sale of the fish, are very exact. The centre of the story is a sad episode in the woman's youth. As a young girl, she brings fish to the market to sell, but there meets a handsome man—a Traveller—and is persuaded to buy a pretty dress with the proceeds of the sale. She has a wonderful day at the fair: 'her mouth still tasted the ice cream and kisses, the kisses and the ice cream, the ginger ale and kisses, the kisses and the ginger ale'. When she returns to the island, her pockets empty, wearing the pretty pink dress, her mother slaps her on the face in anger. She never forgives her mother and 'develops her backbone of steel'. She abandons thoughts of romance, wears grim functional clothes, and runs the farm and fishery with her brother. The story ends with the protagonist in her middle age, buying a pink dress for herself, and declaring to her brother that she will wear it to Mass and forgive her mother. 'Forgiveness was a sweetness that smoothed out lines and quenched her burning looks. It eased the drying bones and lifted the corners of her mouth.'

It is a superb story which encapsulates what is typical of Kelly's writing: the wonderful lyrical, poetic, descriptions of the river and the island; the rich atmosphere of the countryside and country life; plus the redemptive, almost magical power of the beautiful pink dress (a symbol of femininity if ever there was one). All of this combines in a harmonious short story. The theme of loss, lost love, loss of opportunity for a 'normal' life, so standard in Irish short stories of the mid-twentieth century (I'm thinking of William Trevor's 'The Ballroom of Romance'), is counterpointed by the final paragraph. Initially this seems sentimental—the bitter, steely woman is redeemed by a dress, forgives her mother, and the wrinkles of the dress smooth out. But on reflection there is food for thought in this ending. The protagonist might have had a better life had she forgiven her mother earlier. Life itself—poverty, harsh conditions, which are referred to explicitly in the story—is to blame for the mother's anger, the limitations that would not allow a girl to buy a frock. In addition, the sexual puritanism of the time sees romance as a sin which has to be eradicated. But the girl's stubbornness might have also had a part to play in her fate. The story within a story, the central symbol of the dress, the technique employed of looking back on youth from the vantage point of older age, remind me of Alice Munro. It is possible that Maeve Kelly had read the Canadian writer—Munro's first collection came out in 1968, and *The Lives of Girls and Women* (the one most likely to have affected Kelly) in 1971. I am not sure how available Munro's early books were in Ireland. Certainly, the theme of Kelly's collection could be said to be the status of women in rural Ireland. In various ways, her women characters are exploited and punished because they are women, and her stories are fired by protest of this.

Emma Cooke (who was born Enid Cuddy, in 1934) also writes about the lives of Irish women. Her characters, like Kelly's, tend to live in the countryside or in country towns, but they are usually middle class. Cooke was a Protestant from the Midlands. She married a Catholic and some of her best stories revolve around the conflict which a so-called 'mixed marriage' could give rise to. In perhaps her best-known story, 'A Family Occasion', from the significantly titled collection, *Female Forms* (1980), Beattie, pregnant for the sixth time, is treated with a mixture of condescension and puzzlement by her siblings.

> 'Can't you do anything? Can't you be more careful?' she asked, in a dry, matter of fact, tone.
> 'No,' said Beattie. 'We're not allowed.'

The tone of the story is light-hearted and humorous, and it is fairly clear that Beattie is not all that perturbed by her large family and continuous pregnancies. Nevertheless, the story pinpoints the problem which all Catholic married women in Ireland faced until the 1980s, namely the likelihood that they would have numerous pregnancies and huge families, since all forms of 'artificial contraception', as it was called, were forbidden by the Catholic Church and were illegal in the eyes of the State.

'Female Forms', the title story, is about an affair conducted by a middle-aged man, Talbot, and a young schoolteacher who is engaged to somebody else. (The teacher has every intention of proceeding with her marriage, and is well aware that her lover is temporary.) Talbot is a self-centred narcissist who depends on women for everything but doesn't realise it—the story has a back story, a twist in the tail, everything a tight story in a newspaper needs. But what looks radical about it, and other stories by Cooke, is that it treats sexuality head on:

> She had slept with her fiancé several times and knew that he felt sexual intercourse 'had no harm in it' as long as the couple 'knew where they stood'. With Talbot such points were irrelevant. He wanted her and that was that.

What strikes me about all of Cooke's stories is how well they portray a modern bourgeois Ireland, where people are liberated sexually but are still affected by the restrictive rules of the State regarding contraception. Her women characters don't come across as victims. They like sex and they have a lot of it. There is a flow to Cooke's stories, a luminosity in the writing, and a constant wry humour, which makes them extremely readable and engaging. As the blurb says, she is 'one of the most perceptive observers and recorders of life in Ireland's suburbia of the seventies'. Suburbia appears to be used by her as a class rather than as a geographical marker, though, distinguishing Cooke's country town territory from the small farms of Kelly.

But what happened to Cooke, a writer who seems to me as gifted as her contemporaries, Alice Munro, Penelope Lively, or Margaret Drabble, and whose themes have plenty in common with theirs?

Google her and the only mention you will find is a slight reference in the *Oxford Dictionary of Literature* and an obituary (she died in 2015). There is a very brief entry in Robert Hogan's indispensable *Dictionary of Irish Literature*. Unfortunately, that note, which was written by Dorothy Robbie (who perhaps had been Cooke's teacher in Alexandra College), is dismissive, judgemental and subjective.

Emma Cooke wrote three novels, all of which were published by Poolbeg Press—the last in 1994. It would seem that she stopped writing, or at least publishing, then, at the age of sixty. Maeve Kelly published six books, including three novels, one collection of poetry, and two collections of short stories. Like several others who emerged in the pages of 'New Irish Writing' in the 1970s, and whose first collections of stories were published by Poolbeg Press in the late 1970s and 1980s, these two writers are largely forgotten today. It is the fate of most writers to be forgotten, as anyone who strolls through the stacks of Irish fiction in the National Library of Ireland, reading the names on the ageing spines, can quickly observe. But these Poolbeg women, who were nurtured, championed, and above all, published by Marcus, seem to have vanished from the scene faster than one might expect. (Of course, what is lost can always be re-found—Kelly's second short-story collection, *Orange Horses* (1990) was reissued by Tramp Press in 2016, as part of their wonderful 'Recovered Voices' series of books.) All of these writers were good writers. They were innovative, in a sense radical. And they were extremely influential for the next generation of writers—writers like me who also were published alongside them in 'New Irish Writing' but who, thanks to the twenty-year age gap, belonged to the next generation—university educated, accessing contraceptives, illegally and legally, feminist. It was writers like these women, who were put on the map by David Marcus, who showed us the way.

Harry Clifton

The Has-Beens

David Marcus 1924–2009

You who managed your decline
So beautifully, who withdrew
At just the right time—
Or was it luck?—from working the rooms
For talent, seeing the galleys through,
Please, could you help me manage mine?

Crippled with shyness, see me climb
Blind stairs, through the Seventies,
To your high view over the Liffey.
Coat-rack, desk, linoleum—
This, the engine-room
Of reputations, literary heaven…

'You're not married? That's good—
No dependents. Take a look
At the grey desolation outside.
I, too, am writing a book,
Not art, mind you, I'm through with that,
Just pure commercial tat.'

Below in the Scotch House, on the rocks,
A lost generation
Stopped its watches. Cattle-shed, docks,
The 'spectre of emigration'—
If anyone so much as blinked
In that Berkeleyan think-space

Of Ireland, it would all fall through,
The sawdust floor, the national dream,
The *esse est percipi*
Of Seán Lemass's tidal shipping
Sold down the river, unredeemed
Since Nineteen Twenty-Two…

'A word of advice. Stay clear
Of the fool's paradise
Of life in here.
Even the walls have ears and eyes.
You will stop writing. You will disappear
In the depths of the years…'

For Heaven's sake, can that be you
At the intersection
Decades later, as the decals change
And half of Ireland surges through
To its next re-incarnation?
Drooling, self-estranged,

Who once were cruel to be kind,
Do you recognise me
At fifty, a *protégé*
Thrown to the wolves, who takes your hand
On this, our desolate traffic-island,
Sped-through, left behind?

— — —

III

Colum McCann
Expanding the Lungs of Irish Literature

Place him for a moment in the backspin of time. It's 1946. The war is over. The world is concussed. He's twenty-two years old. He's a hyphenated man, Irish and Jewish both. He has moved from Cork to Dublin. And dear ol' dirty Dublin—though much of the world outside doesn't even know it yet—is a town that likes its literature. Here the story matters. The poem matters. The well-placed word matters. Newspapers matter too. And magazines. Even those small literary magazines with single-colour covers. You can find them in the back rack of the bookshop. Or thumbed through in the snug in McDaids. Or roared about in Desmond McNamara's salon. Or peeping out from the torn jacket pocket of Patrick Kavanagh, who mighty be seen walking down Grafton Street still sounding, in his tousled head, the lyrics of a poem soon to be published as 'Dark-Haired Miriam Ran Away'.

These small magazines—like *The Bell*, first published in 1940—are a way to talk back to a country that is drowning in Catholic conservatism. There's no beat generation yet. No rock 'n' roll. No burn-your-bra mantras. So, one of the few ways to get under the skin of the country is to write. The print run of these small journals may be small, but the ideas are not. Enough of the squinting from behind the curtains. Enough of the poisoned narrowness. It's the poem, or the story, or the essay, or even the cartoon, that can pry open the tired national heart.

And so he decides that maybe there's room for another magazine. He's not long out of university, not long shaving even, and he's a polite young man, maybe even reserved, and he's not exactly at the cliff face of the literary scene, but who cares, he's close enough. Let the begrudgers begrudge. The only things worth doing are the things that might break your heart.

It'll take a few bob, and it'll take some chutzpah too, but he sits down at his typewriter—the old hunt and peck—and begins to write letters to his literary heroes for contributions to a magazine that he intends to call *Irish Writing*. The name itself is a form of bravery, since who might even dare to imagine that there's enough good writing out there to fill the pages of another journal. He seals the envelopes on letters to Sean O'Faoláin, Frank O'Connor, Liam O'Flaherty, Edith Somerville and James Stephens for contributions to his first issue.

Nothing worse than waiting for the postman and the drop of the letter on the carpet. But, lo and behold, they nearly all say Yes. Yes, they will, yes. He is not a man to boast or to sing in any unruly way, but we can only imagine how his heart burst out from beneath his careful necktie.

Soon to come were Benedict Kiely, Mary Lavin, Sean O'Casey, Louis MacNeice and two extracts from Samuel Beckett's groundbreaking absurdist novel *Watt*. David Marcus had started what he would do his whole life, expanding the lungs of the Irish literary scene.

My father, Sean McCann, talked about David Marcus with great reverence. They were both literary men with deep aspirations for their own careers, but what they were really good at was finding, recognising and encouraging young talent. My father worked as the literary editor in *The Evening Press* and he knew a good writer when they came along. Over the years he was among the first to publish writers like Dermot Bolger, June Considine, Bernard Farrell, Mary Morrissy, John Boland, Clare Boylan, Nuala Fennell and many others.

He and David were good friends. In many ways they mirrored

one another. Neither were big drinkers, where, in Dublin, on the literary scene, things were often wild and sodden. They stayed away from late nights in the pubs and they kept themselves free from gossip. Instead, they found solace in talking about literature. (Later they also found common ground in horses, wine and, later still, roses.) They were, I suppose, the sort of men who were at the inside and on the outside at the same time. They may have worn neckties and sensible shoes, but they also knew a thing or two about the world and the sentences that help create the edge. I also think that both of them intuitively knew that—although they themselves were very good writers (my father wrote 27 books, David Marcus had three novels, a memoir and over 30 anthologies)—their true talent was in recognising those whose voices might last.

One afternoon in 1968, long after the *Irish Writing* magazine had closed down, they met for lunch in the city centre. David told my father that he wanted to do a 'New Irish Writing' page and he was on his way to the D'Olier Street offices of *The Irish Times* to see if they were interested in publishing a monthly short story. My father argued that it should be a weekly story, and it should be in *The Irish Press* group of papers. So he hurried back to Burgh Quay, to the office of the editor, Tim Pat Coogan, and convinced him that the *Press* would be best paper for this new venture in Irish literature. Coogan immediately—and somewhat out of character—agreed, and Irish writing, once again, took a significant swerve.

David Marcus went on to become perhaps the most important literary editor in the country. Among the writers he published were Desmond Hogan, Neil Jordan, John McGahern, Éilís Ní Dhuibhne, Joseph O'Connor, Claire Keegan, Anne Enright and many others. These were writers who, when you heard them for the first time, you knew things would never be quite the same again. He liaised with literary editors and agents in Britain on behalf of the writers, developing, for instance, a strong relationship with Maggie

McKernan of Phoenix House publishers, and her husband, Giles Gordon of the Curtis Brown agency.

In a way, David was the highest-level scout in Irish literary circles. Publishers trusted his opinion and they listened closely to what he had to say. He wrote letter after letter. He made every introduction he possibly could. He protected his writers and promoted them at the same time. Throughout that whole journey, he was selfless and open to all the new ideas that came his way. But he was also so much more than a scout. He was an inspiration. And he was a mentor. And in many ways he was a muse.

Under his influence, Irish writing—which at the time was still easily dismissed, especially in British literary circles—continued to flourish. In many ways it has never really stopped.

I was one of the lucky ones. In the early 1990s I had left Ireland to try to write. I failed miserably. I found myself in Texas, wallpapering the bathroom of a ranch house with rejection slips. Every day I would open another letter and my heart would do its quick freefall. But then came the note from David Marcus who—with characteristic humility and understated warmth—wanted to see my stories. I sent him three finished pieces and almost immediately he helped turn my career inside-out.

Within a month of sending him my work, David had accepted one of the stories ('Sisters') for the Phoenix anthologies. Not only that but he also got me an agent. Within a year I had a two-book contract. And David published my work in several anthologies.

We seldom know how we lucky we are. And we seldom know how much struggle has gone before us. Nor do we know what sort of sacrifices have been made in order to pave the road. But the truth is that I, and many of my generation, would never have gotten a start were it not for David Marcus. (Others who come to mind as great mentors are Ciaran Carty, Caroline Walsh, Peter Fallon and several others). It takes a certain sort of selflessness to celebrate the work of others. An obvious humility too. But there is also a fierce burning patriotism not only for one's own country, but for the country of literature as well.

In that country, David stamped so many of our passports. It is hardly an exaggeration to say that the Irish short story is as celebrated as that of the Russian short story largely because David helped make it so. By the time the 1990s rolled around, Irish writers were among the hottest properties among publishers worldwide. The way had been paved and the gates propped open.

David was certainly not afraid to push, or become, the edge. Among the anthologies he published were *Alternative Loves: Irish Gay and Lesbian Stories* in 1994 when, lest we forget, consensual same-sex sexual activity had only just been decriminalised in Ireland.

He was, as the Yiddish language would have it, a *mensch*. That is to say that he was a person of extraordinary integrity. In the Irish language he was a *saoi*, or a wise one. He knew that the value of literature is that there's always another story to tell. He had a keen ear. A gentle manner. An ability to anticipate a trend. And he knew that what he was doing would have an effect not only on Ireland's present, but on its past and future too.

All of this praise would embarrass him greatly of course, which only makes it all the more true.

Anthony Glavin
A Treasured Friendship

It would be all but impossible to overstate what David Marcus accomplished on behalf of Irish writing, not least for the short story, which he championed in the weekly 'New Irish Writing' page of *The Irish Press*. For decades, 'New Irish Writing' provided Irish writers of all ages an opportunity to publish their work alongside established figures like William Trevor, Edna O'Brien, Benedict Kiely and John McGahern—figures whose *New Yorker* stories frequently had their second outing in *The Irish Press*.

That literary fiction could find a welcome home in a newspaper speaks to both David's vision and its Irish readership, since a similar attempt by *The Boston Globe* to publish short stories was short-lived, and was prefaced with an advisory comment along the lines of *Estimated reading time: four minutes and fifty-three seconds*. The more than two-dozen short-story anthologies which David edited over the course of his lifetime were also hugely beneficial, given that a writer does not generally sit down to write a volume of short stories so much as see a collection gradually accrue.

A Cork Jew residing in Dublin, David was catholic with a lower-case C in his taste and in the informed literary agenda which underpinned his editorial work. What mattered most were the words on the page, and his precise, enthusiastic feedback when he liked those words was worth its weight in gold to the scores of writers whom he fostered.

My own treasured friendship with David commenced in February 1975 by way of a rejection slip for my first short story, which I had posted to *The Irish Press* from Glencolmcille, Co. Donegal, having arrived from my native Massachusetts the previous autumn. David added several handwritten lines, explaining how the story had failed to sufficiently catch his interest. David also informed me of the eponymous, Dublin-based poet and pianist Anthony Glavin—'A young, regularly published poet. Could be complicating!'—who would also become a cherished friend.

My journal relates how I began to work on a new story, 'Vanishing Boundaries', for which I received an acceptance letter from David that spring. David also proposed that I debut in print as 'Anthony M. Glavin', employing my baptismal middle name of McInerney in honour of my mother's maiden surname to distinguish myself from the eponymous poet.

The reception of my story in Glencolmcille would prove a story in itself, commencing with the parishioner who no longer chatted with me for fear I might put something he said into print. Another informed me how that first story had been fact, not fiction, though he'd read it twice: 'Once before milking the cow, and again before going to bed.' Yet another local remarked how I'd been 'hard on the clergy and could get six months behind bars for that!' For my part, I quickly learned to ask had they read a story, not whether they had liked it. Less inclined now to mention my own writing, I resolved to take on board Henri Matisse's suggestion that those hoping to make art should cut off their tongues (if not literally). I was troubled, however, when told by one neighbour how another was now afraid to talk to me, for fear I might put something he said into the book I was supposedly writing. And I was slightly rattled by yet another who informed me: 'You can take the next bus out of town if your next story's not a good one.'

I recall responding on another occasion to David's suggestion that I avoid a rhythmic repetition of words in another story with a tongue-in-cheek observation of how James Joyce had also favoured that sort of thing. 'Yes,' smiled David, 'but he shouldn't have always been allowed'—speaking as if Joyce might yet be within earshot of *The Irish Press* building beside the Liffey, and bringing home to me how a literary life such as David's doesn't necessarily distinguish between the work itself and the wider world, regardless of reputation or mortality.

His own editorial expertise was itself part and parcel of his character, reflecting the same generosity of spirit, quiet warmth, enthusiasm and positivity, together with a genuine smile. At the same time he never hesitated to tell you if he thought a story had not cleared the bar.

I passed back and forth across the Atlantic several times, from where I submitted stories, a handful of which were published in 'New Irish Writing'. I also continued to correspond with David, who published my first story collection *One For Sorrow* in 1980 with Philip McDermott's and his publishing house, Poolbeg Press. I was also to meet my beloved partner Adrienne Fleming that same year, who also worked with Poolbeg.

October 1986 found our family back in Donegal, where a letter arrived out of the blue from Tim Pat Coogan, editor of *The Irish Press*, asking me to come to Dublin as soon as possible, with all expenses paid, to meet with him and David. Our conversation at a corner table in Coffers Café proved like a scene out of a fantasy film, wherein I was offered the 'New Irish Writing' page on a six-month trial basis. David and I then shared a bottle of house wine with our lunch, the chat spectacular, and myself gainfully employed.

It took the better part of two months for the transition to take place, in which David continued to prove a star, nay a constellation, entirely willing to help me find my editorial feet via remote working (even though the phrase 'remote working' had yet to be coined). Our Donegal postman, Willie Maxwell, went from delivering the occasional letter from family and friends in the

United States to knocking on our door throughout the week with yet another armload of A4 manilla envelopes. I greatly enjoyed the process of selecting stories, working with authors, and liaising with *The Irish Press* staff.

It is a truism that what we do, and how we get on in the world, stems from our character, but it seemed notably true with David whose editorial gifts—the insight, care and honesty he brought to your writing—were but part and parcel of his nature. Quiet, warm and old-world courteous, he had a lovely way of shutting his eyes as he smiled, and was without doubt among the last of our literary gents.

Which is to say, stories, be they short or long, mattered hugely to David. Writing to him from Massachusetts in 1994, where I had met the son of Irish novelist Vivian Connell, I got back a neatly typed aerogramme describing the huge impact that Connell's *The Chinese Room* had afforded him at age nineteen, a novel that after it was banned in Ireland went on to sell over three million copies worldwide. And the joy it was to write to him once back in Dublin in 1997 with word of my first novel, *Nighthawk Alley*, as it was David who had wryly told me that a novel was where the money is! And yes, *Nighthawk Alley* was seeded by a story, 'Transplants', which David had published in 'New Irish Writing'.

However, it was that conjurer of coincidence, W.G. Sebald, who bequeathed us both a pluperfect instance of those vanishing boundaries that can operate between a book and a life. On this occasion, Friday, 14 December 2001, I had posted David a copy of Sebald's first novel, *The Emigrants*, only to receive another of his neatly typed letters, written the following Monday, which told of 'What a morning it was: to read in *The Irish Times* of Sebald's terrible death and then an hour later to get his book from you.' It read entirely, never mind eerily, like something out Sebald's fiction itself—another letter and memory to treasure, together with its sender: editor extraordinaire, generous mentor, dearest friend.

Ciaran Carty
Life with David, Almost

I knew David Marcus years before we actually met and even when we did meet it was almost as if we hadn't. David lived by the pen and tended to communicate in short, handwritten letters, rather than face-to-face. In 1958, while I was still at college, my father, then editor of *The Irish Press*, brought home a proof copy of David's first novel, *To Next Year in Jerusalem*, thinking it might encourage my attempts to become a writer.

I didn't hear of David again until April 1968, when his 'New Irish Writing' page first appeared in *The Irish Press*. Apparently he had been on his way to *The Irish Times* to pitch the idea of a literary journal that could reach a wide readership by appearing in a national newspaper and thus 'cost nothing to print and nothing to buy', but happened to bump into Sean McCann who persuaded him to offer it instead to Tim Pat Coogan at *The Irish Press*. If this had been a few years earlier, my father, rather than Tim Pat, might have been the editor who helped him revolutionise Irish literature.

Ten years later, in 1978, *The Sunday Independent* encouraged me to adapt David's brilliantly simple concept into the format of a weekly feature section called 'Dialogue'—in effect a cultural journal of arts reviews and interviews, that also published a 'Poem and Story of the Month'. This caught the attention of Vincent Browne, who lured me to *The Sunday Tribune* as arts editor in 1985. When *The Irish Press* was forced to drop the 'New Irish Writing' page in 1988, Vincent offered to take it on with me as editor. We shook hands on the deal with David, and *The Sunday Tribune* published our first 'New Irish Writing' page on 30 October 1988.

'I look forward with the greatest anticipation to reading the work of many more new, exciting Irish writers,' David wrote, on the launch of 'New Irish Writing' in *The Sunday Tribune*. David continued to assist us as a consultant, and we were determined not to let him down. The essential idea behind 'New Irish Writing' remained the same, but the annual Hennessy Awards (which were launched in 1971) provided an opportunity to greatly widen its reach. Up until 1988, the Awards were decided each year by two major international writers who did not meet, but who instead scored the entries from 1 to 5 by post, with David totting up the marks to work out who won. The prizes were then presented at a modest reception in the cellars of the Hennessy agents, Edward Dillon and Co., in Dublin.

Brendan Kennelly and Fintan O'Toole helped me get the new 'New Irish Writing' page up and running and to clear a six-month backlog of submissions. I then formed an editorial team, with Dermot Bolger and Anthony (Tony) Glavin, who had edited the last two years of 'New Irish Writing' at *The Irish Press*, as my advisers. When Tony eventually stepped down in 2020, Niamh Donnelly joined the team to bring an exciting younger edge to our deliberations.

We decided from the start to bring the Hennessy Awards judges to Dublin each year to reach their decisions. We also agreed to host a gala awards lunch, where an overall 'New Irish Writer of the Year' would be announced, chosen from the winners of the three award categories: first fiction; emerging fiction; and emerging poetry. The guests included literary agents (such as Peter Strauss and Derek Johns) as well as publishers, established writers and the media. Over the years, several first book deals came about through such contacts. Alan Monaghan, for instance, caught the attention of another agent, Geraldine Cook, and was signed up by Macmillan for a three-book trilogy based on his 2002 award-winning story, 'The Soldier's Song'.

The revamped Awards made headlines right from the start when the 26-year-old Joseph O'Connor, our first New Writer of the Year, and the unanimous choice of the 1989 judges, Brendan Kennelly and Piers Paul Read, was signed up by London publisher Sinclair Stevenson to develop his winning, coming-of-age story, 'The Last of the Mohicans', into a novel. 'Winning gave me the confidence to see writing as a way of life,' Joe said to me. 'When you rang me in London to say you were going to publish my first story, I was about to give up.'

By the time Joe arrived at the following year's Awards in 1990, he had already completed a proof copy of the novel, titled *Cowboys and Indians*. In a virtual repeat of his success, another young first-time writer, Colum McCann, was declared the 1990 New Writer of the Year by judges Clare Boylan and Desmond Hogan. (Des, at twenty-one, had been a winner of the inaugural 1971 Awards.) Colum, however, was unable to attend the Awards luncheon at the Royal Hospital Kilmainham to pick up his winner's trophy and the £4,000 cheque. 'I was cleaning a swimming pool in Texas, paying my way through college,' he recalled. 'When you rang I just dived into the water making a wild splash.'

My other life as a journalist and interviewer enabled me to get to know major authors well enough to persuade them to become judges. Fay Weldon was particularly obliging in 1991, when we had to switch the judging session to London for a morning session at the Atheneum because fellow judge, Neil Jordan, had suddenly got funding for *The Crying Game*, which involved a seven-day-week filming schedule. Of course, not everyone said 'yes' to us. Javier Marías and Kazuo Ishiguro both declined because they didn't believe in judging other writers' work, while Salman Rushdie had to turn down our offer in the summer of 1995 because he was tied up with the imminent publication of his novel, *The Moor's Last Sigh*.

The same year, in 1995, we decided to mark the 25th anniversary of the Hennessy Awards by publishing, with New Island Books, the first of three Hennessy Fiction anthologies. That year also saw us hosting a pre-reception where all of the shortlisted writers were able to meet with the judges. This prompted President Mary Robinson, who was guest of honour at the Awards ceremony, to ask if she could also attend. President Robinson made a point of speaking to each of the eighteen emerging writers who were shortlisted. In 2004 her successor, President Mary McAleese, whose first short story I had published in *The Sunday Independent*, was also guest of honour. The day before the Awards, jihadists had blown up a commuter train in Madrid, killing hundreds of passengers. President McAleese took aside my wife, Julia, who had grown up near the scene of this atrocity, and sympathised with her in Spanish.

Throughout my thirty-five years as editor of 'New Irish Writing', the page has been a particular magnet for emerging Irish writers living abroad. 26-year-old Clare-born Mary O'Donoghue, for instance, was on a day off from her teaching job at Babson College in Massachusetts to read some class essays when I rang her to say she had just won the 2001 new writer of the year award with her first story 'The Byre'. One of the judges, Anne Enright, described her story as 'passionately engaged, tenaciously realised, full of brilliant detail, it creates a complete and intriguing fictional world.' Meanwhile it was mid-afternoon in Bucharest that same day when I got through on the phone to Waterford-born Philip Ó Ceallaigh, winner of the 1998 fiction award, with the news that he had now completed a double by winning the 2001 poetry prize. 'You've really made my day,' he said. 'I've just had another call from the Romanian edition of *Playboy* saying they're going to publish one of my short stories!'

Bringing together the Irish abroad was rooted in the origin of the Awards. Back in the eighteenth century Richard Hennessy left Cork with the Wild Geese to join the army of Louis XV of France. He eventually settled in the small town of Cognac where, in 1765, he produced a beautiful aromatic amber drink that became synonymous throughout the world with brandy. The Hennessy family never lost touch with the country Richard had left behind, and they developed a particular fascination with Irish literature.

Their belief in David Marcus, the grandson of a Lithuanian immigrant who found sanctuary in Cork at the turn of the century, was personified by Maurice Hennessy, a direct descendant of Richard. 'I've been coming to the Awards nearly every year since you took over in 1988,' he told me once. 'Together we've seen a whole new generation of Irish writers emerge.' Maurice would call in to Hodges Figgis bookshop whenever he was in Dublin, and each year he made a point of reading books by our judges. He would also ask me to send him copies of all the shortlisted stories and poems in the hope of spotting the winners.

Today, Hennessy is part of LVMH (Moët Hennessy Louis Vuitton), a multinational grouping of top luxury brands. Maurice was the last family member in the business. Inevitably, with multinationalism, the pride in Irish heritage that had inspired the Awards began to hold less sway. First LVMH withdrew its support from the Hennessy Gold Cup; and, in 2019, the Hennessy Awards were dropped.

Appropriately, that same year, the 48th and final Awards had an international flavour. Colin Walsh, the overall New Irish Writer of the Year chosen by Martina Evans and Eoin McNamee, was living in Belgium, and was working on his first novel *Kala*. This book went on to become a critically acclaimed bestseller when it was published by Atlantic Books in 2023. 'My story started with images, embers coursing through night trees, ice-cream on a lip,' he explained. 'I was lathered in my bed with high fever and realised I should tell the story like a braid of glimpses.' Similarly, the poetry award-winner for that year, Audrey Molloy, also lived abroad, in Australia. 'It is the alchemy of poetry that I really enjoy,' she said. 'Starting with nothing more than an emotion or thought and converting it into first an image, then raw words and finally a poem that I hope will resonate and linger in the reader's mind.'

The Hall of Fame Writer Award was introduced in 2002 to

honour writers launched in the 'New Irish Writing' page who went on to literary fame. The winner in 2019 was Mike McCormack, then a teacher in literature at Villanova University in the US (and now a Professor at the University of Galway), whose first story, 'Thomas Crumlesh, 1960–1992: A Retrospective', won the first fiction award in 1993.

Newspapers come and go, editorial policies alter and editors change, but the beauty of the 'New Irish Writing' page is that it has weathered all the traumatic ups and downs of publishing. It flourished in *The Sunday Tribune* until the liquidators took over the newspaper at the end of January 2011. Three rival papers rang the next day offering us a new home: *The Irish Times*, *The Daily Mail* and the *Irish Independent*. I opted for the *Irish Independent* because it promised to let us run the page with the same editorial freedom as before. This led 'New Irish Writing' to become a separate company and, with Arts Council funding, to publish free with the Irish Independent three standalone magazines—*Hennessy Writers of Tomorrow* (October 2011), and *Hennessy Irish Writing Today* (May and November 2012). These magazines were true to David's original idea of bringing together established and new writers in the same journal.

In 2015 the LVMH group in Paris decided to switch to *The Irish Times*, apparently because they considered it a 'top brand'. Fintan O'Toole welcomed us there and books editor, Martin Doyle, gave us a free hand. After LVMH pulled out of the Awards in 2019, space for the 'New Irish Writing' page was reduced, and in 2020 the *Times* decided to suspend the page indefinitely 'until Covid is over'. Cormac Bourke, editor of the *Irish Independent*, quickly invited us back to his 'Saturday Review' section.

So here we are, one hundred years after David's birth, and 'New Irish Writing' is still a haven for emerging writers thanks to a wonderfully simple idea that captured the support of the editors of four different national newspapers, and that stirred the imagination of generations of readers—and writers—throughout

Ireland and abroad. David lives on for me in a letter dated 8 November 2000. 'Dear Ciarán,' he wrote in that letter (marking a fada on the second 'a'), the day after that year's Hennessy Award ceremony:

> I write to apologise for my absence last evening. Due to the last minute proverbial circumstances completely beyond my control, I had to miss it—the first time in all the 30 years. I was gutted.
>
> I have no doubt it was a highly successful occasion. I'll just have to start looking forward to 2001.
>
> Again, I'm so sorry.

We missed David that night, and always.

Jo O'Donoghue
That Rooted Man

When I began work in Poolbeg Press in 1988 as a neophyte editor/publisher, one of Philip McDermott's methods of induction was to educate me, in a formal sort of way, about 'friends' of the company—as opposed to those who might have become ill-disposed in the straitened years of recession that preceded my appointment. David Marcus was one of the former, although he had ceased to play an active role in publishing short story collections with Poolbeg. Ita Daly's *The Lady with the Red Shoes* and Mary Beckett's *A Belfast Woman* (both 1980) were just two of the jewels in Poolbeg's crown from the David Marcus period. (I mention these titles in particular because they are relevant to the account below.)

Derry writer Sean McMahon had edited *Great Irish Writing: The Best from The Bell* for O'Brien Press in 1978, and it was he who reminded David Marcus of Mary Beckett's early stories, published in *The Bell* and by David himself in his quarterly, *Irish Writing*, in the 1950s. I met Sean almost as soon as I started work in Poolbeg. Freed that summer of 1988 from the shackles of teaching mathematics in St Columb's College in his home town, he was thereafter the most available and obliging of collaborators: he would create an anthology, read a manuscript, even write a children's novel almost as soon as you asked him. Sean reviewed fiction for David when he was literary editor of *The Irish Press* and it was through Sean that I came to know David personally, in his and Ita's home in Rathgar. Sean visited Dublin for work and recreation about once a month for the next five years and a visit to David and Ita was always on his list. I confess I never remember David making the tea or taking credit for the home baking but in every other respect he was the complete gentleman: urbane, courteous, thoughtful and wise.

Many were the favours I owed David both when I worked for Poolbeg and when I set up the Marino imprint for Mercier Press: suggestions, introductions, assessments, particularly of aspiring short story writers. Who remembers that David Marcus edited an anthology called *Alternative Loves: Irish Gay and Lesbian Stories*? I commissioned it for Marino/Mercier—the Marino imprint was then called Martello—in 1994. Homosexuality had been decriminalised in 1993, so it was at the forefront of our minds. David didn't bat an eyelid and it seemed like a progressive piece of publishing at the time, but the word 'alternative' would surely not be used in such a context today.

Publishers are easily wounded by real or imagined betrayals, but I came to admire the pragmatism that was so central to David's personality: despite our friendship and his Cork roots, when he wrote his *Oughtobiography* (2001) he offered it to Michael Gill of what was then Gill and Macmillan instead of Mercier/Marino because he thought Gill would sell more copies. After I had left the company, a sequel, *Buried Memories* (2004), a fictionalised memoir from the viewpoint of a composite character—Marcus himself and 'Cork's last Jew', Aaron Cohen—did come to Mercier, less out of sentiment than because Gill and Macmillan was, rightly as it turned out, not convinced of its saleability.

Two instances of David's benevolence—one of forbearance, the other of generosity—remain with me. I had not been long in publishing when I received a manuscript of short stories from an author known to David (and to me) whose work he had encountered in his 'New Irish Writing' days in *The Irish Press*. I asked him to read it for me and he duly sent me a report that was negative. I forwarded the complete signed report to the author who was surprised by its forthrightness, angry too. When I told David this he was taken aback: he expected, he said, that his anonymity would have been protected and that only significant and not too hurtful extracts of the report would have been furnished to the author. The report was for me, not the author. Nobody had ever explained the protocol to me but I never forgot the lesson. I feared that he would hold it against me, refuse to read for me or work with me again. If he had been a gossip, a type often encountered in the publishing world, I would have feared exposure and public ridicule. But all he said was, 'There's nothing we can do about it now.' Not only did he never mention it again, I believe he put it quite out of his mind as nothing thereafter ever disturbed the harmony of our relationship.

Of his generosity: when I left Poolbeg in 1993 and had ideas of establishing a new imprint, David offered me financial support. He said undramatically but firmly that he would give me what in those days was the considerable sum of £5,000, that he could spare it, that he didn't need to get it back and wouldn't expect to get it back for a long time, if ever. I knew he meant it: he scarcely ever drank so it wasn't a bibulous offer late at night. He said no more than what he needed to say and he repeated the offer in the hiatus between my leaving Poolbeg and beginning work for Marino-Mercier the following year. I tried to thank him but he wasn't interested in thanks. All he was interested in was getting writers into print and the necessary evil of having books marketed and sold. It was much later, in fact the year after his death in 2009, that I finally set up an imprint of my own, Londubh Books. Londubh published Ita's graceful, succinct memoir of David and their life together, *I'll Drop You a Line*, in 2016.

I never heard him playing the piano, although I know he did so every day until he was incapacitated in the final years of his life, but I sometimes met him on his way to or from the bookies during the summer flat-racing season. A man is entitled to one vice, if his sober and methodical approach to gambling could be described as such. He told me he came out more or less even (from the bookies) over the course of a season or at least a few seasons. *En revanche*, he was appalled, nay incredulous, when once, having come directly from the hairdresser's to his house I let slip how much I had spent on my colour and cut!

David was a man to whom extravagance or extravagant displays of any kind were anathema, although his commitment to his authors, to the short story form in particular and especially his devotion to Ita and their daughter, Sarah, the two women with whom he was fortunate to share the second half of his life, ran so deep. He once remarked to me that readers' loyalty to authors, once established, often lasted much longer than the authors warranted. I observed the same kind of loyalty in David, unswerving even if occasionally unmerited. He was the very definition of Yeats's 'rooted man', rooted not in any particular place but in his own sense of who he was and what he was.

David Marcus
The Joyce of Yiddish, the *Oy Vay* of Irish

from Oughtobiography, *Chapter Twenty-Seven*

In 1968 Leo Rosten, an American Jew, wrote a book entitled *The Joys of Yiddish*. What is Yiddish? It is one of two languages I should be able to speak, but cannot. The other one is Irish, in which I was fluent when I left school but that fluency applied only to reading, writing and understanding. I never knew to what extent, or even whether, I could hold a conversation in Irish, because conversing in Irish was never a requirement. Apart from the simplest of sentences, it was not encouraged or practised by any of the different Irish teachers I had in secondary school throughout six or seven years. As a result of such a crass dereliction of duty to schoolchildren and to the native language, and the equally crass accompanying Government-imposed policy of compulsion, Irish was as unloved as Latin, and though not quite as dead, it was in these thirties and for decades afterwards struggling to stay alive. For me, however, although my love of Irish poetry led me to continue translating it for some years after I left school, not having any need or opportunity to speak the language, I never tried to, and so have always had to regard myself as an Irishman who did not speak his own language.

But what about Yiddish? The word means 'Jewish' but is not a synonym for 'Jewish'. It is the name of a language that is almost a thousand years old. Born in the early medieval period, it was a fusion of various tenth-century urban German dialects which became the vernacular of the Jews, and as the Jewish people were constantly forced to move from country to country, Yiddish was colonised by the language spoken in the places where the refugees settled.

Yiddish and Hebrew are entirely different. Hebrew was a sacred language, the medium for holy writings, religious services, theology and *Talmud*, and suitably modernised was declared to be one of two official languages when the State of Israel was founded in 1948, the other one being Arabic. Yiddish had been shunned since the revival of Hebrew, completed before 1920, because although it was 'the language of the heart' and the record of Jewish history, it was also the looking-back language of exile and suffering. Official antipathy to it in Israel lessened somewhat in later years and Yiddish newspapers, magazines and theatre were revived. But the transience of contemporary cultural fashions means that in no area can revival guarantee survival, and so the joke(?) recounted by Leo Rosten in *The Joys of Yiddish*—to which I am indebted for much joy and instruction—may again become apposite.

> On a bus in Tel Aviv, a mother was talking animatedly, in Yiddish, to her little boy—who kept answering her in Hebrew. And each time the mother said, 'No, no! Talk Yiddish!'
>
> An impatient Israeli, overhearing this, exclaimed, 'Lady, why do you insist the boy talk Yiddish instead of Hebrew?'
>
> Replied the mother, 'I don't want him to forget he's a Jew.'

Why is it that although my parents spoke fluent Yiddish, I have only a smattering of Yiddish words and phrases? The reason, of course, is that although in my grandparents' homes in Lithuania only Yiddish was spoken, in Ireland they learned English by reading the newspapers and conversing with their children both in English and Yiddish. However, when two of their children met, married and became my parents, Yiddish—as I have explained elsewhere in these pages—was used by them in the home only as a secret language when they did not want their children to know what they were saying. So for me Leo Rosten's title, *The Joys of Yiddish*, becomes The Joyce of Yiddish, reminding me of the secret language of *Finnegans Wake* which academics and Joyce-worshippers spend years decoding and debating, but cannot speak.

And what do I mean by the *Oy Vay* of Irish? *Oy Vay* means 'Oh, pain', particularly emotional pain in spades, the equivalent of the Irish 'Och Ochón!' It is often used in its fuller form, '*Oy vay iz mir!*' (Oh, woe is me!), a version I was very familiar with at home as it was frequently ejaculated by my mother to express her grief over any of my transgressions. So the '*Oy Vay* of Irish' is a voicing of lament for the Sisyphean strait of the Irish language today. What will be its fate? It is surely as unrealistic to imagine it would ever replace the English language in Ireland as it would be to expect Yiddish ever to replace Hebrew in Israel.

I ask myself what difference it would have made to me, as a writer, if my Irish had never fallen into desuetude. Would I have written in it? I know I wouldn't. Why not? For the same reason that I wouldn't have written in Yiddish even had I been able to speak it. Primarily what mattered to me was not the language I was using, but what I was using it for: my material. And primarily my material was my identity as a Jew and the subjective conflicts that engendered. Not—very definitely not—that I regretted the Jewishness of being a Jew. What I regretted was my inability to transform my material—my identity and its consequential, ever-present feeling of rootlessness—into great literature, and so that material became an incubus I periodically placated by producing novels and short stories which, despite the fact that they were published, sold satisfactorily and were liked by some, were for me irrelevant and forgettable. But nothing is ever forgotten. The deeper it is buried, the longer it lives. Yet there is a twin consolation: I am not a great worrier, living—as I have always tried to live—

by the principle that if you have a problem about which you can do nothing, then don't worry, because to worry is to betray your principle *ab initio*; and I am certain that even if I had been able to write the great twentieth or twenty-first century Irish-Jewish novel about being a Jewish *déraciné*, it would not have solved anything. I would still be a Jewish *déraciné*.

Yet isn't Ireland my birthplace and my home? Yes, I was born in Ireland and, apart from thirteen years in London, have lived here all my life. But as Wellington said, 'Because a man is born in a stable, that doesn't make him a horse'; and while I'm legally an Irishman, and while being Irish may provide the tinder for my everyday passions, the Jew in me is branded on my soul as indelibly as the numbers on the arms of the Holocaust victims and survivors.

I have never visited Israel. I have never desired to go there, a reluctance based on two opposing fears: that I would like it and that I wouldn't. No doubt that makes me some sort of a mixed-up Yid, but I feel sure that to visit Israel must leave me even more mixed-up than before. If I went there and, for whatever reason, did not like it, I wouldn't be surprised or disappointed, because I have always considered the Jews to be like other people, only more so. Individually of course the majority of Jews/Israelis are as civilised as most other peoples. But people in the mass are a different animal, manipulable, as has been tragically demonstrated, and riven by apparently ineradicable traditional hatreds.

If, for argument's sake, I liked being in Israel—but no, even if I did, I cannot see myself as feeling it to be my home. I suspect that for me it is a matter of temperament. Loner-inclined, I would never, like Groucho Marx, want to be a member of any club that would have me, and the ghetto gene, my internal birthmark, would almost certainly rebel at the idea of settling in Israel. Being settled in Ireland from birth has put me in a completely different world, one in which I grew up and was educated and so was able to imbibe it at my own pace, one in which I could feel secure, in which I could become involved on my own bent. What it could not do was make of me a complete Irishman in the sense of that phrase which is now, thankfully, increasingly out of date. I am of Ireland, which is what matters. I know that, because I know that if both Israel and Ireland were taking part in the UEFA Champions League, I would want Israel to win, except if they were meeting Ireland. A draw at full time would, I suppose, be acceptable, but in that event I would look to Ireland to win the penalty shoot-out.

Carlo Gébler
A Story's Worth

In childhood and adolescence, certain names and details were carried into my mind by my parents' talk. The talk, like sediment, was deposited on my mind's floor. Over time the sediment hardened into stratum and became part of my geology.

My parents were the Irish writers, Ernest Gébler and Edna O'Brien. In 1958, when I was four, we decamped from the Dublin suburb of Rathgar to a mock-Tudor semi in the south London suburb of Morden. Our house overlooked a melancholy common where Robert Baden-Powell had spent his summers in a wooden lodge; he had invented the concept of scouting there. By the time we arrived, Baden-Powell's lodge, visible from our front door, had become an ice-cream shop managed by Merton County Council.

In our new domicile (where I lived on and off until 1968) my parents talked a lot about Dublin and the people they had known, particularly in the world of the arts, when they had lived there in the 1940s and 1950s. Their subjects included Brendan Behan (my father claimed he taught him to swim); Valentin Iremonger (a good poet destroyed by services to Irish diplomacy); J.P. Dunleavy (my father said he edited and 'saved' *The Ginger Man*, but was never thanked); Hilton Edwards and Micheál MacLiammóir (they gave the best parties); Peadar O'Donnell (diehard Republican who miraculously evolved into anti-Fascist left-winger); Seán Mac Réamoinn ('In France you have Café society but here in Ireland we have Nescafé society' was his much quoted bon mot); and David Marcus, the writer and literary editor.

I don't know if either of my parents had had any dealings with David Marcus when he was editing *Irish Writing* (1946–1954) and they were both in Ireland; but they both certainly knew of him and they talked about him, and I listened carefully to their talk (I was an ardent eavesdropper), and this is what I learnt.

Marcus was an editor who helped people to make their writing better, which was something most editors didn't or couldn't do. He genuinely liked literature and he knew good writing when he saw it. He wanted the writers who made literature to flourish, as opposed to others who only believed in themselves and their own flourishing and who had not the slightest interest in writers. He stood outside (or 'at a slight angle' as E.M. Forster put it, speaking of the poet Constantine Cavafy) the Dublin literary world. It was notable for hard drinking and backstabbing, for envy and falsity, for philistinism and self-sabotage. But Marcus had absolutely nothing to do with any of this. He didn't drink for a start. He also didn't belittle, gossip or do calumny.

In person he was reticent. He was modest. He was also quiet, serious, respectable, frugal (my father particularly liked frugal), honest, trustworthy and fair minded. He was a person of probity, and a person who acted in good faith, unlike so many, many others.

He was also a good translator, from the Irish, something both my parents approved of. (Both were interested in writing in Irish.) Marcus's version of Brian Merriman's *The Midnight Court* (1953) was in the Morden house in my father's bookcase. However, though he could translate from the Irish, David Marcus was not Irish, not in the traditional Catholic way. For my father, the son of an immigrant (technically an Austro-Hungarian though in truth a Czech nationalist) who was denied a position as first clarinet in what became the RTÉ Symphony Orchestra because he was an alien and not Irish, and who felt for all sorts of reasons (this was my father) that he was an outlier, Marcus's ethnicity was the most crucial fact of all. He wasn't a chip off the old Hibernian block—he was a Jew—and that was the explanation for why he was the way he was.

Since this material was part of my psyche's bedrock, it followed that in the mid-1980s, when I was publishing stories in small magazines and trying to find my footing as a writer, and an envelope arrived at the flat where I lived in London with an Irish stamp, containing a short grammatically precise letter inviting me to write a story (probably for *The Irish Press* or maybe an anthology, I can't remember which) with a signature, in ink, made obviously with a fountain pen, that was neat, sharp, and upward tilting, underneath which was typed, lest I couldn't make out the handwriting, 'David Marcus', I was elated. Of course, I wanted to write for this paragon about whom I knew so much.

In those days I used to go to the Electric Cinema in the Portobello Road a good deal. The area where the cinema was located, which was just below the Westway, was gentrifying but it wasn't fully gentrified yet. There were still boarding houses in the area where single Irish men who typically worked as labourers lodged, and I would regularly see these men, in their cement-encrusted Wellington boots and filthy donkey jackets, a biscuit tin with their lunch under one arm, being collected in the morning or dropped back in the evening by the invariably knackered Bedford vans that construction companies like Murphy's used to shuttle their workers to and from their building sites.

Beside the Electric there was a small supermarket run by a family from Pakistan which was almost always open and stocked Carrolls and Major cigarettes for the local Irish clientele, and here, one evening near Christmas, I witnessed an extraordinary scene. An Irish workman who'd just been dropped off went in with his Christmas bonus, a fifty-pound note, to buy a bottle of Powers, but when he got his change back from the lad behind the till, it was only change for a twenty-pound note. Where was the rest? the Irishman demanded. He'd tendered a fifty. No, he hadn't, said the lad. It was a twenty. Voices were raised. The supermarket owner came over; he was bearded, wore a waistcoat with a lattice design of silver and green, and was emollient. But since he couldn't give the Irishman what he believed he was owed, the row rumbled on. The police were summoned. The till was examined. Plenty of fives, tens, and twenties in the drawer but no sign of a fifty. The Irishman must have been mistaken, said the policeman. It was a twenty which he had thought was a fifty that he proffered. No. The Irishman was belligerent by this point. He knew his bonus was a fifty... He was carted away, eventually, probably to the notorious Harrow Road police station. It was another little London flare-up, which involved the marginal fighting between themselves and the rulers (or their representatives) keeping the peace. But this wasn't the end of the saga and I had the good fortune (coming or going to the cinema again, I practically lived in the Electric in those days) to witness this. Passing the supermarket one evening, I saw the donkey-jacket-wearing Irishman and the waistcoat-wearing supermarket owner shaking hands and laughing. It turned out (as I discovered, eavesdropping again) the Irishman's fifty had been palmed by the lad who served him and slid under the till where the policeman hadn't looked. The supermarket owner had discovered the ruse, tracked the Irishman down and made restitution, and the moment immediately following this was what I had stumbled upon. Oh, here was something to gladden the heart. The marginal reconciling.

I wrote this up as a story and sent it to Marcus. It was called 'The Fifty Pound Note'. The editor replied; he liked it but not enough; it wasn't quite there, he felt. He made some suggestions. I tried to put his suggestions into effect. I sent the story back. The story was returned. It still was not quite there, not quite, he said, so the answer, sadly, regretfully, had to be no.

I'd already collected quite a few rejections by the time I came to show David Marcus 'The Fifty Pound Note' but my interactions with him, unlike so many others who'd said 'No', was different. The others had left me feeling deflated and spurned, but not

Marcus. From our interactions I'd got something. I felt enlarged by our correspondence, and I was learning that in the long term our failures are more important than our successes, they being more helpful to the tempering of our mettle than achievement ever is. (Actually, the truth is most likely that success spoils us while failure—up to a point—improves us.) And what was it I had got? Answer: the encouragement to keep going and to keep trying. This editor didn't think I couldn't write. That was clear. I just needed to write more, to read more, and to persist. I needed to keep on keeping on, but slowly, not rushing. And he left me in no doubt that wherever it was I wished to go, I would get there— eventually; I just had to take it one sentence at a time. I took the counsel about measured indefatigability to heart. I kept on with 'The Fifty Pound Note' and, in the end, it did come right. *The Irish Times* published it. Lessons arrive all through life; some matter more than others and this one, from Marcus, about persistence was one of the most valuable I ever got.

My father died in 1998 and I decided I would write about our curious father-and-son relationship. Marcus knew the world my father was in when my father was trying to find his footing (Dublin in the 1940s and 1950s) and so I got in touch with him. I have his address in the Filofax I kept at the time. I don't believe we met at that time; everything was done by phone or letter. But I do know our interactions were more than merely transactional and business-like. I know, for instance, I needed to know the colours of the different sheets of glass in the fanlight over the front door of 29 Garville Avenue (the house I lived in as a child before we moved to London) because I wanted to write about the day we moved into that house and how I sat on the stairs and stared, utterly transfixed, at these panes of brightly coloured glass in the fanlight over the front door; it was my first experience of aesthetic joy. Marcus lived in Rathgar and I felt sufficiently emboldened (or confident) to ask him to go around to my childhood home to check the fanlight. And he did and then he rang me and in his quiet, clear, precise voice, he reeled off the colours of the panes, going left to right and then asked me to call the details back to confirm I had them right, absolutely right. The exacting precision was delightful and impressive. The book I wrote about my father—*Father and I*—only contains a handful of acknowledgments and David Marcus is one of those I thank.

Sometime in 2005 he asked me for a story for *The Faber Book of Best New Irish Short Stories 2006–7*. I was living in the north of Ireland and the so-called Troubles were over, but those who'd suffered because of the violence went on suffering regardless of the Good Friday Agreement. I decided to write about that, the longevity of misery, and I produced 'Room 303', a story about a couple whose marriage having collapsed, following the murder of their only child by paramilitaries, are obliged, for complicated reasons, to spend the night together in a hotel bedroom.

I'd like to think I was a better writer than I had been thirty years earlier when 'The Fifty Pound Note' landed on Marcus's desk. Unfortunately, I can't find any correspondence about the story; was there any back and forth? Impossible to say. I know from my diary (Tuesday, 25 April 2006) that, 'In the afternoon I went back to my desk… [and] read through "Room 303" the finished draft of which has to go to David Marcus at the end of the week.' It was a great day, I added, because for the first time in a long while I 'gorged on my own work'. The next day, Wednesday, 26 April, I was back at the story, and on Friday (like the obedient writer I've always tried to be), 'I got "Room 303" finally polished and dispatched to David Marcus'.

Almost immediately Marcus was in touch, by phone. We needed to celebrate. He would take me to lunch as he did every writer whom he anthologised. The day was fixed for the following week, Thursday, 4 May; 1pm at the Lord Edward, Christchurch Place, in Dublin. A second call followed. It was his wife, Ita Daly. After lunch, would I take her husband to a bus stop—she described its location—and wait until—she gave the number of the bus—

arrived; and then would I actually put him on this bus, which would carry him back to Rathgar? It was very important I did this because without my careful stewardship there was a possibility that he might never get home otherwise, and if I couldn't put him on his bus some other arrangement would have to be made to ensure he got home safely. Of course, I said, after lunch I'd get him on the bus that would take him home.

I was working in Trinity on the Thursday of our meeting. I was working on *My Father's Watch*, a collaboration with Patrick Maguire, the youngest of the Maguire Seven, the Irish family who were fitted up for the Guildford pub bombings in the mid-1970s. I left Trinity at 12.30, walked up Dame Street, and arrived at the venue. I was looking forward to this not only because I'd be meeting David Marcus but because I was brought to the Lord Edward as an adolescent. I remembered a coal fire glowing in an open grate, red velvet banquette seats and a smell, faint but discernible, of delectable fish stock. Would I find what I remembered? I climbed to the first or was it the second floor, entered, and experienced the rare pleasure of not being disappointed when revisiting a scene from the past. The Lord Edward was unchanged as far as I could tell.

Marcus appeared, thin and formally dressed. There was a quiet smile on his face; the smile was understated, wise, knowing, it reminded me of the smiles on the faces of mystics in Marc Chagall's paintings. It was a smile that suggested its wearer knew something but what he knew was not about this world; his knowledge was about something outside this world.

We sat in the corner at Marcus's usual table, the one he always had for his monthly luncheons with his best friend, Vincent Banville. We ordered and the food was brought: melon for Marcus, crab for me: poached salmon for him, fish pie for me. We established we were born on the same day, August 21; he in 1924, me in 1954. He was the first person I'd ever met who was born on the same day as I was. Here was something synchronous, an augur of something, surely? From our shared birthdays our talk switched to his childhood, his parents, and his father whom he called the Boss and who loved to gamble and who went to Ascot every year, and who paid for him to have piano lessons for which he was eternally grateful. Music was then discussed, which led to another connection. He had vaguely known my great-uncle Hermann, a viola player with the Cork Symphony Orchestra under Aloys Fleischmann in the early 1950s, he said, remembered him taking his tea like a true Mittel-European, black with a slice of lemon, and assured me Hermann went to synagogue in Cork (which was news to me).

Then he told me blood had leaked from the left to the right hemisphere of his brain six years earlier, since when he couldn't remember or recall like he had once been able to remember and recall. The far past was never a problem, but the immediate present, say yesterday, or the day before, that was lost. The shakes had also started, he continued, following on from the bleed, impairing his agility and mobility; yet his ability to type and to play the piano were unimpaired. He did both every day. Then he went back in time again and talked about his siblings, only he couldn't remember where any of them were living now (the immediate present, as he reminded me, being his problem) except that it was in England. He also talked of Ita, his wife, and how they met, and the child they had, Sarah, who, he said, worked for Bloomsbury, the publishers.

'I send her money all the time,' he said, 'but she rings me, and she says, "Dad, don't send me money. I have enough." But if you have money, you might as well give it to the one you love.'

However, he continued, he had no idea where his money came from. He must have got money, he thought, scouting for writers for Giles Gordon, the agent, as he did for years; but he wasn't certain. And he had money from *The Irish Press* for whom he'd worked for years, hadn't he? Yes, he thought so, he said, answering his own question.

But, I said, Faber was paying him for *The Faber Book of Best New Irish Short Stories 2006–7*, surely. There was a source of money.

Oh yes, he agreed, Faber were. But he would be passing his fee onto the authors because he didn't think they were being paid enough. Also, he added, he had reserved the right to decide on the size of fee each contributor to the anthology would receive and each fee would vary according to how much he liked the story. I decided not to press him here (after all, what I might discover mightn't please me: I might discover he liked 'Room 303' less than someone else's story and so was paying me less) and instead I decided to revert to his earlier point, his diverting his fee to his authors. Why should he subsidise our fees, I asked. After all, we were being paid.

'Writers have given me everything,' he said. 'Writers have been my whole existence and now it is time for me to give something back.'

He speared a small morsel of salmon, slipped it between his lips and chewed slowly, meditatively. There was the smile again. The smile of one who knew something. In the silence that followed I felt a confluence of disparate understandings coming together. I was with an old gentleman who was in Ireland in the 1940s and early 1950s at the same time as my parents and in the same world as them. He was a witness and a connection to the world I'd heard them speaking about. Their words had carried a sense of this figure with whom I was sitting into me and decades on I was now being offered the chance to match their accounts with the model. Fabulation is so very often unable to withstand contact with reality, which is why we are invariably counselled to avoid meeting our exemplars (it only leads to disappointment), but not in this case. My parents' accounts were on the money. It had taken a while, a lifetime indeed, to get to this point, when the ideal and the original could be compared, but I'd got there, finally. Yet again, I thought, I was being taught the same old lesson about duration. It only matters that you keep on keeping on.

The bill was paid and I set off with my host for his bus stop. He moved slowly along the uneven paving, fearful of falling. Once at the stop, a change of mood, a feeling of relaxation. It was a warm, moist, spring afternoon and we talked amiably as we loitered. 'Such interesting people,' David said of my story's ill-fated and miserable characters, Anna and Liam, divorced and desolated though years have passed, by the killing of their son, Ciaran, both baffled and both certain they will never reconcile either with each other or what was done to them. A moment after and with impeccable timing, the bus appeared and I helped him to get in. I said something to the driver and the driver waited and watched as Marcus moved gingerly down the aisle and then sank onto the first available seat. The door hissed shut. The bus lumbered off. Through the window a hand and a smile from Marcus and a moment after I was looking at the bus moving away though the traffic, carrying its fragile cargo towards Rathgar. Our first was also our last meeting.

I'm a fairly good archivist. I keep things, important things, the bits of paper that matter, contracts for example. In the course of writing this, I searched my contracts file for the contract for 'Room 303'. It wasn't there. I contacted my agent and he couldn't find it either, which is bizarre, seeing as he has all my contracts going back to the early 1980s. How do I explain this? Simple. I don't think there was a contract. Everything was done by word of mouth. And therefore what I was paid was what David Marcus thought my story was worth, just as he had said he was doing at lunch. And I'm happy with that. Whatever I was paid, I don't doubt it was right.

Mary Dorcey

I first met David at the prize-giving ceremony in the AIB bank in Ballsbridge in 1990, when I had the honour of being awarded the Rooney Prize for Irish Literature. That meeting had a profound effect on my writing life.

My collection of short stories, *A Noise from the Woodshed*, had been published in the UK in 1989 by a feminist press that had earlier published some of my poetry.

I was living then with my French partner, Carole, in a quiet cottage in Ventry. I had started a routine of getting up early and going to a little unheated shed next door to write for an hour. Hidden away as I was, I had no idea that *A Noise from the Woodshed* was picked up by an Irish editor and sent to the Rooney panel, until a well-known voice from RTÉ phoned me in Kerry to tell me that my book had won the prize for that year. I discovered later that Nuala O'Faolain had written to the publisher, Onlywomen Press, and asked them to submit a copy.

Not knowing this, it was with some trepidation that I made my way up from Kerry to Dublin. The period we were just emerging from, the 1980s, had been one of near unrelieved repression, conservatism and belligerent hostility to both the women's and the nascent gay rights movements in Ireland.

So it was with huge pleasure, and immense surprise, that I discovered the warmth and welcome of David Marcus, Nuala O'Faolain and many others that wonderful evening in June.

When I was introduced to David, I was at once struck by the gravity and sensitivity of his manner, the softness of his tone, his alert listening: his head gently lowered as if each word were precious to him. We had never crossed paths before (nor had I ever submitted anything to his *Irish Press* page), but he took me aside at the first opportunity and asked in his grave avuncular manner what I was working on next.

David, of course, was renowned at that time for his passion for literature and his fearless support of writers in his 'New Irish Writing' page in *The Irish Press*. Almost alone in Ireland, he exemplified fairness of judgement, impartiality, combined with a determination to make a public space for writers regardless of class, gender, sexuality, or who they might know. He showed a particular and informed interest in the writing of Irish women.

When he spoke to me that summer evening, he lowered his voice to tell me that he considered my book one of the best first collections he had ever read. He also said that if I had anything else in process to please send it to him. You can imagine my surprise and delight at that greeting from a middle-aged, conventional Irish man, as he seemed. I like to think that his Jewish identity, and his consequent experience of cultural difference, helped to form his understanding of me. I was not accustomed to it, more used to being cold shouldered or openly abused when in respectable Dublin circles. My surname, the only one in Ireland, led to instant recognition by conservatives and bigots alike who marked me immediately as a radical feminist and an unapologetic lesbian.

After that wonderful evening I moved yet again, first to County Wicklow, which I knew well, and then to Dublin. Now at work on a novel, David contacted me out of the blue, wanting to know how my work was getting on. He knew that I had published two collections of poetry with Salmon Poetry during this time: *Moving into the Space Cleared by Our Mothers* in 1991, and *The River That Carries Me* in 1995. 'Very fine work,' he told me, but 'I would like to see more fiction.' I explained my circumstances—my gypsy lifestyle and the need to teach (Creative Writing at UCD and later at Trinity). He asked if I would consider coming to his house in Rathgar and reading a section or two from the novel I was working on for him.

We had a very relaxed, informal session, sitting side by side on his sofa facing the hearth. I think we talked very little of 'the book', but his concentrated interest and clear determination to see me publish a novel was inspiring. After that meeting, a few weeks later, he asked if I would like to visit again, just to talk of general literary matters and see how the book was going.

We had perhaps five sessions together over the next two years. Most of our conversations veered far off course from the work in progress, but our wandering musings on life and literature, were a delight for me, and I hope for him also. On each meeting we sat on the sofa, and he would ask me to read an extract. He paid such close attention I felt as much satisfaction as if the book were already published. I remember the quality of his listening; so intent and alert it felt as if he were memorising the text as I spoke. And of course this acuity of interest, allowed me to hear my own words with a heightened clarity and objectivity. When I finished the page or so I was reading, he would sit back and sigh: 'I think it will be a very fine work, indeed. You must keep going.'

And so I did. *Biography of Desire* was finally published in 1997 by Poolbeg Press and the late Kate Cruise O'Brien. David gave me some words of endorsement for the cover, one sentence of which was published: 'It's a brave, brave book.' Eighteen years before the Marriage Equality Referendum was passed into law, David was an extraordinarily brave and far-seeing man to champion this novel so publicly. Without his encouragement, *Biography of Desire* might never have made it into the light of the new day that it heralded.

Another Glorious Day

When I wake in the morning, if it is the morning, I don't know where I am or who I am. I think, I know, that I have been asleep. And now am awake. But where I have woken to eludes me. And the identity of the I who wonders about it escapes me completely. I cast my eyes around the room searching for a sign, for any indication as to my whereabouts; the time of day or the day of the week. Any concrete fact will do, to provide a foundation on which I can build. A stepping stone against the torrent.

A foothold.

I see a medium-sized pleasant room, some good furniture, a dressing table and chair, a tall window with curtains slightly parted. On the wall at the end of the bed I see what might be a large red and yellow parrot sitting on a wooden perch. Is this likely to be the case? I don't know. Apart from this parrot it appears to be a conventional, well-kept house, wherever it is. Possibly, I am fortunate to be here. It may well cost a great deal to maintain. And who does all the work? I must ask one of the nurses. Why did I say nurses? It is a hospital? Have I any reason to say that? It looks too relaxed for a hospital. A very good carpet and that picture of the little girls with the cat under the table, where have I seen that before? I am beginning to feel hungry; at least I think that's what the feeling is. How long is it since I've had anything to eat? Is there a bell I could ring for attention? I don't see anything resembling a bell.

'Unregarded age in corners thrown.' Where does age come into the puzzle I wonder?

Is there anyone else here who is hungry? Is there anyone else in the house? Is there any way of knowing? Perhaps I'm mad? Perhaps I'm in an asylum of some kind? Have I any means of determining this? I must calm myself. Study the situation. See what I can say for sure. I am lying down, yes. I am wearing a nightdress, yes. I am warm, yes. There is a clean sheet pulled to my chin. A clean pillow under my head. There is silence around me. Is it complete? Can I hear anything? Yes, I hear a clock ticking faintly. Where? I can't see a clock. I am lying on my back with my head on a pillow (yes, a clean pillow I'm glad to say), I'm looking at a ceiling. It is high and white with one large grey cobweb in the far corner (the kind I would have knocked clear with one sweep of the brush). Though as yet there is no spider in evidence. 'Weaving spiders come not here, hence you long-legged spiders, hence.' *Hamlet*, I think.

It is remarkable and at the same time irritating somehow, that Shakespeare has a line to suit every occasion.

When I turn my head to the right I see a smooth wall and hanging on it a large painting in a dark frame. It shows a woman in a yellow cardigan holding a green umbrella. Is this what seemed before to resemble a parrot? I think I remember this painting. Granny used to have it in the sitting room. Is Granny alive or dead? Why did I say that? Who is Granny? Not mine surely? I must try to find out from someone. But who? Is there anyone available to ask? Perhaps it's a hotel or guesthouse. The wallpaper is good; there is a nice chest of drawers and a wardrobe. Should I try calling out? Will anyone answer?

Is it wise to call when I have no idea who might respond?

The light is so sharp it hurts my eyes. I close them for a moment or two. I think. When I open them again I recognise the same daylight making its way across the room. But the light of which day, I wonder? I wish someone would come and tell me, I must at least have the date and the year. Still the ticking of a clock.

Through the window I see a grey sky, white clouds, and below that yellow flowers in a garden. Is there something familiar about it—that garden? There is a cat or, at least, I see a cat walking through tall grass. A black cat. Is this a clue? Who owns a cat? Someone I know? I can't remember. There were cats somewhere else. Black pussy—that's what she was called; black pussy. She must be hungry. I should go home and feed the cats. How am I to manage it? Can I get up unaided? I wonder is there anyone looking after us? Should I call for assistance? I don't hear any sound of life at all. Where could it be? A hospital, a nursing home or a hotel perhaps. Could it be a quiet country house? There is some very good furniture. And the windows are beautifully clean.

A lot of work for someone with a very tall ladder.

Although, now I come to study it, the carpet is a little bit shabby. I never had enough money to replace carpets when they needed it or curtains. I had to wait. But I had sufficient for my needs. Adequate always. I had a hard life. You must remember, Sara; I have had a hard life. Who is Sara? Someone I love. I remember that I have someone I love who comes to see me. More than one person. There is a boy and a girl. I hear the telephone ringing. I hope someone answers it. I don't think I can get up. I'll try. Why is it so hard to stand up? I must ask someone what is wrong with my knees. They don't bend properly and I can't straighten my back. Is the phone still ringing? I should call someone. Will anyone come if I do? Who? A nurse? Perhaps I'm better off without a nurse. I don't think I need her services at present. And I can't know what kind of nurse. Nurses can be very difficult.

'Are you all right, Maeve, would you like another cup of tea?'

I hear a voice calling from somewhere in the house, above or below me I do not know. And who is Maeve? And why does she not answer? I'm sure I heard someone calling her before. Is the voice approaching or receding? I cannot tell. Silence now again. What was I thinking about when I was interrupted? I must concentrate on the important questions, or at least the most immediate. Where is this? Where did I come from? Am I alone?

Some memory is stirring. What was I doing before this? I have a pair of spectacles in my hand. Reading glasses? When did I pick them up and from where? Were they under my pillow? I think I was studying the environment. Making notes. Mental notes. On a low table beside the bed I see a telephone and a photograph in a silver frame. I peer closer but I can't make out who it is a picture of (of whom it is a picture?). I see only that it's a portrait of two young women standing on a flight of stone steps. Good-looking girls, with intelligent faces and good clothes. The kind of girls I would have liked for daughters if I'd had daughters. I wonder why I had no children. I can't think of any reason now. I must ask someone. Daughters, the word rings a bell, some memory is stirring at the edge of my vision. I must wait quietly so as not to frighten it off. I've learned that this is the best way to trap them. Stealthily as one might hunt nervous animals, waiting silent in the long grass until they gather courage, draw closer and at last thrown off guard, come within my grasp.

No sign of the spider as yet.

'Maeve, were you calling? Have you finished your breakfast?'

A woman with a wide moon-shaped face looks round the door. She is smiling. The glass in her spectacles twinkles in the sunlight, which gives her face an impish look. She says my name in a loud clear voice as if doubtful that I can hear her although she is standing now at the foot of the bed. Would you like another cup of tea, love? Oh, it's such a relief to see you, I say, I was getting worried. I thought I was all alone in the house. Not a bit of it, she says, sure we never leave you on your own.

'Oh that's very good news. I wish I'd known that before. And how are you? How is everyone at home?'

'We're all grand, Maeve, all your family and mine.'

'Thank God for that. I was afraid everyone must be dead. There wasn't sound or any sign of life. I thought there must have been some general catastrophe and that by some awful chance I had survived.'

'There's not a bother on any of us.' She has a slight country accent. Somewhere near my part, I think, Tipperary or Limerick perhaps. Munster anyway, which is reassuring. Irish by birth, Munster by the grace of God—who used to say that? She comes closer. She has short blonde hair and arched eyebrows. She is wearing some kind of yellow flannel-like jacket with square pockets and a long, wide zip. I cannot make out whether she's dressed for indoors or outdoors.

I return her smile.

What day of the week is it? I ask to gain a little time. It's evident from her face that she expects me to recognise her and I'm not sure that I do. Though there is certainly something familiar about it. What day is it I find the safest question. Hearing it people seem to assume that I know all the other things I'm not asking. If I make myself patient, whoever is talking to me will, sooner or later, fill in the gaps. Do you want another cup of tea love or will you just not bother? my nice friend says. I recognise this as one of our little jokes. It seems to be a lovely day, Kitty, I reply, and suddenly, like Excalibur, the sword in the lake, her name has risen from the depths in one gleaming piece—Kitty! Kitty O'Neill.

'Did you have a little sleep?' she asks me.

'I think I must have, Kitty, yes. Where am I at present, may I enquire?'

'At home in your own house. Where else would you be?'

'My own house! Are you sure? Well that's extraordinary. I had no idea of that. I don't recognise it at all.' I put my hands to either side of my hips and push myself, groaning aloud, upright in the bed so that my back is propped against the pillows. 'I've been watching the sunlight shining on the grass and the little birds, sparrows, I think. They have amazing courage,' I say to make conversation. 'They swoop down to collect tiny crumbs of bread taking their lives in their hands.'

Not that they have hands, of course.

Kitty is standing now in the doorway, one foot in, one foot out.

I have decided that the jacket is indoor wear so it's likely that she intends to stay for a while. 'I have to go downstairs to answer the telephone,' she tells me. 'Will you say some prayers until I come back?' She disappears as suddenly, I think, as she appeared. Silence follows. Has she left the house? No way of knowing. I look out the window into the garden and see to my surprise what might be a squirrel, some creature with thick greyish fur and a bushy tail, sitting on a tree branch. 'Sometimes my heart hath shaken with great joy, to see a leaping squirrel on a bough or something in a field at evening…' Can it be a squirrel? Unlikely. Is it evening? Possibly. It's gone from sight now so I may never know. And who wrote those lines? It's possible an answer might be supplied to this, at least.

Was it suggested to me recently (by whom?) that I should say some prayers? And when? Well, no time like the present. 'Hail Mary full of grace the Lord is with thee, blessed art thou among women and blessed is the fruit of thy womb Jesus. Holy Mary Mother of God…' Now, how does the rest of it go? Something about sinners. 'On Raglan Road on an autumn day I saw her first and knew that her dark hair would weave a snare that I would one day rue, I saw the danger yet…' There's no need to feel sorry for him then—he saw the danger. But he was always a morose fellow skulking about the canal. Who is it lives on Raglan Road now? A quiet street where old ghosts meet. There were eight in the family. Someone was telling me about them just this morning. What are their names? If I could get the first one I'd know the rest. I have to take a running jump at it. I wonder does any one of them know I'm here. Have I any way of contacting them?

I don't know where I am myself so how could I direct anyone else?

Patrick Pearse, of course, I say aloud in excitement. The answer to some question I was struggling with has just arrived unbidden. I can't remember what the question was.

My nice friend is standing by the window shielding me from the sunlight.

'Kitty, what terrible thing has happened in the world? There's something at the back of my mind. A catastrophe of some kind? Was it an earthquake in India yesterday?'

'Did you say any prayers, Maeve? I thought I heard you.'

'Yes, I think I probably did. On Raglan Road on an autumn day...'

'That's a poem, Maeve, not a prayer.'

'Is it? Well, I don't suppose God will mind. He'll take my great age into account.'

Kitty is folding clothes beside what looks like a chest of drawers at the far end of the room. 'Why is it do you think,' I ask aloud, in reference to some news I can't recall, 'that some of us lead lives of such calm and security while others by a mere accident of geography are fraught with every kind of danger?' Kitty's head is lowered and she offers no solution to this. Instead after a moment she informs me that Jezebel is making her way along the corridor. I ask who Jezebel is when she's up and dressed? She sounds a very unlikely visitor to this respectable establishment. A large striped animal (black and silver stripes on greyish background) leaps onto the bottom of the bed. When she reaches my face she gives an angry cry and shows the extraordinary interior of her mouth—crimson and furrowed.

'Whose the bold pussycat stayed out all night?' Kitty says. I stroke her head and she purrs, and kneads my shoulder with piercing claws. 'Isn't it nice to have one free spirit left in the house?'

'Do you hear the phone, Maeve? I must go down and answer it.'

Down where? I hear nothing but then, that means nothing.

There is something stirring at the back of my mind, some disaster that has happened in the world. Is it the war I wonder, still raging? Not any of the wars I remember, some other one. But there is always a war.

My nice friend with the blonde hair and the matching glasses comes back into the room. That was your eldest son Kevin, she tells me, he rang to see how you are? 'I hope you told him I'm bothered and bewildered?' I answer, having found something sharp in the bed that turns out to be a pair of silver-rimmed spectacles.

'I said you're as fit as a fiddle.'

'Kevin, was it? I wish I'd known that when I was speaking to him. I would have asked him about his work. I hope I wasn't rude to him?'

'Not a bit of it,' Kitty says, 'you were clear and concise as always.'

'I am a very foolish fond old man and to deal plainly, I fear I am not in my perfect mind.'

Kitty tells me not to be worrying about my memory; it's better than hers. I'm a mine of information, she says. I was telling her only this morning, it seems, about the Spanish Civil War, and Franco and the Communists. She is straightening pillows behind my head and pulling back the covers. I see a blue cotton nightdress and two very thin white legs (mine?) protruding from it. She says I was talking about the Second World War yesterday when there was rationing of meat and sugar and the Russian Revolution and the White Army. I am holding onto the bed head with one hand and with the other I grasp Kitty's sleeve. Hey ho and up she rises.

'You're a true scholar,' she says. 'My head is like a sieve.'

'We'll have to be careful to put nothing in it or we'll make a terrible mess of the floor.'

We both laugh when I say this.

I like to see Kitty amused because it must be very dull work taking charge of me.

'I might as well stay in my dressing gown if we have only ourselves to please, Kitty?' She is standing in the doorway holding a tray in her hand. She asks if I can manage for myself while she tidies up below. 'Have you forgotten that Sara is taking you out for tea this afternoon because it's her birthday?' she asks. This comes as complete news but is all the more pleasant for that. 'The jewel in the crown, that's what we call her,' Kitty says. I wonder of what or whom does the crown consist. I decide not to ask or maybe I have asked because Kitty says, 'Your other children, all six of them.'

'Six! Now don't tease me, Kitty—how could I possibly have had six children?'

My friend sets down the tray and comes back into the room. She is proffering one of several small white garments outstretched in her right hand. 'What do we put on first?' she says. 'Underwear. I suppose that's why we call it underwear.' She says she'll get me started and then I can carry on. It's good for me to do as much as I can, so that I don't lose the habit. That sounds very sensible.

'It's very good of you to take so much trouble to explain everything. I must be a terrible trial?'

'Not a bit of it, Maeve. You're an angel.'

'A very earthbound angel, I'm afraid.'

I'm sitting on the edge of a bed. Why? With my feet in large (outsize in fact I would call them) slippers, resting squarely on the floor. What follows next?

The sunlight coming in through the window hurts my eyes. I don't know what day it is or where I am. I close my eyes and count to five. I open them again. Where does this go, for God's sake? There is a piece of white cloth in my hand, which seems to be composed of straps and pockets. It looks like a noose to hang myself. Or a bridle perhaps. To be led like a horse. An extraordinary object. Does it go over the head? Or around my waist? And this? What is this damn thing for? Do I put my feet through these holes, I wonder? That can't be right. Maybe I should wait until I get some help. Is there anyone in the house besides myself? Surely they wouldn't leave me alone. I don't think I'm in a fit state to be left alone. I don't know why. My brain is tired, I think that's what it is. Now if I put this round my waist and then pull it up, it seems to make sense. Then I could put these straps up over my shoulders. Oh, you silly old fool why can't you remember? What is wrong with my head?

Old? Why did I say old? I should call for help. 'Is there anyone there? Does anyone hear me? Am I all alone in the house?'

'Maeve, I'm coming now, don't panic…'
'Oh, Kitty, at last, there you are. I was getting frightened.' In the mirror I'm holding I see a face reflected, an old woman's face with white hair and red-rimmed eyes. Theatrical looking. I don't know who she is and think it better not to ask.
'It's like keeping order in a mad house, Kitty.'
'What is?'
'Managing my brain, effecting the smallest action… I seem to be completely vacant today.'
'Indeed and you're not. Sure, you're a walking encyclopaedia,' she says. 'Now that would be a sight!'
'Would you like me to give you the facts about yourself the way Sara does?' Kitty asks, and begins in the voice of a quizmaster: 'Maeve Kieley, née Roach, born in Waterford 1920, seven brothers and sisters. Moved to Donegal aged eight. Moved to Dublin, Pembroke Road, aged fourteen years. Moved to Seapoint, Dublin, on marriage to Michael Kieley. Six children, all surviving.' All this would be very interesting if I knew whom it concerned. But I don't like to interrupt with more questions.

She is fastening the buttons of my dress, at the cuffs and the collar, and she says I am just myself again. I wonder who I was before.
'With your hair brushed you're beautiful. The contessa—isn't that what we call you? And you'll wear your coat with the fur collar because it's cold and because it suits a countess.'
'Who calls me the countess?'
'We all do because you're just like one.'
'The Hag of Beara, Kitty, I think, would be more like it.'
I put down the hairbrush I am holding in my hand. It has a silver back and short black bristles. 'I think I must need to make a visit to the toilet. I haven't been since yesterday.'

Kitty tells me I was there only half an hour ago.

'Are you sure? I don't think you can be right?'

'Come on now like a good girl. Stand up. Hold onto my arm. You're very steady once you're on your feet.'

We are passing the bathroom door. I see clean towels, green, two hanging on a rail. The blue tiles on the floor look newly washed. 'I think we get on very well, don't we, Kitty?' I say.

'It's because we have so much in common. We were both widowed young,' she says, 'and raised our families on our own and know all about worry and heartbreak.'

'And facing facts, Kitty,' I say. 'And not to kick against the inevitable.' We are making our way laboriously down the stairs. I ask if she knows that O'Neill is one of the great names of Ireland. We are moving one foot at a time and then another foot. And there are four legs to organise on a narrow staircase. The ancient Irish aristocracy, I tell her. Does she know about the Wild Geese and the Flight of the Earls? Kitty doesn't know or doesn't want to talk about them now. She is concentrating on getting down the stairs in one piece. That's what she says. I have to get you down in one piece. When the children were small I was always afraid one of them would break his neck on these stairs, used to dream of a bungalow, I tell her.

'Now, almost there. You're a great girl.'

'Hardly a girl any more, I'm afraid.'

'Do you know how old you are this year, Maeve?'

'Well, now I was hoping you could tell me that.'

'How old do you feel?'

'Well, I'm not sure. I feel very well. But I don't think I'm young. I feel mature. About fifty. Am I right?'

'Here's the birthday girl,' someone says. I am coming, step by step, down a steep staircase. You are standing in the doorway. The sun is forming a halo around your hair.

'Oh, Sara, what brings you here?' The birthday girl, someone says, again, I don't know why. You kiss me on both cheeks and put your arms around me. Are we all ready to go? Kitty is pulling on my gloves. They have jammed at the wrist. 'She needs to wrap up in this cold weather.' You are pulling a hat over my head. Or are you taking it off? 'She doesn't like wearing it so it's always a battle.' I can't imagine that I would do battle over the wearing of a hat but you are both laughing so I laugh too.

'Don't be impatient with me now. Remember I didn't ask to lose my memory.'

The door is thrown wide. Ready steady go. I step out. On one side is a green hedge with yellow flowers on or is it a yellow hedge with green leaves? On the other a blue gate and a huge open sky, full of light. Which way are we going—in or out? If I wait someone will tell me. 'And watch the chocolate!' Kitty calls after us. Why is chocolate to be watched, I wonder? It seems to have threatening properties that have escaped my notice.

There are two pairs of shoes going down the path, two black and two red. Mind your step. I think you must be unsteady on your feet today because you take my arm and hold it tightly. 'What will we do with the drunken sailor early in the morning,' I say.

Concentrate. No singing until we're at the gate.

When we reach the street we pause for what I don't know. A bird with red breast feathers is perched on the gatepost. What are we doing now? I ask. 'We're resting.' My hair or is it my hat is caught in a twig as we pass the hedge. You reach out to untangle it. 'Lean on my arm and use your stick on the other side or you'll fall over.'

'And on my leaning shoulder she laid her snow-white hand.' But it can't have been snow white if she was walking through the Sally gardens, can it? He was always a bit of a poseur, Yeats, but we liked him for it, I say. We used to pass him in Merrion Square. You are holding open the gate and I am inching my way through. I don't know why we are moving so slowly but it seems to be necessary.

We pause for a long time at the kerb and then progress again in our snail-like motion across the road.

'What day is it?' I ask. 'Thursday! Are you sure? I thought it was Sunday, love. It's doing an excellent imitation of Sunday. Are you sure now you're not trying to fool me? I rely on you.' A seagull is standing on the harbour wall. The sun is gleaming on its yellow feet. By the light, I think it must be an afternoon in autumn. A vague picture comes into my head—a woman and a child standing by the harbour wall. They are breaking a loaf of stale bread into small pieces to feed the birds. What day is it, I wonder? I must make enquiries. How are things in the great world, I ask instead. 'Is this terrible war still raging?' 'Yes,' you tell me.

'Isn't it extraordinary,' I say, 'that with all the advance in technology we can do nothing to alter human nature.' The wind is blowing a cold sun over our hands and knees. I see the shadow come and go. Someone I love is walking beside me with her arm through mine. I know the voice but her face is hidden from me. She is bending down now to tie her shoelace, I think. Is it one of my sisters? Or one of my daughters?

A cargo ship is passing behind the island. 'The sky is clearing, it's going to be a lovely afternoon,' you say.

'It's a lovely afternoon, already.'

You look at me with a puzzled (why?) and what seems a tender expression. You ask me if I know who you are today, am I quite clear? You turn your head towards me and I see that you're my daughter Sara.

'Sara, of course,' I say. 'That which we call a rose by any other name would smell as sweet.'

'You didn't recognise me for a while because of my hat.'

'It's a very impressive hat,' I say.

'Do you think I've changed much over the years?' I study your face. There are freckles on your cheeks, above your lip and above your eyebrow, one, two, three, four, and five. Your eyes are sea-green. 'Yes,' I say looking at the freckles, 'a little bit I suppose. Just enough.'

We are standing beside a green car. A little black dog is sitting on the back seat. Where did the dog come from?

'That's Charlie of course. Will we get in now and begin our drive?' You open the door and help me to sit down. 'Put your bottom in first and then swing your legs round.'

'We could do with a giant shoehorn, couldn't we?' I say.

Rain in slow drops is falling on the windscreen; the sun is catching in it, obscuring the view. You turn on the windscreen wipers. They travel to the very furthest edge of the wide screen and then all the way back again, back and forth, in a sing-song motion. Something is stirring in my mind about a child walking on a pier. She is carrying a cowboy hat in her hand. What day is it, I wonder?

'I think they should announce the day of the week when they're reading the news on television. There must be a great many people who need to know,' I say.

You put your hand on my knee. 'Are you all right, now?' you ask, 'are you feeling safe?'

'Well, I'm a bit through other, today, as they used to say in Donegal.'

'It comes and goes, the confusion doesn't it, like clouds over the sun?'

'A lot of cloud,' I say.

The little cat shifts position. Her claws dig into my knees, tearing my stocking but I don't want to give her away. 'Isn't the car a wonderful invention,' I say, 'it gives such extraordinary freedom. Do you remember in the old days waiting in the rain for a bus? I don't suppose you can remember that far back. Have you any memory of your father, at all? How old were you when he died? Six! Oh that was much too young!'

It has stopped raining. You switch off the wipers and turn to look at me. You are wearing black sunglasses. They give your face an unfamiliar aspect. I close my eyes and concentrate on your voice that doesn't change. Unaffected by the seasons or fashion.

'How are you getting on with Kitty these days?' you ask.

'Oh, very well, I think. Is there a reason why I wouldn't be?' I ask. 'Although, I have been worried about her,' I say, 'she seems to have some trouble in the family.' You put your hand on my knee and squeeze it as if to get my attention but I am already giving you my full attention. 'Watch the road, love,' I say.

'If you have any problem, of any kind you must tell me, you know that, don't you?' You pronounce this in a very emphatic tone. I see the anxiety in your eyes but I don't know what the cause is. 'I hope it's not taking up too much of your precious time all this managing of my affairs?'

You smile and kiss me.

The sun is so strong I can hardly open my eyes. I think it must be summer. The island has come into view from a strange angle. It seems to be drifting out to sea as if someone has cut it loose from its moorings.

Crushed shells, extraordinarily bright; red and blue and yellow covered the little beach. The children used to love them.

'If only this could go on for ever. I feel perfectly safe and content sitting here. With the sun shining and the little black cat asleep on my lap,' I say.

'Dog,' you correct me.

'Well, whatever she is,' I reply, 'she's a marvel. So good and so intelligent. And she makes such an effort to please you. But she doesn't want you to know it's an effort.' I stroke the soft hair that grows on her muzzle and she opens her eyes and looks at me sadly.

When I raise my eyes again the sky is filled with movement, white and silver birds. Or is it the shadow of the clouds blown across the hills? 'I wish your father could see this,' I say. Something is making a sound like small pebbles thrown against the glass. What is? Rain? 'He didn't want to die, you know. No man ever wanted to die less. He couldn't bear to leave you all. How long is he dead now? Forty years! I am horrified to hear this. How can that be?' I demand. I stare at you in astonishment. I see from your expression that you are not joking. 'But what age are you then?' I gasp at your answer. 'I thought you were still a teenager.'

There is a girl in a blue frock on a blue bicycle near a high white wall. A grey van goes past us at great speed. The car is buffeted as though by a strong wind. You are telling me about your childhood, about sunny days on the beach, about picnics and outings and trips to the pictures. There couldn't have been a better time or better setting. 'Did we go all the way to Glendalough?' I ask. 'How did we get there?' You tell me that I filled the car with children and drove you. This must be an exaggeration, surely? Petrol, perhaps, not children.

A flurry of blossom, pink and white (spring?) is blowing along the black tarmac of the road ahead. I remember the smell of the tar melting on a hot day as we walked to the beach. And did I have anything to do with this happy childhood? I ask in connection with something you have been telling me. 'You were the platform on which everything else was built.' The little black dog licks the back of my hand with a small rough tongue. She looks at you enquiringly and back again to me.

'I know I tried my best. That's all any one of us can do, Sara,' I say, 'I couldn't make up for your father of course because he was devoted to you. But he had more free time than I did. I had so much to do. I don't know if any of you realised that.'

The water is choppy, dark grey with purple streaks across it, beautiful and cold. The wind is rising, I think. You're not lonely at all, these days? you ask.

'Oh not a bit. There is some very pleasant friend who comes to help me in the house. I don't know who she is but she knows me. She seems to have some little difficulty, though. Some trouble in the family. I'm concerned about her. And she needs do things slowly. I think she might be hard of hearing.'

'Kitty you mean.'

'Yes, Kitty. Why did I forget that? She must be one the carers. Isn't that what we call them? A silly name, I think, carers. But that's not their fault. For the most part, they are very good people; kindly and considerate.' I see that the gorse is in full bloom on the hillside, buttercup yellow. It used to stain our fingers when we tried to pick it.

'And they are tactful,' I say, 'they take pains to conceal from me the fact that I'm a prisoner in my own home.'

I have saddened you now.

We round a bend and suddenly the whole sweep of the bay comes into view at once, a beach and hills and trees and white houses. You stop the car at the side of the road. Your face is pale when you turn towards me. 'I'm sorry they've started to lock the front door,' you say. 'I've spoken to them about it but it's an insurance thing—standard procedure. You never do anything foolish or careless but they don't know that.'

'Well, if they think it's necessary I don't mind,' I say, 'and you know sometimes I can be very confused. I don't think I should be on my own too much, unsupervised.'

'You're not; there's somebody with you all the time.'

'Oh that's a great relief to hear. Because my brain can be unreliable, you know. It comes and goes you see, the forgetfulness, for no reason I can think of.'

The clouds are flying along the sky and the waves are flying almost as fast below them. 'It would be a fascinating condition if I was well enough to study it,' I say.

You put your hand on my shoulder. It feels warm and soothing.

'Are you tired, love?' I ask you.

'I'm fine, I just worry about you a little.' I turn to look at you. It's an effort to concentrate. But I see that you are pale and there is a furrow between your eyebrows. 'Cease thou thy worrying, as

Shakespeare would say. There is nothing to be concerned about. I'm splendid most of the time. And after all, at my great age I can't expect to be perfect.'

I count one, two, three bridges over the railway. Stone I think brought from the quarry in Victorian times. The boys used to ride to school along the disused railway.

'The mind is a mysterious organ, isn't it? Or the brain, should I say? Was it Boswell or Swift, when asked about the purpose of life, said a chicken is the egg's way of making another egg? Confusion worse confounded.'

I close my eyes. The words of a poem stir in my memory, 'Better to sleep than see this house now dark to me...' I open my eyes. 'In my own case I could quite happily forget about purpose if I had the least idea what my function is.'

'Don't worry about it,' you say. 'You remember everything you need to. There's only so much room on the shelves, you see.'

'Oh that's a comforting idea,' I say. 'I hope it's true.'

'Imagine a big house with all the precious things stored in the basement. You can't always get down because the stairs are worn but when you get hold of the ladder you find everything is just where you left it.'

When they were all growing up there wasn't a basement to store things in. Never enough room to put anything away for long. I see a tall man walking past on the pavement. He has a shaven head and thick black beard. He looks as if his face is upside down. I must make an effort. I must pull myself together. I must not keep asking questions.

'Anyway, I'm perfectly content now, sitting here with you. Perfectly safe and perfectly happy.'

'Good,' you say. 'That's what I like to hear.'

I read the names that are written on the gates along the roadside: 'Seaview', 'Seacrest', 'Seamount'. Does it make more or less work for the poor postman? I wonder. 'We joined the navy to see the world. And what did we see? We saw the sea.' Some child used to love that song.

'And tell me, how is life treating you these days?' I say, to change the subject, whatever it was. I would like to ask about your career but I'm not sure what it is. 'And your work—does it bring in much in the way of money?' Enough, you tell me and smile.

'I play the violin in the symphony orchestra.'

'Oh, isn't that wonderful.' I am delighted by this news. Although there is some faint picture in my mind. A girl by a window, a violin in her arms that is almost bigger than herself.

'It doesn't pay as much as I'd like but I like it so much it doesn't matter.'

I say that sounds like a tongue twister. 'But I think you're very wise, to be following a passion.' You are wearing a plain silver band on your ring finger. Does this mean you've become engaged without my knowing? But I remember then something of your situation and I put out my hand, touch the ring and say, 'Engaged to life.'

You glance at the driving mirror and then open the door on your side. 'I have to get something from the boot. Will you be all right for a moment on your own?'

'Yes, love but don't be too long will you?' The little dog jumps out after you, wagging her stub of a tail. There was some other dog with a thick-fringed black tail like a fan, long ago. We always had spaniels at home.

'Only a minute. Just sit here and keep your eye on me and you'll be perfectly safe.' I see you standing at the side of the car. You are walking backwards so that your face is turned towards me. You are smiling. Now you are behind me, almost out of sight. Your back is to me now. I try to turn my head. Suddenly, you have disappeared. A cloud must have gone across the sun blocking everything out.

My face is cold and my hands. There is a strange pressure in my chest.

A tall man with a shaven head and thick black beard is walking along the footpath. He is carrying a silver-topped walking stick. Why am I here? I wonder. Am I alone? I have the feeling that I shouldn't be alone. I can't remember why. I wonder do I know any of these people? Where am I? How long have I been here? Are there any clues? It's obviously some public place. There are people about and a lot of cars. There are houses and gardens with high gates and tall dark trees. Menacing looking. I wonder how I got here? Where was I before this? I can't remember anything before this moment. Where do I live? What is my name? Do I have any family or am I quite alone in the world? The wind is growing louder. The sea is purple, the waves look mutinous. 'My grief on the sea, how the waves of it roll...' There are so many people passing on the road and none of them seems to know me. Have I to drive home? Do I know how to drive? I remember the handbrake start, the three-point turn. I didn't start to drive until I was forty, after Kenneth died. The hill start was the most difficult thing of all to master. Is there any possibility that I could manage it now? How far have I to go? Did I come with someone? Where is she? I'm sure it was one of the girls.

Who are the girls? What am I talking about?

That man has a strange air about him. I don't like the look of his cane. And his smile has something ominous in it. He is talking to a young woman in a black hat, a hat with a wide brim. I cannot see the face. Where am I? I wonder, and what am I doing here? The place looks completely unfamiliar. What time of year is it? What time of day? That path leading towards the sea looks vaguely familiar. How do I get home from here? I have no idea. Where is my home? If I knew my address I could ask someone. Come on, you silly old fool—just think now, think! What is your address? Name and address—old fool! Rank and serial number? Keep calm and think. Think! Someone must have brought you here. Who was it? Think! If you sit here quietly whoever it is will come back. You must keep calm. Say a prayer, that will help you to stay calm. 'Hail holy queen, Mother of mercy. Hail our life, our sweetness and our hope. To thee do we cry, poor banished children of Eve, to thee do we send up our sighs, mourning and weeping in this valley of tears...' I close my eyes and count to ten. I open them again.

Someone I was with was here and is gone.

Who was it? Someone I love. I know that much. Someone I love who loves me. If she loves me she will come back to find me. If I wait calmly she is bound to come looking for me. I must control my fear. I must try to organise my mind. If one of the children got lost long ago we told them to wait quietly until someone came looking. Just stay still. Don't cry. Someone will find you. Not lost but waiting to be found. Somebody who was here was telling me about a lake, a place we used to visit together. When was that? Why did we go there? And who was telling me about it? Something is hovering at the edge of my mind about a lake at evening. 'She stepped away from me and she moved through the fair, and fondly I watched her go here and go there, then she went her way homeward with one star awake, as the swan in the evening moves over the lake.' Where is she now?

I close my eyes. I count one, two, three, four, five, six, seven, eight, nine, ten seconds before I open them again. Dark purple clouds are gathered over the mountains. It looks like rain. My hands are cold and my feet. I am hungry, at least, I think that's what the feeling is. Who am I waiting for? What am I waiting for? 'Turn then, most gracious advocate, thine eyes of mercy towards and after this our exile show unto us...'

The wind must be rising; I hear it knocking against the windowpane. I look up. The door opens. A young woman in a black hat is standing looking at me. She is holding a small black animal in her arms. She gets into the driving seat beside me. She puts her arms around my shoulder. 'I'm back now,' she says. 'I'm here. Everything is all right.' Her face is smiling broadly as if there's nothing whatever the matter with the world.

I reach my hand and grasp yours.

'Oh Sara, I was never more pleased to see you. Your arm is trembling or is it mine? I thought there had been some terrible catastrophe,' I say, 'and that by some awful chance I had survived it.'

You kiss my forehead.

'Where is everyone? I've been sitting here on my own for hours.' You put your arm around my shoulder.

'I'm sorry,' you say. 'Your old friend Tom Mulcahy passed by and I stopped to talk to him.' You are speaking very softly and looking into my eyes. 'I was watching you all the time and you were looking at us.'

'Was I?' I fix my gaze on the black tarmac of the road ahead. It seems to be the only constant feature. 'I don't remember any of that, at all,' I say slowly, 'you can't imagine what it's like. I was terrified.'

You place a small shivering bundle on my knee. It feels warm and soft.

'I know,' you say, 'hold Charlie and he'll help to calm you.'

Your arm is around my shoulders. Your cheek is close to mine. You are speaking very gently, as adults do to children. Do you have children? I wonder. I don't think you do.

'You must be patient, Sara. It's the most terrible sensation. My mind is a complete blank. I don't know where I am or how I got here. I can't remember anything at all. And nobody can help me.' You reach behind you and take a red and green plaid blanket from the back seat. You wrap it over my knees and under the small dog.

'I'll help you,' you say. The dog sits upright on my knees balanced precariously. She is panting. A small red tongue hangs from the side of her jaw. 'And Kitty when we get home again.'

I close my eyes and open them again slowly. Nothing seems to have changed. Nothing has become familiar.

'Oh yes, let's go home. Because if you don't mind, love, I'm very tired. Have we far to go?'

'Just down the road,' you say, 'we only stopped to admire the view.' 'My home is down the road!' I say astonished. 'But I've never been here before!' I try to make myself be patient. To wait for this mad confusion to clear. We are evidently at cross-purposes.

'You've been living here for sixty years,' you say with unsettling calm.

'Sixty years!' This is the most appalling news. 'I must have been in a dream the whole time then because I don't remember anything about it. Who lived here with me? Children? Oh, you'll have to stop telling me, Sara. I can't take in any more now. It's all a complete shock, I didn't know I had ever been married. I'll just have to take your word for it.'

I look around me, searching for any recognisable object or person. The trees and the houses and the gardens look equally strange. They might belong anywhere. There is nothing visible that means anything. If I live alone here how do I manage? Surely I'm not fit to be trusted to my own devices. You seem to imagine I'm quite sensible. Should I tell you the truth? But you look so pale and tired. I know you have your own worries. I can't remember if you have anyone to cook a hot meal for you when you get home. You seem exhausted. I am exhausting you. If only I could remember facts for myself. I must put a brave face on things. I must not be a burden. I must not be a worry to anyone. Especially my children. I will try not to be a nuisance. I will do whatever you tell me to do. I think I do that anyway.

You start up the engine and pull out onto the smooth black road.

'If we say some poems, will it help?' you ask.

'I don't know,' I say. 'I was going over a poem in my mind while you were gone. Something to do with a lake. "The Lake Isle of Inisfree", I think. Music has charms to soothe the savage breast, they say, and so has rhyme and narrative. I don't know why.'

'I think your brain is held together by poems and songs, isn't it?'

I am keeping my eyes fixed on the white line that divides the black tarmac of the road. It seems to be the only unchanging thing.

What will become of me, if I go on like this? I will end up in the mad house. How will I bear it? If I can't remember anything I'm helpless. And if I'm helpless I can't defend myself.

A soft drizzle is falling on the windscreen. You take a bar of chocolate from the glove compartment and break off four squares.

'Have some,' you say, 'as much as you like.'

Sunshine in a narrow shaft pierces the side window. It lights the air between us. It glistens on your hands that are holding the steering wheel and on the side of your face. The chocolate is delicious. It melts in my mouth.

'Aren't we extraordinarily fortunate in the weather, Sara?' I say. 'What they have to endure in other countries! The poor people in Pakistan at present, I can't stop thinking about them.'

The little dog leans forward from the back seat, panting with excitement. Her breath is moist and warm. She is resting a confiding paw on my shoulder.

'Charlie loves you,' you say. I have no way of telling if this is true but it's a very pleasing notion. Her paw is resting on me for support, I think.

'Do you know, Sara, I count my blessings at night and Charlie is one of them. And I think too I'm blessed in my health. I have the usual aches and pains, of course, but mercifully, I can still rely on my brain. You are smiling now, I'm glad to see.

'I always had a good memory, though I say it myself who shouldn't.' Some picture comes to me, a picture of children on a stony beach. And a story about a sword rising from a lake. 'When I was young, someone used to say that there was no resource like a well-stocked mind,' I say, 'and do you know, I think they were right.'

The windscreen wipers are washing back and forth in their singsong motion. On either side of the road the hedges are ablaze with gorse. It must be April or May. I turn to look at you.

'It would be the very worst thing, wouldn't it, to have any condition that affected the mind.'

You are looking straight ahead concentrating your eyes on the road.

'Yes,' you say.

'You must take me out and shoot me, Sara, if anything ever goes wrong with my head. Promise me that?' You are still watching the road attentively.

'Yes,' you say. 'I promise.'

You lift your left hand from the gear stick and take hold of mine. 'But before any of that,' you say, 'can we have our tea first? We're on our way to Avoca, you know?'

I put another square (the last, is it?) of the delicious, dark chocolate into my mouth and lick my fingers.

'Of course, who wouldn't remember that name?' I say. '"There's not in this whole world a valley so sweet..." Thomas Moore made sure we could never forget it even if we wanted to.'

You pass a white paper tissue to me. 'Wipe your fingers,' you say, 'and blow your nose.'

'Vie did the viper not vipe her nose?' I ask. 'Do you nose the answer?' I touch your nose with the finger of my glove.

'Because the adder 'ad 'er 'ankerchief,' we say in unison and then we both laugh aloud, delighted by our joke. 'Because the adder 'ad 'er 'ankerchief.' I see a woman standing at the side of the road facing us. She is leaning on a wrought-iron gate. The full skirt of her red dress blows out in the breeze. Some friend of ours, it must be because she smiles as we go by and lifts her hand to wave.

'I think he must have written it on a day like this, Sara. In sunshine and in shadow. A glorious day.'

William Wall

Remembering David

What I sometimes think of as David Marcus's first miracle occurred in the Unitarian Church in Dublin on the day of his funeral. Only David could have persuaded several hundred, mostly Dublin people, mostly writers, editors and sundry other hardbitten literary and journalistic types, to sing 'The Banks of My Own Lovely Lee' on their home turf. If there is a life after death, something neither I nor David believed in, then David was sitting on Parnassus that day, smiling his sly smile with the glittering eyes and nodding his head with satisfaction. I could imagine him boasting about it to the dead writers whom he admired so much, William Saroyan perhaps, or James Stephens. Stephens at least would understand.

At the age of fifteen I sent David Marcus some poems for publication in 'New Irish Writing' in *The Irish Press*. My father was a staunch Fianna Fáiler and the paper was read cover to cover in our house, and it was either he or my mother who suggested I send the poems. Being fifteen I probably attached a query as to whether the esteemed editor thought I was a poet or not, and his response came back, typed on headed paper, a rejection of course, and in reply to my question, that he couldn't tell from the poems I enclosed whether I was a poet or not but I was certainly 'a romantic introspective fifteen year old'. It was quite true in every respect but it rankled. Who was this arrogant Dublin mandarin with his imperious headed paper and his lofty dismissal? I was probably all the more irritated because I knew the poems were no good. Don't we all—all the time! It was years later before I understood that David didn't like modern poetry and didn't understand it. He told me so himself. He liked his poems to rhyme and to have a regular metre. He told me this with that self-effacing shrug that said 'I know I'm old fashioned and out of date, but there it is ...' Where prose was concerned, however, he was anything but backward looking, a fact attested to by the huge range of writers whose talents he nurtured and admired.

Many years later, after David had published several of my stories, I finally got to meet him. It was at a festival in Cork, organised by the late Mary Johnson and Paddy Galvin, and David was reading in The Loft theatre. I remember that he read the title story from his collection *Who Ever Heard of an Irish Jew?* By then we had corresponded quite a bit. I was used to his gentle prods about edits and his stilted, almost nineteenth-century style of writing. The man, when I met him, was exactly as his 'notes' suggested. I came to think of him as essentially a *belle époque* gentleman in his tweed jacket and cavalry twill trousers.

My wife, Liz, and I quickly became friends with David and Ita, and in due course they would come and stay at our house in Cork whenever they were down here. In turn we visited them in Dublin, often for a book launch or a reading. The conversation was always interesting, David at his best talking about books, whereas Ita and I shared politics as well as literature. David was never comfortable talking about politics. Books and sport were his passion. I remember arriving on a Saturday afternoon at his house and having to sit through a Munster rugby match. He loved Munster and was a big fan of Ronan O'Gara, partly because both he and O'Gara went to Presentation College. There was no question of conversation. The game was sacred.

I had, of course, read David's novel about the Cork Jewish community at the beginning of the twentieth century, *A Land Not Theirs*. He was inclined to disparage it as a 'tale'. I disagreed if only for the social significance, the fact that it chronicled the life of a small Jewish community at a time of turmoil and change.

David's Jewishness was never in doubt. He was happy to talk

about it but, being an atheist, he had forgotten a good deal of the ritual, or perhaps he chose not to speak of it with me. He had become an atheist as a teenager, another rite of passage we shared. Even our motives were similar—the ridiculousness and injustice inherent and often explicit in the theology of, in his case Judaism, in mine Catholicism.

David's family was part of a small wave of migration, Jewish families and groups of families fleeing pogroms in eastern Europe. They used to joke that they were going to America but the ship landed them in Ireland and they didn't know the difference—it's an urban legend that you also find in Italy and other places with high levels of migration. In these times of rising rightwing rhetoric and hostility to people in need of international protection it is salutary to remind ourselves that the extended Marcus family gave us one of our most important literary editors and a fiction writer of importance, two film makers (David's brother, Louis, and his cousin, Louis Lentin) and a Lord Mayor of Cork city (Gerald Goldberg, David's uncle). That's aside from the economic and other cultural benefits that immigration brings to any country.

As well as his editorship of 'New Irish Writing', David also edited anthologies for various English publishers and he was a scout for Giles Gordon, an agent with Curtis Brown. He was responsible for first publishing many of the most famous names in Irish literature, but his great passion was the short story. He believed the best way to read a story was in a single sitting. He would return to them later, but that single sitting was the best way to get the effect of the story, the import, to sense the shape and emotional power of it. When you sent him a story you knew it would have his full attention, a fact that was both consoling and unnerving. And he could refuse stories even from well-established writers. Just because he published your first or second didn't mean your third would go equally well.

In his later years the honours fell to him. Some, as often in these cases, came too late, after his mind had strayed, but the honorary doctorate presented by his old alma mater UCC was timely and much appreciated. Liz and I were his and Ita's invited guests, along with the late Vincent Banville (brother of John) and his wife, Róisín. Vincent was probably the only person whom David met on a regular basis, perhaps his only really close friend. It was a crisp, sunny day and the ceremony and lunch were held at the then brand-new Glucksman Gallery, a little architectural jewel in what is a beautiful campus and set on the very path that David took from his home on the Mardyke to the Quad on his first day in UCC. It was on that path that he first met Jack Lynch.

I remember his broad smile and Ita's pleasure to see him so happy. By the time the next honour from his native city came he was already in the throes of the dementia that blighted his last years. On this occasion he was honoured by the City itself, a belated recognition of a much-loved scion of its ebbing Jewish culture.

But my happiest memory is of the night of the Cork launch of his *Oughtobiography*. He liked to introduce the book by recounting how his friends had been telling him for years 'that he *ought* to write an autobiography'; hence the title. The book is an important account of the life of a key figure in modern Irish literature and it has all the hallmarks of the personality that wrote it: his delicacy, his reticence, his unwillingness to blow his own trumpet. Nevertheless a picture emerges of a daring young man with a deep love of literature who chanced his arm to write to all his literary idols and whose daring paid off. I remember the gasps of shock when someone asked what happened to all the letters from those early contributors (people like Saroyan, or George Bernard Shaw, who famously replied in the negative, with a postcard saying simply 'NO, GBS'), and David, matter of factly, explained that after he moved to London his mother cleaned out the attic... The hall was packed full of well-wishers, an audience that recognised David's genius, that admired his historic nurturing of Irish literary figures, that loved his own writing and that, above all, loved the man and were as proud as he was of his Cork origins.

IV

Angus Cargill
David and Faber

Sometime in 2003, David Marcus got in touch with us at Faber to ask if we would consider doing a volume of his 'New Irish Short Stories'. He had previously edited seven collections published by Phoenix, but was looking for a new home and I think had come my way because I was by then working with Sebastian Barry, Claire Kilroy and other contemporary Irish writers. I'm guessing too, of course, that David was aware of Faber's long history of publishing Irish writers—novelists, playwrights and poets—as well as our pedigree for publishing short story writers from around the world, from Flannery O'Connor to Lorrie Moore, and Hanif Kureishi to Junot Díaz.

I didn't then fully know of David's long history of championing and supporting the short story in Ireland prior to this—via his many anthologies of stories, and his 'New Irish Writing' page for *The Irish Press*—but his knowledge, passion and love for the form was instantly clear and infectious when we spoke. So, it was an easy commission, one which was to follow his own suggested brief – the only condition being that the stories would have to be new and previously unpublished. David alone would identify and write to the authors he wanted, to ask if they had stories ready or would like to write something new.

That first volume, published as *The Faber Book of Best New Irish Short Stories* in 2005, had a stellar list of contributors, from established names such as Roddy Doyle and Colm Tóibín to younger, emerging talents like Gerard Donovan and Claire Keegan. It also featured Edna O'Brien's tremendous story 'Love's Lesson', which anticipated, by six years or so, her eventual place on the Faber Fiction list, which began, appropriately, with her story collection *Saints and Sinners* in 2011.

The publication itself was a happy and extremely well received one, its tone and the spirit of the whole enterprise driven by David. As he noted in his short, passionate introduction, this was 'frontline' publishing designed to support the creators, the writers themselves, and to help sustain and breathe life into the form. Perhaps, above all, it continued and embodied 'his own life's journey' to read, recognise and champion writing which would enrich readers' lives as he felt it had done so for him.

So, a second volume was discussed and agreed on for 2007. While this collection opened with a story from John Banville (again, anticipating his arrival on the Faber Fiction list many years later) and closed with one of the very few published short stories by Sebastian Barry ('A Russian Beauty', well worth checking out), it was conceived by David, as he noted in his introduction, to support and showcase female Irish writers, including stories by Anne Enright, Éilís Ní Dhuibhne, Emma Donoghue and Mary Leland, among others.

Once again, David's selection was well received and supported on publication. After his death in 2009, we decided to honour his memory and work by continuing with the series. I would invite a guest editor each time to make the selection, and while they were free to bring their own taste and spin (and titles) to each one, they would broadly follow the spirit of David's collections, and mix established writers with new and emerging talents. So far, Joseph O'Connor, Kevin Barry, Deirdre Madden and Lucy Caldwell have all stepped into those nurturing shoes and delivered fascinating and nuanced collections, with two of them including the first publication of stories which went on to win the prestigious Sunday Times Short Story Award, Kevin Barry's 'Beer Trip to Llandudno' and Danielle McLaughlin's 'A Partial List of the Saved'.

Those years have also seen an explosion in Irish fiction writing, further fanned by the work of The Stinging Fly and Tramp Press, among others, often including writers of short stories as much as novelists, and supporting David's sense that Irish women's writing was long overdue wider appreciation. In terms of legacy, David's two collections certainly helped bolster our belief and conviction in continuing to publish short stories. For our 90th anniversary in 2017 we curated a set of thirty individual stories from across our history, and across countries and languages. It had, of course, a strong Irish showing, with stories from Edna O'Brien, John McGahern, Julia O'Faolain, Sally Rooney, and Anna Burns, as well as Claire Keegan's 'The Forester's Daughter', a version of which first appeared back in David's 2005 collection.

Having worked at Faber for nearly twenty-five years now, the introduction to David was an important one for my career too. As mentioned, I had already started working with Claire Kilroy and Sebastian Barry, who I continue to edit today, but David helped further connect me to the Irish writing scene. I've enjoyed working with Peter Murphy, Eoin McNamee and many others, and have visited Ireland at least twice a year since. Before then I had only ever been once, but in the strange circular way of things, this linked me back to some of my own roots—my Dad having lived and grown up in Bray, and later Dublin, with his Irish mother before her death when he was seventeen.

People sometimes ask about the act of editing, which is always hard to answer—being so bespoke to the particular writer you're working with at the time, the nature of their writing and their own process—but what I would say I observed and have tried to take forward from David is his attentiveness and respect for the work, his belief in the importance of long-term relationships with writers, and also his quiet, unobtrusive, but determined sense that championing good writing was both a responsibility and a privilege.

Our most recent guest editor was Lucy Caldwell, whose 2019 collection, *Being Various*, was conceived to only feature writers who had started to publish since the Good Friday Agreement. Fresh and diverse, it deliberately sought to pose the question 'What makes a writer Irish?', and among others featured Yan Ge, a Chinese-born writer, whose first story to be written in English, the Dublin-set 'How I fell in love with the well-documented life of Alexander Whelan', opened the collection. After that, I read more of Yan's work and in 2023 we published her first short story collection, *Elsewhere*, a journey and path to publication I think David would have been—to borrow a word he often used in our correspondence—'delighted' about.

The Covid pandemic has slightly put us behind schedule for the next collection in the series, but I'm sure in some iteration we will commission and publish another volume of 'New Irish Short Stories' in the near future. Watch this space.

Claire Keegan

In 1996 I won fourth prize in the Francis MacManus Short Story Competition for a story called 'Storms' and I met David Marcus. He said to me, 'Do you have any more?' I had about half a dozen. He said, 'You have to get a collection together and you must send them to me.' He explained that he was the literary scout for Giles Gordon at the Curtis Brown Agency in London. I went off to Achill then for a while and finished the manuscript. David published 'The Ginger Rogers Sermon' in *Phoenix Irish Short Stories 1997* and he sent the manuscript of my stories to Giles. Giles accepted it and he sent it to Faber and they in turn accepted it. That was the process of getting *Antarctica* published. I just found David Marcus's encouragement to be greater than anyone else's. He was so generous and genuine in both his criticism and his interest in the stories.

— — —

The Ginger Rogers Sermon

Don't ask me why we called him Slapper Jim. My mother stamped his image in my head, and I was at an age when pictures of a man precede the man himself. The posters verify; Thin Lizzy with a V of chest exposed. Pat Spillane's legs racing across my bedroom wall, his hurley poised. I was the girl with the sweet tooth and a taste for men. And pictures.

I have a photographic memory. I can see every tacky page of my cousin's wedding album, the horseshoe on the cake with the man slightly taller than the woman and their feet sunk in the frosting. I parcel out my life in images the way other people let the calendar draw a line around them every month. That time of Slapper Jim was the time of the strangest pictures.

We killed pigs then, ate pork cracked in its own fat with a pulpy sauce. Plasticine grey and apple green, those were the colours of my home. Ma held my dinner plate with the tail of her skirt and talked through the day while I tucked in.

'You should see the new lumberjack your da hired. Slapper Jim, they call him. A great big fella he is! Walked in here and I'll tell ya nothing but the truth, he leaned up against the partition there and I thought the whole yoke was going to cave in.'

My brother, Eugene, quacks his hand behind her back. I spear a slice of pork and in my mind I see a giant, the earth tremoring where he walks. A man who doesn't know his own strength. That can be dangerous. I've seen my father crack a cow's ribs with his fist. Just trying to slide her over in the stall.

'I gave him his bit of dinner and he reached over for the handle on the saucepan without getting up. Ate eleven spuds. Eleven spuds if ya don't mind! Yer lucky there's aer a one left.' Ma rummages in the cutlery drawer for a spoon.

Tapioca and stewed apples, I suppose. I hope for sherry trifle, gooey caramel, dollops of ice-cream.

'What's for afters?'

They leave me here alone on Saturday nights. Eugene goes too, even though he doesn't dance. Him staying home with me is a sissy thing to do because he's so much older. Seven years older. I was made out of the last of my father's sperm. I found that out just recently. My mother says I am The Accident in the family. My father tells people I am The Shakings of the Bag, which I suppose is much the same thing.

Dance mad, my parents. Ma says a man who can't dance is half a man. She's taught me the harvest jig and the wake, the quickstep and the Siege of Ennis in the parlour. She says dancing is good therapy, makes her feel like she's in time with the world. Mostly we move where we're put, stooping under the rain and such, but dancing frees her up, oils her joints, she says. Everyone should know how to move in their own time. She puts the record on, I shake Lux across the lino, and we whirl around the parlour floor like two loonies. I am the man loony. I pretend I don't see her watching her reflection in the mirror of the sideboard as we pass. The Walls of Limerick requires two-facing-two, so we hold our hands out to imaginary partners and move them into their places. I like this knowing what Ma will do, where she'll go before she does, not having to think about it.

Saturdays smell of girls: wet wool, nail polish and camomile shampoo. In the kitchen, Ma sets her hair. We call it The Salon. I hold the pins between my lips and roll her hair around the spiky curlers, stiffen them with setting lotion. Her head goes into the net and she sits in under the hood of the dryer we bought down at the auction. I hand her an old *Woman's Weekly* and imagine it's *Vogue*. The last page is ripped out so Da can't read about women's problems.

'Do you want a coffee!' I shout above the noise.

There was never any coffee in that house. She stays under there, deaf and talking loud like an old person and I hand her a cup of frothy Ovaltine and an hour later she's out, relieved and pink.

Then the daubs of shoe cream, the shush of the steam iron smoothing out the creases. The shuffle of the entertainment pages and Da working a lather for his face and sticking the headlines on his chin to stop the blood. Ma wriggling into her flesh-coloured roll-on, a big elastic knickers to keep her belly in. Pot Belly, I call her.

'Are you going dancing now, Pot Belly?'

'Where's the beauty contest, Pot Belly?'

'Where did yer pot belly go, Pot Belly?'

She calls me The Terror. 'Shut up, ya terror.' She dots Lily of the Valley behind her ears with the glass stopper and slides her tapping feet into her dancing shoes, ready to take off.

'You won't fall into the fire now will ya?' Da always having the last word, jingling his keys like they belong to the only car in the parish.

'No, Da.'

Eugene pulling on his corduroy jacket, giving me a look like I shouldn't be alive.

The film comes on after the nine o'clock news. I change into my pyjamas and find the biscuit tin. She hides it in the washing machine or the accordion case or the churn. Once Eugene left a note that said, 'Find a better hiding place next time,' but Pot Belly went mad, so now we leave nothing and she says nothing. That's the way it is in our house, everybody knowing things but pretending they don't know.

I turn off all the lights and sit with my feet up and play with myself in the dark and hope the actors take off every stitch and go skinny-dipping in close-up. *The Birds* is the name of tonight's film. Crows line up on the wires, watching the children with their black eyes. Ready to swoop. Even the teachers can't offer them protection. I think of the grey crows picking out our ewe's eyes. I hear a noise but it's only the milk strainer hammering the glass in the wind. Looked like a metal claw, a wiry hand. I slide the bolt across the door and let the setter up on the couch. I squeeze my eyes when the birds dive on the town.

It's after midnight when the headlights cross the room. Ma wobbles in, opens the fridge, its light shines pink on her cheeks.

Da slides the kettle over on the hot-plate and warms his hands, ready for a feed. 'Saw the Slapper down in Shillelagh. He was out on the floor with a one.'

'And the size of her,' Ma chips in. 'No bigger than a bantam hen she is, sitting up beside him. And neather one of 'em has a step in their foot. Fecking useless.' She bites into a tomato with a vengeance and Eugene heads for the stairs before she starts her Ginger Rogers sermon.

'How's the bantam?' is the first thing I say when I meet Slapper Jim. He laughs a big red laugh that sounds like the beginning of something. He has plump lips and blond hair and standing beside him is like standing in the shade. He's as big as a wardrobe. I feel like opening all his shirt buttons and looking inside. 'Haw' is the word he uses all the time.

'Who's this bantam now, haw?' Sounds like he's talking down a well.

My father sits at the head of the table and rubs a wedge of tobacco between his palms and packs his pipe. He has no teeth to distract the smile away from his eyes.

'Ma says your one is like a bantam,' I say.

'Haw?'

'Do ya leave her sitting on the nest all week?'

'Maybe she's not nesting at all.'

'Pluck her.'

The bantam jokes went on until the end. The hatching, plucking, sideways-looking, gawky jokes carried us through summer and beyond.

Slapper doesn't wear a belt. If he pulls his trousers up on his hips, the hems almost reach his ankles. On real wet days, the men stay home and do odd jobs around the yard. The fence, pare the sheep's feet, weld bits and pieces. On Saturdays Eugene watches *Sports Stadium* and bites his nails. I help Slapper split the sticks. I am a girl who knows one end of a block from the other, knows to place it on the chopping block the way it grows, make it easier for Slapper. But I don't suppose it would make any difference. That axe comes down and splits that wood open every time, knots or no knots. Even the holly, which my father calls 'a bitch of a stick to split', breaks open under his easy strike. We have a rhythm going; I put them up, he splits them open. With other people, I take my hand away fast, but not with Slapper Jim. He and I are like two parts of the same machine, fast and smooth. We trust each other. And always he gives his waistband a little tug when I'm putting them up, and that waistband slides down with the swing of the axe and the crack of his arse shows every time.

I too am a lumberjack in summer. Pot Belly says it is no job for a girl. Girls should flute the pastry edge or wash the car at best is what she thinks. I should wallpaper my room, practise walking around the room with a book flat on my head to help my posture.

'Keep her away from the saws. If that girl comes home from that wood with no feet, don't come home here.'

We've all seen such things. Toes sawed off, an arm mangled in a winch, and once, a mare gone mad with the sting of a gadfly, pulling the slig out on to the road and scrapping the car. But when morning comes I'm up and ready, watching for Slapper's Escort on the lane.

Following the mare is the job for me. A grey Clydesdale with a white face, she's seventeen hands if she's an inch. And the smell of her, the warm earth smell like the inside of a damp flowerpot. I put my nose on her neck and breathe in. And she's smart too, knows how to stop when she snags and hikes up without putting out your shoulder. No dirt in her, but still she'll give you a lash with that tail if you're not quick. We're clear-felling every second line on the slopes. Slapper and Da fell and trim, sitka spruce mostly, and larch, the trimmer's dream. I hook the chain around the slig and follow the mare down the lines on to the car-road, drawing the timber as close together as I can, keeping the butts even. I unhook the slig and lift the swing back up on the hames and then my favourite part—holding on to the mare's tail and letting her pull me back up the line after her. Slapper says I have brains to burn, thinking of that. Da says I should give some to Eugene because he does nothing, only sit around on his arse with his nose in a book all day.

We drink mugs of tea from a flask at nosh-up, and milk from an old Corcoran's lemonade bottle. Soda-bread soggy with the tomatoes and sardines in red sauce. The tea tastes bitter towards the end of the day. Slapper dents the bumper where he sits, talks with his mouth full.

'Uckin' lies,' he says when he swats the flies. They light on the horse dung and the bread. They chase me up and down the lines and drive the mare cuckoo. I sit on the mare backwards with my feet up on her flanks while she grazes the bank and wait for somebody to open the biscuits. Jim lifts me up there. Peaches, he calls me but I am nothing like a peach. My father says I'm more like a stalk of rhubarb, long and sour.

'Ya have a way with that baste, Peaches. She bites the arse off me.'

'It's always hanging out anyway, Slapper. Here,' Da says, handing over a wad of baling twine, 'until ya can buy yerself a real belt.'

'Haw?' Slapper smiles but he doesn't tie his trousers up. He just looks at the twine in a way that makes Da put it back into his pocket, and gives his waistband a tug the way another man might push his glasses up on his nose.

Slapper teaches me the tricks of the trade. He holds his big finger up but doesn't stoop when he says these things. 'Don't open the slig until you've unhooked her; if she takes off, yer fingers will be dogmate. Don't stand in front of the saw, if there's a loose link and the chain breaks, you're fucked.' He opens up that forbidden world of adult language and invites me in. Then he leaves me alone to be capable.

We stay at it until dusk. The foresters come around with their kettles in the evenings and paint the stumps with the pink poison. We hide the saws and the oil and petrol cans under the tops up the line and let the mare loose in the field down the road. The lorries drive up with their robot claws and load up the lengths. Twenty-five tons is a load for them, a cheque for us, and a pound of wine gums and a *Bunty* and *Judy* after Mass and two choc-ices and gobstoppers for me.

'What do they learn ya in school?' Slapper asks as we're driving the mare down to the field.

I know trigonometry. 'I know the square of the hypotenuse is equal to the sum of the squares on the other two sides.'

'What's a highpotinuze?' Jim pushes back the passenger seat to make room for his legs, but his knees are snug against the dashboard. He holds the mare's reins out through the open window as she trots next to the car.

'Go on, ya lazy cunt ya! Whup! Whup! Ya hairy farting fucker ya. Go on! He claps the outside of the door with his hand.

'The child, Slapper. The child!' Da admonishes.

Slapper looks back at me. My father's eyes watch me in the rear-view mirror. I pretend I haven't heard a bad word.

'What's a highpotinuze?'

Those are the pictures of that time. Three dirty lumberjacks sligging out timber, the wood slick and white beneath the bark. Eating packets of coconut creams, spitting, listening to Radio 1 in the car when it rained, sharpening chain, files grinding on the rakers, the cutters shining all round like some deadly necklace. Slapper asking what they learned me in school, his file sharpening smack-on with the slant of the cutters every time. Da says Slapper's a great man with a saw. The last fella Da had working with him slid a matchstick in between the spark plug and the petrol tank so she wouldn't start, but Da found out and gave him his walking papers. I tell Slapper Jim the things I learn in school. I know that Oliver Cromwell told the poor people 'To hell or to Connaught' (I can see him on his black horse, pointing west), that Jesus lost his temper. I can recite William Blake 'Tiger! tiger! burning bright/In the forests of the night. What immortal hand or eye/Could frame thy fearful symmetry?' I can see it on the page, the curve of the question mark at the end. Slapper holds my hand and stands me up on the bonnet of the car in the rain, telling me to say the poems. I read them off my memory. He asks me what 'immortal' means but I don't know. He says I am the morbidest child in Ireland.

'Get that child in out of the rain!' Da putting a damper on it from the driver's seat. 'Do ya hear me, Slapper? She'll catch her end and you can be the one to bring her home!'

But Slapper just smiles. 'Say the poems, Peaches.'

I shoot up like the rhubarb stalk Da says I am, and the transformation begins. I take an interest in my cousin's old dresses. Flowery things with thin patent belts and matching pointy shoes that pinch my toes. I limp home from school and make the announcement. Ma says Shusssssh! and gives me the elastic belt and towels. I think it's the equivalent of Da's newspaper for his chin.

'Don't let your father see them,' she says. Her always hiding women away, like we're forbidden.

Now that I am thirteen, I am sectioned off from the men. It happens in school too, in gym class, I play basketball and jump over hurdles and come back all red-faced and sweaty and talk non-stop in class. Nobody sits beside me because I smell like an afterbirth. I wear the pads and the Lily of the Valley and go dancing down the pub. Slapper Jim is always there with the Bantam. I waltz around in the cigarette smoke with old men my father knows. Watch Sam Collier prancing across the floor in his patent shoes, swinging Pot Belly around, and him with his left hand up so high, she can barely reach it. Foxy, we call him, with his head of slicked-back silver hair, his horse's eye. The men's hands grip me by the waist and swing me around, same as if I'm a bucket of water. They hold me close as an excuse not to let me go. The backs of their shirts are wet. I drink Babychams out of long-stemmed glasses. They taste like warm honey and soften the pictures. Eugene sits with his elbows on the bar, watching the dancers, his shoe tapping in perfect time on the rung of his stool.

Slapper cannot dance. If his feet move on the beat, it's an accident. He doesn't catch the rhythm. He takes me out on to the floor and puts his arms around me and shifts his weight from one leg to the other, taking huge strides for the waltz. My head comes up to the fourth button on his shirt. I could almost see past him if I stood on my toes. I can smell him, get the whiff of the mare, the hair and the warmth under his shirt, the big feet moving over the floor. I try to lead him into the rhythm, exaggerating my sways, but he does not feel the music, and I wind up stepping on his toes.

'Should have worn me steel toecaps,' he says.

His Bantam isn't even as tall as me, a dark, plump woman with a mouth like his. She wears a royal blue blouse with gold sequins blown across the bust. He could scrape her sequins with the buckle on his trousers, if he had a buckle. That's how funny-looking they are.

At closing time, the couples stand against the gable wall: women with their backs against the wall, the men leaning against them, both hands against the bricks, kissing. Snogging, we call it at school. I want to see Slapper snogging the Bantam. I don't know why but I want to see what that looks like. I think he'd have to put her standing on a beer barrel. I look for them, but they're never there at the gable wall. I wonder what it would be like to kiss Slapper, to have the tough, hard hands inside my dress and his mouth on my mouth. Ma puts her arm around my shoulders and leads me to the car, shielding out that world of romance and men and women and touching.

The winters are dark here. I shiver from the chill behind the curtains, piss without touching the toilet seat. Downstairs, the paraffin oil heater throws shapes like tears on to the kitchen ceiling. Ma turns up the wick, making the shapes dance when Slapper comes in. I think of the way she turns up the oven when she puts the second loaf in. She braids my hair in two long plaits while I eat spaghetti hoops and a fried sausage. She wets her thumbs on her tongue, catching up the stray hairs. I listen to the suck of Slapper's pink mouth slurping tea, the cast-iron pot swinging on its hinge outside the window. I don't want to go to school.

I crack wafer ice on the puddles in the lane and smoke twigs until the bus comes, blow my breath out white. I bring home nits from school. Da holds me down with his farmer's grip while Ma douses my head with turpentine-smelling lotion. She pulls the comb along my scalp and catches the nits between the teeth and crushes them with a crunch beneath her thumbnail, saying, 'There, we've got him.'

The snow has come this Saturday. I have taken everything but the blinkers off the mare, left the men to pack the gear. I am riding her the whole way home to keep her in the stable until the weather improves. When the car passes me on the road, the mare whinnies and trots on after them, but soon we are left behind. Slapper's hand waves from the passenger window. Sometimes you'd think he was the Pope or somebody. The road is quiet, but the mare's ears are up. Then further on, I see three yearling colts leaning up against a field gate, waiting. I try to pull the mare to the far side of the road, but there's no bit in her mouth, and it's impossible. She puts her nose to theirs, and squeals. I dismount. The colts have their willies out, the pink and black hoses almost reaching their girth lines. They snort and push the gate until I think it will fall over on to me. The mare kicks out with her hind leg and squats to piss on the road. I pull the reins down hard but she is oblivious of me now. Her snorts deepen and the colts bite each other, their mouths fast and open. They scrape the bars with their hooves. I throw stones at them and they eventually launch into a farting gallop down the field and back again, trotting inside the ditch beside the mare as I pull her home. I am afraid to mount her until I get well away from the colts, knowing she will canter back given the slightest chance.

When I reach home, Slapper's grey Escort is still parked in the yard. He comes out of the barn and reaches up and pulls me down into his arms.

'Are ya frozen, Peaches?' he says.

'She's horsing, Slapper!' My teeth chatter. My hands are stiff.

'Haw?'

'I'm not joking ya. Them colts nearly climbed over the gate to get at her.'

Slapper says nothing but smiles as he rubs her down.

We walk across the frozen mud towards the house. Pot Belly has made beef stew with the bone from the round steak sitting in the soup. Dumplings bobbing on the surface. Eugene's reading a book called *Seven Deadly Nights at the Edge of the Universe*. His eyebrows have grown together since the last time I looked at him. Pot Belly gives out and tells Slapper he's not to be going home in this weather. He's staying the night.

We make up the extra bed.

'I hope the shagger doesn't snore and keep me and Eugene up all night.' I try to put her off the track.

'Your mouth's getting worse, young lady. I'll have to have a word with Slapper about that.'

But she never would. She, like the rest of us, thought the sun shone out of Slapper's arse.

He doesn't know I'm watching. He stands where the slant of the blue light partitions the room. I am glad of the snow. Slapper closes the door behind him and doesn't bother to open the buttons on his shirt. Instead, he holds the back of his collar and pulls it over his head. He doesn't wear a vest like Eugene. There's hair all over his chest and more on his back. His stomach is a plank of muscle. He slides the zip down, exposes his legs, sits down, pulls the waistband down over his feet. I imitate Eugene's breathing in the far bed. Slapper comes over to my bed in his navy-blue underwear. He bends down and I close my eye. His breath fans my face. I am just about to let him kiss me when I hear the creak of the other bed.

His feet hang over the mattress. I know by the quiet that the snow is still coming down outside. The light gets whiter. We are safe inside the drifts. Snowed in. Tucked up. Perhaps the drifts will come and he will have to stay another night.

'Are ya asleep, Slapper?'

'Haw?' For a long time he says nothing and then says, 'It's a cold fucking house.'

I go over to him, wrapped in my blankets. I pull his bedclothes down and get in, compounding our warmth. I lie up against his back and breathe on his neck. My hand slides around his waist, wanders shyly down through the curls of his pubic hair. I feel him stiffen. I think of the colts. He moves to the edge of the mattress but I follow him. When he turns over, his hands are cold. Big and gentle and precise. 'Jesus, Peaches,' I hear him whisper before his will subsides. Eugene's breathing is steady in the far bed and I am thankful that the bed does not creak.

Three feet of snow has fallen over Ireland, the wireless says. I find a bonnet from an old Volkswagen and Slapper and I spend the afternoon sliding down the top field, right over the ditch, across the lane and into a nice curve in the field below. The track gets a little longer every time, but when we get off at the bottom and look back up, I cannot resist doing it again. He pulls the bonnet in one hand and mine in the other and hardly says a word. Suddenly, I am somebody no one is supposed to know about. At last I know the reasoning behind my mother's secrets. Men are weak and women must hide themselves to keep them strong, must rip out problem pages of the women's magazine, must hide the flow of blood, be sexless.

I saddle the mare and take her the full circuit through the snow, down the lane and up past the bog field. The moon brightens the dark sky like a fake sun, but the land is white. The world's turned upside-down. The evening is edged in blue like TV light. All the chainsaws have stopped. I listen to the puff of the mare's breath and her hooves compressing horseshoe tracks through the snow.

The smell of the pines is everywhere for the snow has bedded down all else. We have just eased into a canter along the car-road when she shies. A pheasant flutters out over the trees. Horses frighten easily at night. Especially when there's wind. I pull her up and listen. It may be deer. I dismount and lead the mare down between the trees. The ground is dry, the moss smooth underfoot, and the mare stumbles. It's black beneath the branches. And then I get the smell. The mare pulls on the reins. I stop and listen. The wind pheews through the treetops like somebody learning to whistle. We walk towards the smell and then I see the source. Slapper's boots are at eye-level. They are resting on nothing. As I draw closer, I see his face, darker than bark. Christ, the smell. The wind spins him gently on the rope. I can't even cut him down. I leave him there, hanging in his own dung, and gallop home.

That was the hardest part, taking the others up there, letting them see him like that. The way they stood and looked and cursed and said Jaysus and Holy Mother of Divine Jaysus and Why in the name of Jaysus? and took their caps off and carried him down the hill on the bonnet of the Volkswagen we had used as a sled, my father's coat draped over his body. I was sorry I hadn't stayed longer with him among the trees.

Eugene stood there looking at me like I did it.

We come home from the wake and sit in the parlour. The room is like a second-hand furniture shop, the walls painted lime green, a border of faded roses creeping below the ceiling. Pot Belly produces a bottle of Bristol Cream from the sideboard and fills four glasses to the brim. The padlock on the yard gate beats its clasp, hammering down the silence of the room. My father watches the sparks lifting into the soot. Eugene has no nails to bite: they are bloody to the quick. When his eyes meet mine, they are full of accusation and blame. I am aware of my own breathing.

Pot Belly brings candles down out of the kitchen, white blessed candles she got at Easter, and lights them from my father's match. She stands them upright in their own grease and places them about the room. She takes a record from its sleeve and turns the light off. The room is lit by a flame. On the mantelpiece stand trophies, silver-plated couples frozen in mid-swirl. They quiver in the firelight. Pot Belly catches Eugene's hand and pulls him upright. He does not want to dance, but her pull is steady. I know what she is doing, and from my father's evasive eyes, that look he has when Ma is changing her dress. I know that something's going on, know my parents have spoken of this. They have it planned. Ma has always thought a man should know how to dance. The only flaw she could see in Slapper Jim was his leggy, graceless motion on the floor. She is teaching Eugene, as a precaution, as if him knowing these steps will carry him through, prevent him from tying a noose around his neck later on.

She begins the slow waltz and he follows her reluctantly, shifting his weight, his body stiff, his feet imitating hers. My father keeps his eyes on the fire. Pot Belly takes Eugene around the furniture whispering one-two-three, one-two-three until the music stops. The stylus crackles in the groove and the rhythm changes to a quickstep. Da stands up and pulls off his overcoat and takes my hand. The steel of his suspender digs into my side. The voice of a travelling woman, clear and stern, pushes us together. Pot Belly counts the beats into Eugene's ear. One, one-two, one. We dance around each other, cautious of the space we're taking up. And then the song changes to a reel and there is nothing but the primitive da-rum of the bodhrán, the sound of wood pounding skin. Da-rum, Da-rum. The near screech of a fiddle, the pull of hair on string, the melodeon, the wheeze of bellows catching up, and the slight imprecision of the live instruments playing. We lift the furniture to the edge of the room, and I shake the Lux across the floor. We swig our drinks and exchange our partners. Eugene starts moving with the beat, throwing himself in time. Ma removes her shoes. A V of sweat darkens the back of my father's shirt. The music is raucous, ornamented. Our shadows are larger than we are, doubling our statures, bending us up on to the ceiling. It is two-facing-two. We face each other. Eugene jumps up and down like a highland dancer and although he does not know the moves, he has found the rhythm. We move him into the places he should go. First the ladies exchange places, then the men. We take the man facing us and go right for seven and back again. We swing our partners and begin over. The fire heats the room and I peel off my cardigan when the tune ends. We gulp the sherry. Ma gets the stand from the hair-dryer and sings into it like it's a microphone. Eugene puts his hand up very high, imitating Foxy, sticks his belly out and we move around in circles.

'Do ya come here often?' he says.

'I do when the ewes aren't lambing.'

'Do ya live in a disadvantaged area?' he belches.

'Yeah, I get the subsidy.'

'God, you're lovely. There's nothing like the smell of a hogget ewe.'

He breathes me in with his sherry breath. We move with the squeal and squeeze of the uileann pipes, we are pulled in with the bellows. The quavering lilt and sway of a tin whistle curls through the dark room. The long swathe of hair that covers Da's bald patch falls down and almost touches his shoulder. Ma pulls off her roll-on and swings it like a hula hoop on her index finger, keeping her left hand at her waist. The last picture I remember is the roll-on flying across the room with the snap of elastic and Eugene asking, 'Can I interest you in a snog at the gable wall?' as he swings me in a perfect twist.

Declan Meade

More is More

It was hearing David Marcus speak about the need for there to be more outlets publishing more short stories that emboldened me to become the founding editor and publisher of a literary magazine. This was in the Irish Writers Centre in Dublin, back in September or October 1997, at the launch of *Dog Days and other stories*, a book that featured, as per its cover, fourteen new short stories from the Fish Short Story Competition. David Marcus was the guest speaker that night, but he wasn't meant to be. Joseph O'Connor had written the introduction for the book, and he was supposed to speak at the launch, but he was unwell. David took O'Connor's place, and he praised Fish Publishing for running the competition and for publishing the winners, but he made it clear that he would like to see more happen for the short story. Whatever was being done was not enough.

*

I know I listened intently to David Marcus that night and his words made a deep impression on me. I left the Writers Centre with my friend Aoife Kavanagh and—in my memory of it at least—by the time we'd got to the bottom of Parnell Square, we'd agreed that we were definitely now going to go ahead with the idea we'd been discussing for the past number of months: we were going to set up a literary magazine. I also know that I really didn't know who this man, David Marcus, was. Nor did I in any way appreciate just how much of a champion of new writers and new writing he had been for the past fifty years.

*

I moved to Dublin in 1995 when I was twenty-four. I had just spent ten months in Atlanta, Georgia, working in a family-owned bookstore. I'd travelled to the US on a Morrison visa, which I'd won in a lottery, and which would have allowed me to get a green card and to stay in the US, but I decided I wanted to give living in Dublin a go. I'd also decided I was going to try to be a writer.

In Dublin I got a part-time job through a community employment scheme at the James Joyce Centre. I joined a couple of writing groups and did a couple of evening classes at the Irish Writers Centre. I met a lot of people who were also trying to write. Many of them had been doing it for longer than I had. They had written poems and stories, or they were working away on novels. Some of these people had had work published, but many of them hadn't and I started to hear story upon story about how difficult it was to get published, how frustrated people were by the dearth of opportunities for new writers.

*

I do not come from a literary background; very few people do. I don't recall ever seeing a literary magazine while I was growing up in County Louth, in the countryside outside Ardee. My father read *The Irish Press*, but not every day, and it seems he didn't buy it on a Saturday. I'd taken to reading early, so I'd like to think I'd have followed the 'New Irish Writing' page, had I known it existed.

I was still only 15 when David retired from the newspaper.

*

We received about 100 submissions for the first issue of *The Stinging Fly* in late 1997 and ended up selecting five short stories and twenty poems for publication in our first issue, which we published in March 1998. We hadn't thought about what would happen next, but the response to the first issue was positive enough for us to carry on and publish a second one. Aoife moved on to do other things after this was done, while I decided to keep going.

The Stinging Fly now receives well over 5,000 submissions each year. These are read by a panel of readers and contributing editors and by the magazine's editorial team, led by Lisa McInerney. We publish two issues a year with short stories and essays and poetry by writers from all parts of Ireland and from around the world.

*

Editing and publishing, first the magazine and eventually books, became my life. Any interest in writing myself—or in trying to write—gradually waned and I was happy to let it go. I've been lucky enough to meet so many people who are more talented as writers, more driven to get the work done, and who have much more interesting things to say.

*

David Marcus clearly understood how important it was to support new writers and new writing. He recognised talent and did his best to nurture it. This is what he spent his life doing, from setting up *Irish Writing* and *Poetry Ireland*, through his work with *The Irish Press* and with Poolbeg Press and the numerous anthologies he edited.

*

There is no going back in time, but if I could I'd want to tell David Marcus that night in the Irish Writers Centre about the many good things that were coming down the track. I'd tell him about all the magazines of new writing that are flourishing in Ireland in 2024; so many that I would not attempt to name them all. He'd be happy, I'm sure, to hear that Fish Publishing is still going strong and that writers can still submit poems and stories to 'New Irish Writing'. I could tell him about increases in government funding for the Arts Council and how this directly benefits writers and the various people and organisations (including The Stinging Fly) who support them. I could tell him too of the remarkable successes Irish writers have been enjoying in recent years, including many of those who'd received that all-important early encouragement through his endeavours.

Of course, despite all this good news, it has to be acknowledged that writers continue to face huge uncertainties and challenges. Becoming a writer is not easy. Sustaining oneself can still require massive levels of determination and tenacity. There's still a genuine risk that some voices could go unheard. There's plenty more of David's important work to be done.

Kevin Barry

I started writing short stories in a serious way in the early winter of 2000. I was thirty-one years old and had just returned from a month in the US turning out colour pieces on the Bush-Gore election for the *Irish Examiner*. During the trip, I visited a branch of Barnes & Noble in Santa Barbara and saw a section given over entirely to small literary journals. Realising there were many places to send stories, I decided I'd try my hand at some, and I began to write in the form with some relief—a long attempt at a novel was in the process of forlornly ending.

My first acceptances were from tiny American journals: the *Adirondack Review* and some operation in North Dakota. Over the course of that same winter I saw a copy of the Phoenix Irish Stories anthology in Easons and there was an address for David Marcus in the back of it, I think a PO box number. I sent him the story that lies ahead of us now...

I have just read it for the first time in almost a quarter of a century. It's sentimental and bluff and often has a gauche note to it. Its clear and boyish ambition is to make the reader blush. I did not yet have a knack for titles. I did not do any research on chicken farming, and I think the reader can sense that the writer has never been near a rural setting in his life: there are lines that have a giveaway Limerick city accent to them: 'It was true for him.' The child is good, the mysterious child who is calm only in the chickenhouse. The line, 'I don't know if I'd miss her if she was away because she had never been away,' is good, too, if suspiciously close to Philip Larkin's, 'He married a woman to stop her getting away, now she's there all day,'—I was reading Larkin a lot at that morose age. I think the story also shows an embryonic writer who has a natural feel for the rhythms necessary to make a piece of short fiction seem whole. It goes into a weird lyric reverie in the closing paragraph, a kind of dying swoon, as if I've decided it's time for John Updike to arrive on the page. Eerily, I have indeed ended up in County Sligo, just like the unfortunate narrator, and at the time of writing I'd never been to Sligo. Be careful what you write your fiction about—it has a habit of coming true in life.

The most important aspect of the story was its acceptance. I was in Barcelona in February 2001 when I rang Olivia at home in Cork from a payphone in the Barri Gotic and she read out a letter that had arrived from Mr Marcus. It remains one of the most memorable moments from my writing life—I was going to be in a book, and I had at once a new confidence about my work.

I met David Marcus late in 2001 at the café upstairs in Hodges Figgis. He was a lovely man, and very pragmatic about publishing. He said I had lots of talent but I might have a difficult time getting published, because my stories were all sex and drugs and chaos. He said what the English publishers wanted from Irish writers were stories about family and ideally with rural settings.

In the early summer of 2006, when I was living in Liverpool, I revised the story for inclusion in a collection that Declan Meade had suggested might be put out by the Stinging Fly Press. I've just reread that version, too, as it appears in *There Are Little Kingdoms*. It's gone from first person to third, and much of the gaucheness has been removed. It's retitled 'Animal Needs', which is not much better than the original, but the story itself is much better, in the way that it opens out to its world, and there is even a little swagger to the narrative line. I have begun to exert some control on the page, and that was a long battle. It strikes me now, with some amazement, that in the intervening years between the story's two publications, I must have been working like an absolute dog. I also think it's a good job I didn't publish a book until I was thirty-seven.

Miami Vice

The whole wife-swapping thing can arrive out of nowhere and before you know it, there it is. On your plate.

We were living in the bungalow outside Birr and it was bleak enough at the best of times. The four walls and a few old fields. I don't know about this stuff where the countryside is supposed to be relaxing you because I nearly went out of my mind. Of course the child was sick half the time. I had fixed up the operation pretty good. I had it lickety-split. People said there was going to be a problem with the chickens but there was no problem with the chickens, none. The problem was a long way from chickens.

They were living inside in the town on a small terrace. It was fairly cheerful. She used to get all done up. She'd be going up to Dublin and coming back in all the gear. He was the man for the jokes and the winks. The wife thought they were the greatest thing since sliced pan but basically they were about the only people we knew. The wife knew her since she was a child and they had been at the afters of the wedding and on a couple of visits for weekends when we were above in Sligo. She was a nice-looking woman and there was plenty of her there. He sold combination socket wrench sets at the markets. We'd go for a few drinks of a Saturday inside to Dooley's. There'd be music and baskets of cocktail sausages and that sort of thing. It was grand, I suppose. After that, we'd go back to their place on the terrace with a curry. It was always the four of us, the two couples, and nobody else. He started making cracks about it. 'They'll think we're wife-swapping, John! They'll be saying, who's with who?' My Mary, God love her, would blush to her ankles. Margaret thought that it was all great sport.

He was one of these men who always seems to be red in the face. Breathless-looking, with watery eyes and thick hair combed back off the skull, always in great form, but kind of like a man trying to make out he's in great form. He was from the North originally and he used to wear cheap copies of flashy watches. Rolexes and that sort of get-up. Contacts coming out his ears, he said. He liked to make out that he knew loads of criminals.

Maybe six months of the going to Dooley's and the curries and it was coming up again and again, the same old line. And then one night he took me aside in the jacks. We were after a few. 'Listen to me,' he whispered, 'what about it? Grown adults, so we are, and whose business is it only our own? There's no objections on our side of the fence, John. Margaret thinks you're a very attractive man and don't be saying you haven't seen her putting the eyes on you, you rogue! And God forgive me but I'd get up on that wee Mary as quick as you'd look at me!'

I tried to laugh it off. 'Ah come on now, Frankie, go handy,' I said. I jabbed him in the arm with my fist and gave an old laugh out of me. He gave an old laugh back but as he went out of the jacks he leaned in to my ear and said, 'Sure ye can have an old talk about it anyway, friend.' Cuffed me on the back of the head with the big mock Rolex.

To be honest with you the whole thing kind of spoilt the night on me. He kept throwing out comments. Like about the watch. He turns around to Mary and says, 'There's links to go on there yet, it's a bit tight on me.' 'Sure you're a big man,' says Margaret. 'Oh I am that,' he says, giving Mary a look. She doesn't say much, only laughs kind of quiet and looks down at her shoes.

I was a happy man to get back to the bungalow. We cried off the curry side of things. The babysitter drove away home. The child was asleep at nine o'clock, he told us. Which meant she'd be up at four. Seven years of age and bawling in the middle of the night. Did you ever hear the likes of it? Myself and Mary sat down and got out the gin.

'They're getting worse by the week,' I said.

'They are,' she said. 'But I suppose they're lively at least.'

'You won't believe this,' I said, 'what it is he said to me inside in the toilet.'

'What?'

'Doesn't he start going on about the wife-swapping thing again! In all earnest.'

'Ah he's only pulling your leg.'

'He's serious. He says Margaret would have no bother going with me and he'd go with you. He was full in earnest, Mary.'

I'll never forget what she said next. She said, 'Ah sure, what harm in it?'

I had some week the week after that. Couldn't get it out of my mind, do you know that kind of way? I'd be going around trying to look after chickens and it would be haunting me. Thoughts about Margaret. She was a very handsome woman and you'd be seeing plenty of her. Skirts that went up to there and tops that came down to here. Between myself and yourself and the four walls, she had come into my thoughts many a night. Of course now, Frankie and Mary was a thing I could in no way deal with. The very thought of it made me sick to the pit of my stomach. And I could not get over herself: what harm in it! What harm in it my eye. There were chickens kept waiting for their grub that week. I didn't know whether I was coming or going. I said nothing to your one but by the looks on her you could tell that there was something on the agenda. After a while when you're married there's no great need for things having to be said out loud.

But by Saturday, somehow, I kind of felt that nothing would come out of anything, that everything would be just ignored or something and we wouldn't be going to Dooley's. I finished up as usual about three o'clock and in I come for the few sandwiches. She's looking at the television and turns around and says, 'What time are we going to Dooley's? What time will I get washed?'

There was never any formal meeting arrangement or anything like that. It was the kind of thing where we'd see them inside in Dooley's around teatime. Half the town would be in there after the bit of shopping, but the four of us would always land back at the same table. On this particular Saturday I felt that us showing up at all was like a signal or something. Of course I had no doubt themselves would be inside. And sure enough and yes they were, tearing into the chicken wings and packages of Bacon Fries. Frankie all kitted up in a purple shirt. Bright purple, now, not a maroon kind of thing. And jewellery on him like something out of *Miami Vice*. Margaret in the shortest skirt yet and a face on her like she's after eating a bar of lipstick. Chatty as you like, the two of them. What are ye having, and all the rest of it. And I suppose I started to relax after a few minutes—maybe he was pulling my leg all along. The night passed easily enough and there was no mention of anything, just the usual old talk about football and the television, and half eleven we're all saying, grand so, curry.

Back on the couch in the front room on the terrace. Curry boxes everywhere, vodka and beer. Frankie messing with the stereo and singing along, red in the face. Margaret and Mary skitting and nudging. Myself getting the bad feeling again. Then he's up and he's up the stairs and back down the stairs with a huge pile of sports jackets in all the colours under the sun. 'My new line,' he says, 'selling like hotdogs so they are.' 'Cakes,' I said, and I probably sounded kind of bitter. 'Will you do a spot of modelling for me, Johnny boy?' he says. And I didn't want to seem like the sour puss. So the next thing the two of us are parading up and down in front of the stereo in jackets, pushing the sleeves up and play-acting.

'Crockett and Tubbs!' roars Margaret.

And then of course The Eagles is gone on and we're all dancing. And Frankie takes me in his arms, messing, and he says to me, 'What about it, Tubbs?' And Margaret comes in behind me and puts her arms around my stomach and what can I say only she rubs her crotch off my backside. 'What about it?' she says.

The next thing I can remember I'm sitting on the couch with my head shaking back and forwards in my hands and I'm going 'Ah no, no.' And Mary says, 'Ah, John.' And I say, 'Ah Jesus lads, it's wrong.' Margaret sits beside me and rubs my thigh inside and says, 'Still and all, Johnny.'

And this is how it happened that Frankie and Mary walked out of the living room, him looking back over the shoulder and saying, 'Well, we'll see ye in the morning.' Not as much as a peep out of herself. 'Come on, John,' says Margaret, 'we'll head for the bungalow.' 'What about the child?' 'Sure, we won't be waking any child,' she says.

You'd imagine that the wife-swapping kind of thing would take four decisions, but really it only takes three.

'I swear to God to you, John, it wasn't the same,' says Mary. Half eleven the next morning aud I was sitting in the kitchen trying to eat a sausage sandwich. And you know there is no bite to eat I like better in the week than the sausage sandwich of a Sunday morning. And I couldn't eat it.

'No, honest to Jesus,' she says, with a big old grin on her face that would shame a scarlet whore, 'it was not the same, it was just all different. I'm telling you, John, all I wanted was to be back at the usual thing. Never again!'

Well, I thought, I either believe her or I go mad. So I tried to believe her and I felt a little better. I took a bite out of the sausage sandwich and squirted another bit of brown sauce in it. I'm a martyr to the brown sauce. Then: I decided there was one thing I had to ask straight out.

'Did you come, Mary?'

'Oh, I came about six times!'

Now I did not believe that Mary was a malicious woman. I am not a fool and I know that there are women who have malicious streaks. My mother, now, was a malicious woman, you could even say an evil woman. I'll never forget the night I goes into her room after she's unbeknownst to me after being with O'Donnell and the way she was lying on her stomach and the way she turned around to me and the way she kind of... *writhed*, is the only word, like a snake, and the look on her face. Pure hate. But Mary, I felt, was just the sort who says things without thinking about them.

All the same. Six times. I don't want to get deep into this kind of stuff but we might have gone at it twice a week and if she came twice a year it was nothing short of a miracle. There was walls in that bungalow painted more often than Mary came. I don't know how I finished that sausage sandwich but I finished it. Then I went out to the chickens.

The worst of it is when you lose the control of your thoughts. Do you not find? It doesn't happen all that often in life I suppose, but it happens. When you fall in love or when there's a death. You cannot decide for yourself what you're going to think about, it's all just there, first thing in the morning, last thing at night. And that was about the way of it the week after the night of the wife-swapping. I couldn't get past it.

The worst of it, actually, for me, wasn't connected with the sex angle. The worst of it was that I had crushed two Valium into hot milk and fed it to my crying child to conk her out. It was all Margaret's idea, and they were her tablets to begin with, but what kind of a way is that for a father to be acting? Jesus Christ almighty above on the cross. I'm not ashamed to say that I shed tears myself over doing that with the Valium. Poisoning a small child with drugs because I had a horn on me. All this was worse than the sex angle, but of course there was the sex angle as well.

I'll be totally honest with you, I went close to insane with jealousy. Jealousy is one of the big boys when it comes to the suffering. You hate her and you hate yourself even more. And I felt in my bones that we were only at the start of the thing, I felt in my bones that she'd be sneaking off with Frankie all of the time for her six comes. They'd have to be doing it on the sly because let's face it, there was no way that Margaret was coming next nor near me again. So that deal was off.

Oh it was an absolute disaster. I mean, I suppose we *did*, technically speaking. But it was an out-and-out joke. It had taken some amount of a build-up to get in the gate in the first place. Whether it was nerves or drink or what I don't know. We were there a good two hours before there was any bit of a stir out of the thing. It is an awful curse of a thing when it lets you down like that and only for she started taunting me I don't think we'd have got anywhere at all. But of course as soon as it went in it went and exploded on me. She lay there for the rest of the night yapping nonsense out of her, smoking her cigarettes, saying 'Ah it doesn't matter love, no harm done.' Talking about her tablets. 'That young miss will sleep now sweet as a dream for you, John, you have nothing to worry about there. Those are the English Valium now you know, the old Valium we used to get all along. Until they starts making them below in Clonmel. Clonmel! Oh yeah, they're making them down there now, only they're not the same at all and I'm not the only one saying so. Honest to God, John, you might as well be eating Smarties. But I have an arrangement about the English Valiums with the man in the chemist, the man of the Laffertys. Have you ever noticed, John, the way every single last one of the Laffertys has the big teeth?'

I never put down a night like it.

Poultry management is no joke at the best of times. And it's not as if I have background in it. I come from a town myself. But when the father-in-law had the seizure there was only Mary and the business was there and what were we going to do? It wasn't like we were setting the world on fire above in Sligo. And how much can there be to do with chickens, I was saying to myself. I got a queer land when I realised the reality of the situation. And listen, I'm the last one would ever criticise family but I have to say that

Mary's father, God rest him, was some devil for letting a place go. If you've ever lived out the country you'll know there is such thing as a dirty farmer, and I hate to say it but the father-in-law fit that bill.

It was not a pleasant set-up, really, by any stretch of the imagination. I mean it was cleaned up a bit and all the rest of it and there was money gone into it, who are you telling, but it was not a nice kind of thing on an everyday basis. To make it worth your while you really have to pack them in. There was a young lad in town wore one of the long coats was forever buttonholing me with rants about cruelty. 'What about the quality of life?' he says, getting himself all worked up, 'What about my quality of life?' I says. 'Do you think I'm outside in a palace?' But it was true for him, of course, it's not a way you'd want to see any creature treated. But what could I do?

The main chickenhouse was bad, now, it was bad. It was dark only for the ultra-violet and the smell was brutal and they weren't, you know, the healthiest looking chickens. They cannot move around in the cages and you have to kind of tie the legs into them when they grow any bit. And the feed then is not good stuff at all by any description. But it's funny the way I have mixed feelings about the chickenhouse. I have mixed feelings because it is the one place my daughter was calm, it is the one place she never cried or screamed. She'd pull at me to take her there and I'd go. She'd sit there on an old pail in her little red coat and it was like she was in a chapel.

To look at now I wouldn't be much. I'm fairly low-sized and I'd have a bit of a gut on me. I wouldn't say I'm ugly but I'm no oil painting. The only thing out of the ordinary is one of my eyes is blue and the other is green. And as things turned out that was the ice-breaker when I met Mary. She was about eighteen years of age and very shy, very gone into herself, I wasn't much older and as it happened I hadn't too much to be saying for myself either. How we ever managed to get a bit of talk going between us at all is one of the divine mysteries. But she mentioned the eyes and that got some bit of a spark flying, I suppose. I wouldn't know anything, now, about love or any of that kind of thing. I wouldn't have the faintest idea about what it might be exactly or whether I've ever actually had a lash of it myself. I know I love my daughter of course but I'm talking about the romance thing, with a woman. There was never anyone much apart from Mary. And we got on grand, you know. We wouldn't be the sort for fireworks. We'd never even really be doing the holding hands or any of that crack, not even when we were younger. I didn't know if I'd miss her if she was away because she had never been away.

And she did go away, of course, not long after the night of the wife-swapping, upped without a word and off to the sister in Hartlepool with a suitcase. She's living with a fella runs a B&B. I was embarrassed more than anything. I couldn't say exactly that I missed her so I cannot say if I ever actually loved her. But you would miss the heat of a woman in the bed at night. She's very thin, Mary, but there was some heat off of her, it used be like she was on fire.

I had enough of chickens, and me and the child are in Sligo again and scraping by one way or the other. I have never seen such a change in a child. She has really come out of herself.

And Frankie and Margaret? We could picture them in Birr, still, ageing slowly in the beautiful light that lingers now on these summer evenings, a little happiness in their faces, even, maybe after a good day at the market in Roscrea and a feed of steak in Shinrone on the way home, and the promise of an evening's drinking opening before them and the interest coming alive in their faces when the doorway is filled with new shadows because after all, you would never know who might walk into Dooley's.

Lucy Caldwell
On Being Various

I sometimes wonder how different life would have been with a Belfast accent.

I get asked if I'm American, or Canadian—the assumption is often vaguely transatlantic. South African I've had too. Australian. Sometimes, when I tell people, 'Northern Irish', they will concede the Irish part, but say they'd never have guessed the North. Other times, once they know what to listen for, they'll claim to hear the rhythms, the inflections—especially, it seems, if I'm angry, or speaking passionately.

There's an irony, of course, to saying this on the page, where you can't actually hear my voice. But on the page I feel a great freedom—my characters can speak in the voices and accents I hear in my head, and the reader can hear them unimpeded. When I read aloud, I'm often painfully conscious of the disparity between my own accent and that of so many of my characters. It's something I've felt for the whole of my published life. In the first interview I ever gave, to a prominent Irish newspaper, the journalist described me as speaking in 'a breathy, upper-crust English accent.' The shame I felt, that my own voice should be lampooned, rather than the focus being on the words that I had written, or the stories I was trying to tell of teen suicide or familial alcoholism. It felt exposing in a way that was hard, as a very young writer, to recover from. For years, I began interviews, conversations, events, by pre-emptively explaining and apologising for my voice, which would almost inevitably be questioned. And it continues. Another profile of recent years, also for a major Irish newspaper, in which I thought

I'd had a good conversation about literature with an intelligent journalist: he chose to open with a pejorative description of my voice and accent, which in his opinion 'sounds breathy, as if she's just run up a flight of stairs'. On the receiving end, it feels like people questioning your right to tell certain stories, and your right to speak—or write—at all.

But I was born in Belfast; grew up in Belfast; my parents still live in the same East Belfast house they moved into when I was 11. I love the Belfast voice. I love it because it is so familiar to me, so deeply ingrained in me. But I love it because it's a gift for a writer, too, so supple in its range, in its demotic, so vivid in its imagery. I love its rhythms and its darkness and its abrasive humour. I keep a running list of phrases on my phone that my dad remembers his Gran Robinson saying—'That's the tune the auld horse died to'—'She ran away like a liltie'. I was working on my own version of Chekhov's *Three Sisters* a few years ago when I found myself sitting next to a Russian scholar at a dinner who said, categorically, that Chekhov did not work in English. He gave the example of a typical Russian toast, which might translate literally as, 'I want you to know, my friend, how much I esteem and value our companionship.' It would sound stilted in English, he said, which is a language of the ironic, the repressed, the pared-back, understated; the toast translated would have none of the soul or guts of the original Russian. Aha, I said: but in Belfast English you can say, 'I fucken love you, you're sound as a pound.'

My dad is an Ulsterman, of Scottish ancestry, christened into the Church of Ireland, who grew up on a council estate in south Belfast. My mum was born in Bristol into an English Catholic family of humble means and Irish descent—her father's family comes from Mayo, from Limerick, from Cork, and fled Ireland during and after the Famine. My mum has a soft and non-specific English accent—unlike the broader Bristolian accents of her siblings, because she was the only one of them to pass the Eleven Plus and attend the local convent school, where the nuns used to insist they spoke 'properly'. My mum left school at sixteen, left home shortly afterwards, and moved to Belfast when she met my dad. Belfast is her home, the place she's chosen, and she is upset when people insist, even all these years later, on aligning her with the place she happened to be born in, the place in which she was unhappy, the place she chose to leave.

As children, my sisters and I, close in age, and very close to each other, adored my mum. She was entirely devoted to us, and we all spoke like her, and none of us has ever changed our accent. I wonder now how much this was a choice, at some unconscious level—a way of protecting her, a sort of solidarity with her. Because I think we were aware, in that keen and instant way that children can be, of how often people misread her, were suspicious of her, or were cruel to her. An English accent in 1980s Belfast was freighted with so many assumptions.

There were cross-currents. This was a time when 'Speech and Drama' lessons were basically elocution. You stayed after school, going into the P6 classroom, and took it in turns to stand at the front of the room and recite the poem you'd memorised that week. If you said it 'nicely', the teacher would give you a lemon or a toffee bon-bon or a strawberry sherbet from the paper packages she kept in various pockets. 'Nicely' meant more than loudly and accurately—she would be pleased if you said, in that phrase notorious to elocution lessons, 'haow naow braown caow', with rounded dipthongs, /aʊ/, rather than the flatter, quicker, 'hoy noy broyne coy', and you definitely wouldn't get a sweetie if you said 'high nigh brine cigh'. My sisters and I were often praised and held up as examples for our nice, clear voices. But at secondary school, one particular teacher would always ask me to read aloud any section of prose that contained the word 'eight', /eɪt/, so that she and the class could laugh at the way I said 'ayt' in one round, long syllable, rather than 'ee-ut' in two flattened bursts. I would know the word was coming and I would try to steel myself, the laughter breaking out already. I was often bullied for sounding English, or for considering myself 'posh', the two things being synonymous then—and why would you not be, if even the teachers took the lead?

Another cross-current: being of a generation which was, as Northern Irish poet Nick Laird puts it, 'reared for export'. For my whole childhood, people said: work hard at school and then you can get away. Teachers said it, family friends said it, even my mum, who had chosen to move to Belfast in 1975, said it, all the time. Our elocution lessons, our exam results—we were being educated to leave. My sisters and I all left. Some of the places we have collectively lived: London, Nottingham, Essex, Kent, Aberdeenshire, Mexico, Australia. Of all of us, I've come back most, but never for longer than a few weeks at a time. I have never lived, as an independent adult, in my home city—not even with my fiction's compass so firmly set there.

I was always happiest at home, with my sisters, in the imaginary worlds that were entirely our own—we would sometimes act them out with toys, or build them from Lego, would sometimes write them down, making miniature books, or chronicling genealogies of characters down through the generations in huge bundles of paper which we'd beg our dad to spiral-bind in the machine at work. It still feels the greatest psychic rupture of my life, having to grow up, and it's my saving grace that I found a way back to those places.

Maybe it's useful for a writer to feel like an outsider, to feel that there's somewhere that you more truly belong. Or maybe I've got causality the wrong way round—and it's a temperamental thing, some more fundamental fracture of the soul, that a writer should feel so different from the world around them, so set apart. Whichever way it works, I never felt that I belonged in the world around me, nor that I was entitled to. At university in England—I went to Cambridge—I was known as 'Irish Lucy' to differentiate me from the other Lucys in my year. My friends back home cracked up when they heard that—me, with my English voice? I was the least Irish person they could imagine. But it was at Cambridge, and through writing, that I discovered myself to be Irish. It was while writing my first novel, in my garret room overlooking the rooftops and spires, that I applied for my first Irish passport—under the terms of the Good Friday Agreement, which I'd been too young by a year to vote for, you were allowed to hold British and Irish passports simultaneously. My Irish passport was both an act of defiance, and sanctuary.

I never met David Marcus. I don't know anything of him beyond the anthologies that he edited. But before I considered myself an Irish writer, or Irish enough to be considered an Irish writer, and even before I was officially Irish by dint of that passport, I had his anthologies on my bookshelf. Re-reading them now, his short, self-effacing but sharp introductions, I feel all over again the spirit of plurality, of variousness, of generosity, of inclusivity, that felt so crucial to me then. His *Faber Book of Best New Irish Short Stories 2004–5* talks of contemporary Irish writers 'choosing plots and characters that aren't inked in green', and his anthology from 2006–7, the year my first novel came out, insists on the significance of Irish women writers, something that, for a twenty-four-year-old debut novelist navigating a literary world that often felt very male, was so important to me.

I felt that pressure as I was editing *Being Various*, published in 2019 and to date the latest in the series of Faber anthologies that David Marcus began. The series, incidentally—or maybe not incidentally at all—was the first acquisition at Faber by my own long-term editor, Angus Cargill, who was born and raised in the north of England with a father from Dublin. As I said in my speech at the launch event at the Irish Embassy in London:

> The act of anthologising is a deeply political one. The mid-century anthologies of Irish writing on my shelves invariably have just a handful of women writers, and usually the same three or four names. I have anthologies of contemporary Irish fiction that do not include a single Northern writer. 'New' is too often a synonym for 'young'. And too few, even those that

purport to be twenty-first century collections, include work by Irish-born or currently residing writers who have mixed cultural heritage. When you're putting together an anthology, you are, literally, making and shaping the canon—you are choosing writers and giving the seal of approval, in this case the mighty Faber colophon, to their work.

It remains a great regret that I didn't manage to include a story by a writer of Irish Traveller heritage, though in subsequent years Skein Press has published beautiful collections of stories and essays by Traveller writers Oein DeBhairduin and Rosaleen McDonagh.

But I am glad of the ways that I did manage to break open, to expand, the canon a little. When Melatu Uche Okorie, who came to Ireland from Nigeria as an asylum seeker, heard that her story, 'BrownLady12345', a subtle and nuanced account of a refugee exploring his sexuality, would be published in the anthology, she wrote an email to me that resonated a lot: 'Would you believe, I have three editions of the *Faber New Irish Short Stories* series? And now I get a chance to be a part of it? This is MY Irish dream come true!'

I had a very moving conversation with Arja Kajermo at the Dublin launch, where she talked about how, despite Ireland being the place she chose to come to, the place she got married and raised a family in, the place she chose to stay in even after that marriage ended and those children had grown up, she is almost never referred to as an 'Irish' writer, only ever a 'Finnish' one.

And when Chinese-born Yan Ge received her copy of *Being Various* in the post, and saw that her story opens the anthology, she tweeted: 'I feel like a real Irish *cailín*.' When Yan moved to Ireland in 2015, the first book she read was *Town and Country: New Irish Short Stories*, edited by Kevin Barry, a previous volume in the series. Now things had come full circle. It was, she said, 'magical'. In a further magical twist, her first English-language collection, *Elsewhere*, was acquired by Angus at Faber and published last year; my own stories are due to come out this year in Chinese, with a Foreword by Yan. The David Marcus spirit is generous—and generative.

*

The personal is always political, and vice versa: I think of all the times I was asked as a child, 'Where are you from?' and how, when I'd say, 'Here,' the response would invariably be, 'No, but where are you really from?' I think of the ways that for so long, I was ashamed of my voice, or didn't feel it counted. I still feel the pang of it sometimes. A taxi driver will pick me up from George Best Belfast City Airport and say, 'First time visiting, love?' and even if he means it kindly I'll feel mortified explaining that I was actually born here, grew up here; as if I've moved away and changed my voice because it wasn't good enough. But then I think of all of the Irish writers—Irish readers—Irish citizens—who feel or have been made to feel that because of something like their accent, their accident of birthplace or parentage, they somehow count less, are insufficiently Irish to make a contribution; and I think of what a gift it has been to have known and to have surmounted that myself.

Within weeks of the publication of *Being Various*, I found myself having conversations with a British-Trinidadian writer who, had I known she had an Irish mother, would have been in this anthology. With a young London-born London-Irish writer who said it had spurred her to finally start writing the novel she has long wanted to write, the novel she's been ashamed to write because she doesn't feel properly Irish. With a Belfast-born woman of Chinese heritage who was struggling to tell her story because there were no stories like hers out there. And, perhaps most movingly of all, with an Indian-born Northern Irish mother who brought her two young daughters, aged nine and six, to meet me after an event. The younger girl excitedly showed me her first novel, written in a school exercise jotter. Her voice, I was able to tell her, truly was the future.

I spent much of this weekend watching YouTube footage of Kneecap, the Belfast-based hip-hop trio who rap in an addictive blend of Irish and English, and who are, at the time of writing, much in the news. I thought I was just putting off writing—I knew what I wanted to say, about my voice, my childhood, and it was something I'd never said in public before; I thought I was reluctant to begin. But then I realised it was more than that, too: I was watching the music videos and interview segments with the sort of obsessive intensity that usually means there's something else going on. I finally understood what it was. As I thought about voices and Irishness and the future, as I watched Kneecap's videos, I was feeling a complicated and bittersweet sort of joy—at the fact of these young people so unapologetically using their own voices, using them playfully, wittily, defiantly. When someone is telling the stories they should be telling, in the voice only they could tell them in—you can feel it, and it's galvanising. Mo Chara, Móglaí Bap and DJ Próvaí talk often in interviews about how they couldn't see their own experience represented in their own language, so they started doing it themselves. They talk about the things that unite and the things that are used to separate us: for instance, how they have far more in common with working-class kids on the Shankill than middle-class people in Dublin. Of the generation that Lyra McKee called the 'ceasefire babies', they offer a new vision, a new version, of Irishness. They talk of how Irish is a language belonging to everyone on the island, and their Belfast Irish accents are electrifying.

I have no way of knowing what David Marcus the man might have thought of Kneecap. But the David Marcus sensibility—which searches for new ways of telling old stories, and for stories entirely new, that sees the energy of creative change as being brought about when the traditional meets the cutting edge—would love the notion of a language being used anew to describe not just turf on the fire but drug-taking on the Falls.

You make the space for yourself—you fight the psychic battle to feel entitled to that space—and it opens up space for others, too, and it creates new ways of being. Your voice is the only one you have, and you have to use it.

V

Sarah Marcus
Love, Always

My father did not believe in God. Or so he professed. But my mother always wondered why, if he did not believe in him, Daddy was often very angry with God.

I think he was often angry with God because he cared so much about the vulnerable of the world and he wanted them to be helped. He always said that pets should be cared for and fed before humans, because they couldn't feed themselves. (Our cats were woefully poor mousers, although I'm not sure that's what he was referring to.)

He saw all the incomprehensible injustice in the world and I think he found it quite unbearable, and perhaps that was another source of his anger with God. As a Jew, I wonder if he couldn't reconcile the Holocaust with the existence of God, or certainly not with a responsible, benevolent God.

He did not live lightly in the world; it was in many ways not an easy place for him to be, I think. Some people do not suffer fools, my father did not suffer unkind people, or thoughtless people. He trusted a small number of people absolutely, and he was unwaveringly loyal to them.

My father was someone held in huge esteem, but also in great affection, by a great number of people. He is often remembered as an absolute gentleman, and it is true that he was. But he was more than that—he was a person of the greatest integrity. He was honest in every word and deed, from the core of his being.

I think it was this honesty, along with his huge kindness and gentleness, which left a mark on people. I think it was the presence of these traits in my lovely father that have made me value them so deeply.

He was dishonest, I think about one thing, and that one thing was me. I'm pretty sure he thought I was perfect, and of course he was quite wrong there! But he loved me and my mother so deeply, and I think that love was fundamental to his passage through the world he found so difficult in many ways.

And he had his other great loves: sport, of all types—he was a great sportsman and his recurring piece of sporting advice to me could be applied in many other areas of life too: keep your eye on the ball! Biscuits. Absolutely nothing wrong with that. Horse racing. The short story, of course.

But his greatest love of all was classical music. One of my friends once said to me that she thought that not being able to express oneself through music was a deep lack. I don't find I can express in words what music meant to my father. It was his core, his soul.

Before you've lost a loved one, you worry about how to talk to people who've been bereaved. You think you maybe shouldn't mention the deceased, lest the person who has suffered the loss is managing to have a bit of time not thinking about it.

But of course once you've lost someone you love deeply, you don't want time not thinking about them. Quite the opposite—thinking about them and remembering is how you can be with them again. It's how you keep them alive, somehow.

My father reminisced a lot about his childhood and youth in Cork, about his years in London, about playing football and cricket on the Mardyke, cycling to Cobh and back in a day, writing speeches for Jack Lynch for the Fianna Fáil Ard Fheis, about meeting my mother with her beautiful red hair for the first time. He had so many memories, until slowly but surely, he started to lose them all. It was the cruellest end for a man whose identity was rooted in reflection, memory and narrative.

But he had music to the very, very end. My wonderful mother brought a portable stereo into St James's Hospital in Dublin, where he spent his last six months so beautifully cared for, and played him the piano music he loved so deeply. Tchaikovsky, Chopin, Mozart, Beethoven…

I hope that the music transcended the lost words and the lost memories and comforted him and rooted him to his past, as he left this world.

He left, but I can't let him fully go. When I want to be with him again I listen to some of the indescribably beautiful music that he introduced me to, and in my heart we are together still.

Ita Daly
Still Beautiful

from I'll Drop You a Line

As we get older, most of us begin to forget things, then start worrying that it is the beginning of Alzheimer's. But David's memory was always better than mine. It was something else that I was picking up: increasingly, he didn't seem to understand what I was saying, even when I said it a second time.

For example, I'd tell him I had cooked salmon for our dinner and he'd reply that he hadn't bought any salmon that day. This was harking back to his bachelor days when tinned salmon was one of the staples in his diet. Or if I suggested that he take his umbrella as it was looking like rain he'd reply that there was no need for me to buy an umbrella as he already had one.

At first I tried to convince myself that all this was nothing, that David's hearing was causing problems or that he hadn't been listening to something I said. Eventually, however, I had to admit it—David was having difficulty in processing what was said to him. I was frightened and this led me to deny what was happening, in the hope, I suppose, that it would disappear. It didn't get any worse but it didn't go away. He got a hearing aid but it made no difference and I began to discuss my worries, telling his family and one or two close friends what I feared. Dementia is hard to spot in the early stages and everyone told me that David was fine and that I was worrying unnecessarily. He *was* fine, most of the time, but the lapses in understanding continued and eventually I had to take my head out of the sand. When I disclosed my worries to our family doctor, a supportive man who had seen us through all sorts of crises, he didn't dismiss them but referred us to the gerontology department of our local hospital so that David could undergo tests.

The initial tests were the crudest you can imagine. We were ushered into a sort of long hall, one side of which was lined with small cubicles. Inside these cubicles old men (I saw no women), deaf for the most part, answered questions put to them by junior doctors. Or didn't.

It went something like this:
Who is the President of Ireland?
What?
What city are we in?
What?
What day of the week is it?
What?
The doctors shouted at the old men, who shouted back.

David passed the test with flying colours. He knew who the President was; he knew what day of the week it was. Surely there must be some other tests he could undergo? Sure enough, when a doctor saw him later on and talked to him and gave him shapes to look at and name, he told me what I already knew: David was in the early stages of dementia, a progressive disease for which there was no cure.

There is a psychological difference between suspecting something and suddenly knowing it to be true. I wasn't particularly upset but I began to live my life differently. For the first time since childhood, I began to live in the present; the future was somewhere I didn't want to go. There were no dramatic changes. David continued to search for talent but now, from time to time, he would ask me for help with his correspondence. He was having difficulty typing and his handwriting was becoming smaller and smaller and more indecipherable so I offered to type his letters for him.

I don't know if he thought there was anything wrong with him: certainly, he behaved as if he didn't. The only acknowledgement he made was that he would tell friends who called that his memory had got very bad. His difficulties in understanding what was said to him didn't seem to increase but I began to notice small changes in his personality, the sort of changes I would never have expected. He had always been anti-social but suddenly he wanted to accept every invitation that fell through our letterbox—poetry readings, novel launches, lectures. When he got to these events he talked. If he saw a writer he would make a beeline for them, usually beginning with, 'I was going to drop you a line…'

This change might be considered a good thing—that, at this late stage David was becoming more engaged with life. It should have pleased me that he was easy enough in himself to be able to approach people freely, such a change from his earlier, shyer self. But there was something wrong with the way he greeted people and I could often see that they thought so too. There is always a restraint in human intercourse and David could seem overpowering now, especially with someone who was an acquaintance rather than a friend.

I also saw a shift in power that I found upsetting. In the old days, when David, with reluctance, attended a party or launch he would stand somewhere at the back of the room and people would approach him. His shyness held him back but writers, young and old, wanted to talk to him. Now, he seemed to be making the running and the writers were backing off. I thought I might have been imagining this because I had become protective of him but I don't think this was the case.

Luckily David saw none of this. He was happy most of the time although, occasionally, he seemed to sense that there was something wrong. Momentarily he would look confused, then upset, but this never lasted long and he was back to his busyness, reading or dropping some writer a line.

I knew that this was a temporary slowing down of the disease but it was one we both benefited from so I refused to think of what lay ahead. Life wasn't all glum and Sarah's regular visits home were something we both enjoyed. It was lovely to see the love between father and daughter and the pleasure each could still take in the other's company, sitting together in silence or listening to music.

***

David Marcus was ill with dementia for five years before his final demise.

One morning after I had got David up and dressed and sitting in his usual chair he suddenly slumped sideways. I straightened him up but he slumped again and I saw that he was unconscious. Pushing his chair against the wall so that he wouldn't fall on the floor I went to phone for an ambulance. He was taken to the accident and emergency department of St James's Hospital where he was quickly assessed, then admitted to a ward of noise and bedlam with each patient looking at an individual television set. It made no difference to David, the man who had loved quiet. He had regained consciousness on the journey to the hospital but kept his eyes closed and didn't respond as I talked and held his hand. As I looked at him in the hospital bed, in a blue hospital gown, he seemed to have shrunk and taken several steps closer to death.

After about a week he was moved to a four-bedded ward. The three men with whom he shared it were also suffering from dementia and were more or less the same age as him. They were to become his final companions. He had had another bleed into the brain; we were entering the home straight.

A year ago I went back to St James's to see a consultant. I had been dreading it, driving my car into that familiar car park and getting the lift up to the concourse with its bustle and colour. I feared being returned to those days when the hospital had become a home from home for me.

My experience was quite the reverse. I felt a calmness, a loosening of tension as I waited to ask for directions at the reception desk. This was the hospital where David had died, where I had watched him grow thinner and weaker by the day. But none of this came back to me then. What I was remembering was the all-encompassing care and love he had received—we had both received—in this hospital.

David moved further and further away. He had stopped talking for some time before being admitted to hospital and now he seemed completely cut off from the outside world. He didn't really react when I came in to see him; he would stare at my face but his expression of puzzlement never changed. His reaction to all his visitors was the same and I was almost sure that by now he could not tell one person from another. Yet, as I watched him, I saw this expression change when a nurse or care assistant approached, to be replaced by one of fear. He didn't seem to know me or Sarah or Louis; yet, at some level, he seemed to recognise that we were familiar, while the hospital personnel were strangers.

At such moments I wondered if I should try to bring him home but in reality I knew that there was no question of it. He had to be washed and fed and lifted in and out of bed, a task that needed a minimum of two strong people. As I lay in bed at night I would come up with impossible plans, calculating how long our savings would last with round-the-clock care for him at home.

I tried to visit him every day and every day as I walked home I wondered how long he would live. I couldn't say that I wanted him to die but I didn't want him to live, either—not as he was. His heart and lungs were still strong. I began to revise my opinion and to think that this might be a long goodbye. But the disease moved forward inexorably. He began to refuse his food. At first I tried feeding him and when that didn't work I started bringing him food from home, things I knew he liked. But nothing seemed to appeal to him: he couldn't be tempted even by sugar and he grew quite gaunt. His poor arms, emerging from the sleeves of his pyjamas, were like sparrows' legs.

I bought a little portable CD player and when I visited him I played him Mozart—sunny, happy Mozart. I also read his own poems to him, written when he was a young man and reissued in a slim volume some years previously. Before I left him, I always brought my face close to his and said, 'I love you very much, David, and I'll see you tomorrow.' As I watched his eyes, I thought I saw fear and was very aware as I walked out the door that I was leaving him to the care of strangers.

As time passed by, I did want him to die. He was getting thinner and thinner; he seemed frightened and maybe in pain; he was not going to get any better. I was afraid that the hospital would start feeding him through a tube and I thought of the extra discomfort that would cause him. I walked to and from the hospital every day and at night I slept, in a suspended state now as life continued on around me.

David had very faithful visitors during those months in hospital—I remember especially his brother, Louis, and his friend, Tony Glavin. Some good friends found it more difficult or even frightening and didn't repeat an initial visit.

It was difficult to visit him, even for me. He lay in bed, his bones visible through a gossamer-thin skin. His eyes were enlarged and staring, frightened. But his strong heart kept beating and his lungs kept drawing in the warm hospital air.

I settled into a rhythm of hospital visits bookended by long walks. It seemed as if this could go on for many months. And then, when I was least expecting it, I got that call from the hospital. David was beginning to fail; I should summon any family members who lived abroad.

I phoned Sarah and went into the hospital. David's eyes were closed now and his breathing audible. I sat and prepared to wait. I knew the drill as I had been through it with my parents, who had both died within a fortnight of each other in Doctor Steevens' Hospital. I was familiar with hospitals at night time when patients have been sedated into sleep and the lights are dimmed and the nurses' station forms an oasis of life and warmth at the end of the ward. They are eerie places but there is something tranquil about them too.

The next morning Sarah arrived and we sat with David throughout the day and night, taking turns to go out and get something to eat. Towards dawn, a nurse suggested that one or other of us go home and get some rest but neither of us wanted to move until the sun was properly up in the sky. As a species we may have conquered darkness but not our atavistic fear of it. Everything somehow seems better, more hopeful, once the sun is up.

As it turned out, our wait was not to be long. David died at the next dawn, signalling his departure with a strange, guttural sound as if the heart, the spirit, was escaping from the diminished body. We said goodbye and kissed his already cooling forehead. All his life he had raged against the dying of the light but that light was now, after eighty-four years, finally extinguished.

We left the ward that had in some senses become a second home for me. Down below we met the consultant and signed papers and thanked various people for the care they had given David over the previous six months.

It was a beautiful May morning. By then, Sarah's husband, Tom, had arrived and the three of us went for a walk out into Dublin port along the length of the South Wall. The sun was shining on the water and seagulls swooped. The pulse of life was strong everywhere and I could only be glad that David's sufferings were over. I looked around me, out towards Wicklow where the mountains were visible, backlit by an early summer sun, and I thought, as I often do, how beautiful this world is. Nothing made much sense but the world was still beautiful.

David Marcus: Bibliography

Fiction

To Next Year in Jerusalem (London: Macmillan, 1954)

A Land Not Theirs (London: Bantam Press, 1986)

A Land in Flames (London: Bantam Press, 1987)

Who Ever Heard of an Irish Jew? and other stories (London: Bantam Press, 1988)

Poetry

Six Poems (Dublin: The Dolmen Press, 1952)

Cúirt an Mheán Oíche / The Midnight Court, by Bryan Merriman, newly translated into English by David Marcus (Dublin: The Dolmen Press, 1953)

Lost and Found: Selected Poems and Translations, with an introduction by George O'Brien (Dublin: New Island Books, 2007)

Autobiography

Oughtobiography: Leaves from the Diary of a Hyphenated Jew (Dublin: Gill & Macmillan, 2001)

Buried Memories (Dublin: Marino Books, 2004)

Edited Anthologies

New Irish Writing 1: An Anthology from 'The Irish Press' series (Dublin: The Dolmen Press, 1970)

Tears of the Shamrock: An anthology of contemporary short stories on the theme of Ireland's struggle for nationhood (London: Wolfe, 1972)

The Sphere Book of Modern Irish Stories (London: Sphere, 1972)

Modern Irish Love Stories (London: Pan, 1974)

Irish Poets, 1924-1974 (London: Pan, 1975)

New Irish Writing: from 'The Irish Press' series, with a preface by V.S. Pritchett (London: Quartet Books, 1976)

Best Irish Short Stories (London: Paul Elek, 1976)

Best Irish Short Stories 2 (London: Paul Elek, 1977)

Best Irish Short Stories 3 (London: Paul Elek, 1978)

Body and Soul: Irish Short Stories of Sexual Love (Dublin: Poolbeg Press, 1979)

The Bodley Head Book of Irish Short Stories (London: The Bodley Head, 1980). Reissued in two volumes as *Irish Short Stories* (London: New English Library, 1982); reprinted in one volume as *Irish Short Stories* (London: New English Library, 1986)

The Poolbeg Book of Irish Ghost Stories (Dublin: Poolbeg Press, 1990)

State of the Art: Short Stories by the New Irish Writers (London: Sceptre, 1992)

Alternative Loves: Irish Gay and Lesbian Stories, with a foreword by Ailbhe Smyth (Dublin: Martello Books, 1994)

Listowel Writers' Week: Award-Winning Short Stories, 1973-1994 (Dublin: Marino Books, 1995)

Irish Sporting Short Stories (Belfast: Appletree Press, 1995)

Irish Christmas Stories (London: Bloomsbury, 1995)

The Irish Eros: Irish Short Stories and Poems on Sexual Themes (Dublin: Gill & Macmillan, 1996)

Phoenix Irish Short Stories 1996 (London: Phoenix, 1996)

Phoenix Irish Short Stories 1997 (London: Phoenix, 1997)

Irish Christmas Stories II (London: Bloomsbury, 1997)

Phoenix Irish Short Stories 1998 (London: Phoenix, 1998)

Mothers and Daughters: Irish Short Stories (London: Bloomsbury, 1998)

Phoenix Irish Short Stories 1999 (London: Phoenix, 1999)

Irish Ghost Stories (London: Bloomsbury, 1999)

Phoenix Irish Short Stories 2000 (London: Phoenix, 2000)

Phoenix Irish Short Stories 2001 (London: Phoenix, 2001)

Phoenix Irish Short Stories 2003 (London: Phoenix, 2003)

The Faber Book of Best New Irish Short Stories, 2004–5 (London: Faber & Faber, 2005)

The Faber Book of Best New Irish Short Stories, 2006–7 (London: Faber & Faber, 2007)

Contributors

Kevin Barry is the author of four novels, most recently *The Heart In Winter* (2024), and three story collections, most recently *That Old Country Music* (2020). He also works as a playwright and screenwriter. He lives in County Sligo.

Sebastian Barry was born in Dublin in 1955. He has twice won the Costa Book of the Year, and twice the Walter Scott Prize. He has been nominated five times for the Booker. He was Laureate for Irish Fiction from 2018 to 2021. 'The Beast' was his first published story.

Dermot Bolger is a poet, playwright and novelist whose early work was published by David Marcus in 1976, when Bolger was still a Finglas schoolboy. His fifteenth novel, *Hide Away*, is published in September 2024, and his twentieth play, *Home, Boys, Home*, is staged in the 2024 Dublin Theatre Festival.

Lucy Caldwell was born in Belfast and is the author of four novels, several stage plays and radio dramas, and three collections of short stories, most recently *Openings* (2024). She is also the editor of *Being Various: New Irish Short Stories* (2019), the sixth and most recent volume in the Faber series begun by David Marcus.

Angus Cargill is an Editor and Publishing Director at Faber, where he has worked since 2000. His authors include Kazuo Ishiguro, Sebastian Barry, Claire Kilroy, Lucy Caldwell, John Banville, Laura Lippman, Peter Swanson, David Peace, Peter Pomerantsev, Angie Kim, Adrian Tomine and Willy Vlautin.

Ciaran Carty has edited *New Irish Writing* since 1988 and curated the Hennessy Literary Awards. As film critic and arts editor at *The Sunday Independent* and *The Sunday Tribune* he helped end censorship in Ireland. His books include *Confessions of a Sewer Rat*, *Citizen Artist*, *Intimacy with Strangers* and *Writer to Writer: The Republic of Elsewhere*.

Harry Clifton was Ireland Professor of Poetry from 2010 to 2013. His lectures were published as *Ireland and its Elsewheres* by UCD Press in 2015. His most recent collection of poems is *Gone Self Storm* from Wake Forest and Bloodaxe Books (2023). He teaches at Trinity College, Dublin, and he is a member of Aosdána.

Tim Pat Coogan is a writer, historian and journalist. As editor of *The Irish Press*, he worked with David Marcus—whom he hired as literary editor—for thirty years. His passion for the story of Ireland produced several books, including biographies of Michael Collins and Éamon de Valera, and a bestselling history of the IRA.

Ita Daly was born in County Leitrim but has lived in Dublin most of her life. She has written several novels, a volume of short stories, two books for children, and a collection of Irish myths and legends. She is also the author of the memoir, *I'll Drop You a Line: A Life with David Marcus* (2016). She was married to David for thirty-six years and she has one daughter. She is a member of Aosdána.

Mary Dorcey is an award-winning poet and fiction writer. She has published seven collections of poetry, including most recently *Life Holds Its Breath*, and three fiction titles: *A Noise from the Woodshed*, *Scarlet O'Hara*, and *The Biography of Desire*. She is a member of Aosdána.

Carlo Gébler was born in Dublin in 1954 and lives outside Enniskillen, County Fermanagh. He is a writer, novelist and occasional broadcaster. He teaches at the Oscar Wilde Centre for Irish Writing at Trinity College, Dublin, and HMP Hydebank. He is a member of Aosdána.

NOTES ON CONTRIBUTORS

Anthony Glavin is a Boston-born novelist, short-story writer and editor. Published works include his novels *Nighthawk Alley*, *Colours Other Than Blue* and *Way Out West*, and short-story collections *One For Sorrow* and *The Draughtsman and the Unicorn*.

Katrina Goldstone is an independent researcher, writer and cultural historian, focusing on minorities and cultural diversity. Her recent work includes the monograph *Irish Writers and the Thirties* (2020) and essays in *Reimagining the Jews of Ireland: Historiography, Identity and Representation* (2024), eds. Zuleika Rodgers and Natalie Wynn.

Michael Harding is the author of numerous plays, novels and memoirs. He is a columnist with *The Irish Times*, chronicling stories of ordinary life in contemporary Ireland. He has been the recipient of numerous awards for his writing and is a member of Aosdána.

Desmond Hogan was born in Ballinasloe, East Galway, in December 1950. He is the author of five novels, several volumes of stories, and a book of travel writing. Some of his earliest work was published in 'New Irish Writing', and his awards include an inaugural Hennessy Award (1971). *Larks' Eggs: New and Selected Stories* (2005), *Old Swords and other stories* (2009), and *The History of Magpies* (2017) are published by Lilliput Press.

Neil Jordan is a multi-award-winning film director, screenwriter and author. His first book, *Night in Tunisia*, was published in 1979 and won the Guardian Fiction prize. His most recent book is *Amnesiac: A Memoir* (2024). His films include *Angel*, the Academy Award-winning *The Crying Game*, *Michael Collins*, *The Butcher Boy* and *Interview with the Vampire*.

Claire Keegan's works of fiction are critically acclaimed, international bestsellers and have been translated into thirty languages. *Antarctica* won the Rooney Prize for Irish Literature. *Walk the Blue Fields* won the Edge Hill Prize. *Foster* won the Davy Byrnes Award. *Small Things Like These*, a *New York Times* Best Book of the 21st Century, was shortlisted for the Booker Prize, the Rathbones Folio Prize and won the Orwell Prize for Political Fiction and The

Kerry Prize for Irish Novel of the Year. *So Late in the Day* was published in the *New Yorker* and shortlisted for the British Book Awards. Keegan was awarded Woman of the Year for Literature in Ireland in 2022, Author of the Year 2023, the Seamus Heaney Award for Arts and Letters 2024 and most recently the Siegfried Lenz Award.

Mary Leland is a Cork-born journalist who has published two novels and a collection of short stories. A recipient of Arts Council bursaries and several awards, her stories have been frequently anthologised and she continues to work as a creative writer.

Colum McCann is the National Book Award-winning author of a dozen books, including *Let the Great World Spin*, *Apeirogon* and *American Mother*. Born in Dublin, his work has been published in over forty languages. He is the co-founder of the global storytelling non-profit, *Narrative 4*.

Frank McGuinness was born in Buncrana, County Donegal. He contributed poems and short stories to 'New Irish Writing' from 1974. The author of many plays, he worked in the University of Ulster, Maynooth College, and University College Dublin, where he is Emeritus Professor of Creative Writing.

Eoin McNamee was born in Kilkeel, County Down. He has written seventeen novels, including *Resurrection Man*, *The Ultras*, *The Blue Trilogy* and *The Vogue*. He has written for radio and television. Works for cinema include *Resurrection Man* and *I Want You*. He is the Director of the Trinity Oscar Wilde Centre. His latest novel, *The Bureau*, will be published in 2025.

Louis Marcus was born in Cork in 1936. His film career began as an assistant editor on Gael Linn's *Mise Éire*, and he made his own first film in 1959 on the sculptor Seamus Murphy RHA. He proceeded to direct almost eighty documentaries for cinema and television, winning twenty festival awards, including two Oscar Nominations. He is a member of Aosdána.

NOTES ON CONTRIBUTORS

Sarah Marcus is the only child of David Marcus and Ita Daly. She works as a teacher in London, where she lives with her husband and three children.

Declan Meade is publisher and CEO of The Stinging Fly, a registered charity, with a mission to seek out, nurture, publish and promote the very best new writers and new writing.

Mary Morrissy is the author of four novels, *Mother of Pearl*, *The Pretender*, *The Rising of Bella Casey* and *Penelope Unbound* and two collections of stories, *A Lazy Eye* and *Prosperity Drive*. Her story 'Bookworm', first published in *New Irish Writing*, won her a Hennessy Award in 1984. A member of Aosdána, she is a journalist, teacher of creative writing and a literary mentor.

Eiléan Ní Chuilleanáin was born 1942 in Cork. She has taught at Trinity College, Dublin since 1966, and she was Ireland Professor of Poetry from 2016 to 2019. Her latest book of poetry, *The Map of the World* (2023), was shortlisted for the T.S. Eliot Prize. Her *Collected Poems* appeared in 2020 from Gallery Press.

Éilís Ní Dhuibhne, a Dubliner, has written over thirty books, most recently *Selected Stories* (2023) and *Fáinne Geal an Lae* (2023). Recipient of many awards for her work, in autumn 2020 she held the Burns Scholarship at Boston College. She is a member of Aosdána, and President of the Folklore of Ireland Society.

George O'Brien's publications include an autobiographical trilogy: *The Village of Longing* (1987), *Dancehall Days* (1988) and *Out of Our Minds* (1994). He was a recipient of a Hennessy/New Irish Writing Award in 1973 and is Professor Emeritus of English at Georgetown University, Washington, DC.

Jo O'Donoghue is a publisher with Londubh Books. She is also a writer, both in English and in Irish, based in Dublin, with a particular interest in history and Irish studies as well as literature and books. Her works include a critical study of the Belfast-born writer Brian Moore.

Mary O'Malley has published ten books of poetry, most recently *The Shark Nursery*, (Carcanet 2024). She lectures and teaches widely in the US and Europe. In 2019 she was Writer Fellow in Trinity College Dublin, and was awarded an Honorary Doctorate by Galway University in 2021. She is a member of Aosdána.

Gerard Smyth's most recent, and tenth, collection of poetry is *The Sundays of Eternity* (2020) with Dedalus Press. He is a former Managing Editor of *The Irish Times* and since retirement has been the paper's Poetry Editor. He is a member of Aosdána.

William Wall is the author of eight novels. His most recent, *Ti ricordi Mattie Lantry?*, will be available in English in 2025. He has also written six volumes of poetry and three of short fiction. He was the first European to win the Drue Heinz prize for Literature in the USA and his 2005 novel, *This is the Country*, was longlisted for the Man Booker Prize. He was Cork's first Poet Laureate.

Editors

Paul Delaney is Associate Professor in the School of English and a Fellow of Trinity College, Dublin. He has written widely on Irish literary culture and on short fiction, and his recent books include *The Edinburgh Companion to the Short Story in English* (2019, co-edited Adrian Hunter) and *Dublin Tales* (2023, co-edited Eve Patten).

Deirdre Madden is a novelist whose works include *Molly Fox's Birthday* and *Time Present and Time Past*. She is the recipient of a 2024 Windham Campbell Award for Fiction and is a member of Aosdána. She is also a Fellow of Trinity College, Dublin, where she taught Creative Writing for over twenty years. A study of her work, *Deirdre Madden: New Critical Perspectives* (eds. Anne Fogarty and Marisol Morales-Ladrón), was published in 2022 by Manchester University Press.

Acknowledgements

While editing this book, we were struck by the number of people who remarked, 'I'm so glad you're doing this.' The respect for David Marcus, and the affection in which his memory is held, was evident time and again. Thanks to all the contributors who responded with such generosity, by giving stories, poems, essays, and personal reflections.

Particular thanks to Ita Daly. When we first approached Ita with the idea for this celebration, she responded with warmth and enthusiasm; we are deeply grateful to her for her help and encouragement. We are also grateful to Sarah Marcus and Louis Marcus for their contributions, which bring unique insights into David's private life.

Thanks to Declan Meade of *The Stinging Fly* for rowing in from an early stage and agreeing to publish the book. As Declan has previously noted, the seeds for *The Stinging Fly* were sown in October 1997 in the Irish Writers Centre in Dublin, when David Marcus decried the lack of publishing outlets for short-story writers in Ireland. Since then, *The Stinging Fly* has played a pivotal role in the fortunes of Irish writing, and its maintenance of an open submissions policy, and its commitment to the work of new and emerging writers, is an honourable extension of David's core beliefs. All of this made The Stinging Fly Press a natural home for this book. We are extremely grateful to Deirdre O'Neill for her careful attention to the text, and to Eimear Gavin for her beautiful cover design.

Pat Collins, Tom Coogan, Antony Farrell, Clíodhna Ní Anluain, Eve Patten, and Zuleika Rodgers were especially helpful at critical points in this venture, and we are indebted to each of them for their knowledge and assistance. Paul is enduringly grateful for the love and support of Finola McLaughlin, and Katie Rose and Joe Delaney. Thanks also to the staff of the National Library of Ireland and the Library of Trinity College, Dublin.

It is a very generous thing for a writer to allow early work to be reproduced. We are particularly grateful to Kevin Barry, Sebastian Barry, Claire Keegan, and Eoin McNamee for doing just this, as they each gave permission for the inclusion of early versions of stories and poems which were first published by David either in *The Irish Press* or in the Phoenix anthologies of short stories.

We are also grateful to the following who have granted permission for the reprinting of material: Ita Daly for permission to reproduce extracts from *I'll Drop You a Line: My Life with David Marcus* (2016); Mary Dorcey for permission to reprint 'Another Glorious Day' from *The Faber Book of Best New Irish Short Stories, 2006–7* (2007); Antony Farrell and Lilliput Press for permission to reproduce Desmond Hogan's 'The Mourning Thief'; Harry Clifton for permission to reprint 'The Has-Beens' from *Gone Self Storm* (2023); and Ita Daly for permission to include extracts from David Marcus's *Oughtobiography: Leaves from the Diary of a Hyphenated Jew* (2001) as well as an excerpt from David's translation of *The Midnight Court* and 'A Jolson Story'.